# VM/CMS

## Commands and Concepts

# VM/CMS

## Commands and Concepts

Steve Eckols

**Mike Murach & Associates, Inc.**

4697 West Jacquelyn Avenue
Fresno, California 93722
(209) 275-3335

**Development team**

| | |
|---|---|
| Technical editor: | Doug Lowe |
| Production editor: | Judy Taylor |
| Book designer/Production director: | Steve Ehlers |
| Production assistant: | Carl Kisling |

20 19 18 17 16 15 14 13 12 11 10 9 8 7 6 5 4 3

Library of Congress Catalog Card Number: 87-62576

ISBN: 0-911625-44-5

# Contents

Preface                                                                                      vii

**Section 1    Introducing VM and CMS**                                                      1

Chapter 1    An introduction to IBM mainframe computer systems                               2

Chapter 2    An introduction to VM environments and commands                                 23

Chapter 3    An introduction to virtual machines                                             37

Chapter 4    An introduction to VM's Conversational Monitor System (CMS)                     54
  Topic 1    How to access CMS and issue commands in the CMS environment                     55
  Topic 2    An introduction to CMS minidisks                                                62
  Topic 3    An introduction to CMS files, file management commands,                         69
             and procedures
  Topic 4    How to use the XEDIT command                                                    81


**Section 2    Disk file handling**                                                          95

Chapter 5    How to manage your CMS disk files                                               96
  Topic 1    How to use the FILELIST command                                                 97
  Topic 2    How to use the TYPE command                                                     117
  Topic 3    How to use the COPYFILE command                                                 124
  Topic 4    How to use the COMPARE and SORT commands                                        139

Chapter 6    How to manage your minidisks                                                    145

Chapter 7    How to use the VM File Storage Facility                                         159


**Section 3    Tape file handling**                                                          179

Chapter 8    Basic tape concepts and commands                                                180

Chapter 9    How to store and retrieve tape files: The TAPE and DDR commands                 196

Chapter 10   How to process non-CMS tapes:                                                   214
             The MOVEFILE, FILEDEF, and LABELDEF commands


**Section 4    Spooling**                                                                    229

Chapter 11   VM spooling concepts                                                            230

Chapter 12   How to print and punch data                                                     241

Chapter 13   How to use your virtual reader                                                  259


Index                                                                                        275

# Preface

VM and CMS are acronyms for operating system software products that support thousands of IBM mainframe computer systems. If you work with an IBM mainframe system, the chances are good that it runs under VM and CMS now, or that it will in the future. To make the best use of your system, you need to understand the concepts that underlie VM and CMS and the commands you issue to request VM services. That's what you'll learn in this book.

Actually, CMS is a part of VM, but because much of the interaction users do with VM is through CMS, it can often seem to be the more important of the two. The fact is, though, they work together. Currently, IBM supplies VM as a package called VM/SP; that stands for Virtual Machine/System Product. Don't worry for now what "virtual machine" means. You'll learn that soon enough.

What you *should* know now is that VM and CMS provide an interactive computing environment that (1) lets large numbers of users access IBM mainframes and (2) is easier to work with than IBM's other mainframe operating systems. If you're familiar with either of IBM's other two major mainframe operating systems (MVS or VSE), you know that to provide support for interactive computing requires complex add-on products like CICS, IMS, TSO, ISPF, and ICCF. That's not the case with VM.

Not only is VM easier for you to use than other IBM mainframe operating systems, but it can also make more efficient use of a system's hardware. As a result, even though VM has been available for over ten years, it's in wider use today than ever before, and it's still growing in popularity.

All of IBM's current mainframe systems, from the smallest 9370 models to the largest 3090s, can run VM. This range of support reflects IBM's support for VM. In fact, VM is one of IBM's "strategic" products. In other words, IBM will continue to develop and support VM and will base other products on it.

Reflect on these points for a moment: VM is easier to use than other IBM mainframe operating systems, it can make better use of expensive hardware, and it's a "strategic" IBM product. Taken together, these considerations paint a rosy picture for VM. And they should encourage you to learn as much as you can about it. You can be confident that the VM skills you learn today will be in demand for a long time.

In spite of the fact that VM is easier to use than IBM's other mainframe operating systems, it's still not a snap. After all, tapping the power of a mainframe computer system and making it available to a range of users is complicated business. So the concepts you need to know to use a VM system and the commands you issue to interact with it are complicated too. Making them easier for you to understand is the purpose of this book.

## Who this book is for

If your current job—or the job you want—involves working with a computer system that runs VM, this book is for you. Unlike the situation with some of IBM's other mainframe operating systems, you don't have to be a "computer person" to use the facilities of VM. In fact, because VM puts computing resources in the hands of a wide range of users, you're likely to need to know how to use its features regardless of your job title. Whether you're a programmer, a systems analyst, an administrator, a data entry operator, or a manager, if you develop a good understanding of VM, you'll find that your job will be easier to do, and that you'll get more out of your system.

## Required background

You don't need much background in data processing to benefit from this book. However, you should have at least a basic understanding of the parts of a computer system and how they work together. If you've used a personal computer, or simply know the functions of a processor, disk drive, and printer, you have all the background you need. (The first chapter of this book introduces IBM mainframe systems; if IBM mainframes are new to you, you should certainly read this chapter.)

If you already have experience with IBM systems, don't automatically assume that this book isn't for you just because it starts off with basics. You'll find that this book is not intended only for novice users. It provides a balanced presentation of the VM features all users really need to know.

## How to use this book

This book is the first of a set that covers a range of VM skills. It introduces the fundamentals of VM and how to use the commands that are common to nearly all applications. Then, in subsequent books, you'll learn how to use other more sophisticated VM features most effectively: the text editor, program development features, and VM's procedure language REXX.

You should probably read this book from start to finish. But don't feel like you have to master every point as you go along. Of course, you should feel free to refer back to the book as often as you need to refresh your memory on points that you've forgotten or that weren't crystal clear to you as you read them the first time.

Although I recommend that you read the chapters straight through, you can certainly adopt a different approach if you like. For example, if you're already familiar with IBM mainframe computer systems, there's no reason for you to read chapter 1. And if you're not interested in how to do tape processing, you can skip section 3. Or, if you really want to learn the details of VM's unit record support, you can skip ahead to section 4 after you've read the chapters in the first section. In other words, you can decide what you want to study, and when.

## Related reference manuals

IBM's library of VM/SP manuals is extensive. But frankly, much of the material they contain is just not very helpful for day-to-day use of the system. That's what this book is for! However, because VM/SP is a broad and complicated topic, you'll probably need to refer to the reference manuals from time to time.

The two you'll find most useful are *CMS Command and Macro Reference* and *CP Command Reference for General Users*. Keep in mind, though, that these are strictly *reference* manuals. Together, they represent nearly a thousand pages of material. Although they're not as hard to use as some other IBM reference manuals, they're still formidable. Most of your VM/CMS questions will be answered in this book and its companion volumes.

## Conclusion

I'm convinced that you'll find this book to be an effective and interesting tutorial that will make learning VM easier for you. And after you've learned VM, I think you'll refer back to this book again and again as you use your system. Of course, I welcome your comments. If you have suggestions on how I can improve this book, please share them with me. You can use the postage-paid comment form at the end of this book. Good luck!

Steve Eckols
San Diego, California
October 1987

# Section 1

Introducing VM and CMS

VM/CMS stands for the IBM mainframe system software product VM/SP (Virtual Machine/System Product) and CMS (the Conversational Monitor System), one of the central components of VM/SP. The four chapters in this section lay the foundation for your VM/CMS training.

Chapter 1 introduces you to IBM mainframe computer systems. If you're new to the mainframe world, you should certainly read chapter 1. On the other hand, if you have experience with IBM mainframes, you may be able to skip ahead to chapter 2.

Chapters 2, 3, and 4 introduce you to essential VM/CMS concepts and commands. Chapter 2 describes the VM environment and shows you how to issue basic commands to VM. Chapter 3 introduces virtual machines, the mechanism VM/CMS uses to let you access the resources of the computer system. And chapter 4 introduces you to CMS, the software component you're likely to interact with most when you work with VM.

# Chapter 1

## An introduction to IBM mainframe computer systems

This chapter presents what you need to know about the hardware components that make up IBM mainframe computer systems, the kind of systems that support VM. If you've had significant experience with IBM mainframe computers, you can probably skip this chapter; much of it will be review. To check your knowledge, review the terminology and objectives listed at the end of this chapter. If you're comfortable with them, you can go on to chapter 2.

A *mainframe computer system*, or just *mainframe*, is a large collection of computer hardware devices, like the one illustrated in figure 1-1. Just what "large" is depends on your perspective and experience. Clearly, a national computer network with thousands of users is a large system, and a single-user PC is a small system. In general, though, a mainframe system, regardless of its current size, is one that can be expanded into the largest of systems.

This chapter has four parts. The first two describe the types of hardware components that make up mainframe computer systems: *processors* and *input/output devices* (or just *I/O devices*). In the third part, I'll describe two typical configurations of mainframe computer equipment. That will give you an idea of how the various components are used together. Finally, in the fourth part, I'll introduce the systems software used to support IBM mainframes; this is where VM enters the picture.

### Processors

The central components of mainframe computer systems are processors. VM runs on processors that are members of the *System/360-370 family*, a group of IBM

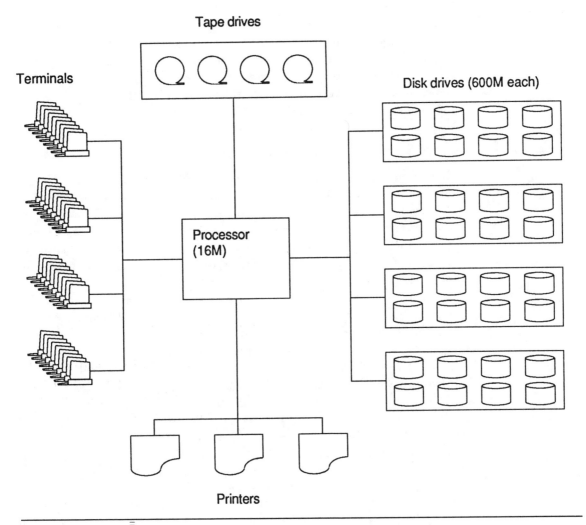

Tape drives

Terminals

Disk drives (600M each)

Processor
(16M)

Printers

**Figure 1-1**    A typical mainframe computer system configuration

processors that has evolved over a 20-year period. The System/360-370 family
includes the System/360 models of the mid-1960s, the System/370 models of
the early 1970s, the 3030 models of the late 1970s, and the 4300 and 3080 models
of the early 1980s. The most recent entries in the System/370 series are the large
3090 models, sometimes called the Sierra systems, and the small 9370 models.

As IBM has developed new models of its System/360-370 processors, it has
used contemporary technologies to create better, faster, and cheaper machines.
But even though the technology has changed significantly, the basic operating
characteristics of the processors have not. As a result, the System/360-370 family
has maintained a high degree of compatibility over its 20-year life, in terms of
both the hardware and software that can be used with its processors. That's why

although the older System/360 and System/370 models are obsolete, the current 9370, 4300, and 3090 processors are still generally called System/370s.

Since the first System/360 models were introduced, thousands of users have invested billions of dollars in software for systems built around System/360-370 processors. As a result, we can expect that future members of the System/360-370 family will maintain that compatibility as well.

### Basic System/370 architecture

IBM maintains compatibility among various System/370 processors by designing each with the same basic architecture. Although the details of the System/370's architecture are far too complex to describe here, I want you to know how the major components of a basic System/370 processor are arranged. Figure 1-2 shows that arrangement. As you can see, the processor consists of three main parts: the CPU, main storage, and channels, which provide control functions needed to connect I/O devices to the processor.

The basic configuration shown in figure 1-2 applies to all System/370-type processors, including the 9370, 4300, 303X, 308X, and 3090-series machines. As you'd expect, the number, size, and arrangement of these basic components is more complex in processors with greater processing power.

The *central processing unit*, or *CPU*, contains the circuitry needed to execute program instructions that manipulate data in *main storage* (or *main memory*). Although figure 1-2 doesn't show it, most System/370 processors include a special high-speed memory buffer between the CPU and main memory. This relatively small amount of storage operates at speeds even faster than the storage in main memory, so the overall speed of the processor is increased. Special circuitry constantly monitors accesses to main memory and keeps the most frequently accessed sections in the high-speed buffer.

### Multiprocessing

In the more advanced models of the System/370 family, more than one CPU is included in the processor. In those *multiprocessor systems*, two or more CPUs share access to main memory and can be utilized in different ways.

*Multiprocessing* provides two benefits. First, the overall instruction processing rate of the system is increased, because two or more CPUs are available to execute program instructions. Second, the system's overall availability is increased because if one of the CPUs fails, another can take over its work.

In multiprocessor configurations that contain four CPUs, the processor can be run in one of two modes: as a single four-CPU processor, or as two independent two-CPU processors. When operating as two independent processors, resources such as main storage and channels are split between the two processors. Depending on operational needs, the installation may switch from one mode to another.

Processor

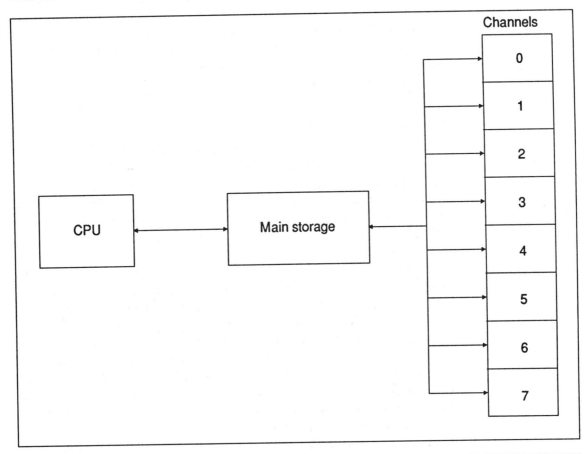

Figure 1-2    Basic architecture of System/370 processors

## Channels

Perhaps the most interesting components of the System/370 processors are *channels*, which provide paths between the processor and I/O devices. In figure 1-2 there are eight channels, numbered 0 through 7. As a result, there are eight different paths along which data can pass between the processor and I/O devices. The actual number of channels that can be included in a system depends on the processor model; the largest 3090 processors can include up to 128 channels.

Actually, a channel is itself a small computer; it executes instructions called *channel commands* that control the operation of the I/O devices attached to it. As a result, the channel frees the CPU to execute other instructions. Since channel processing overlaps with CPU processing, overall system performance is improved.

| Processor | CPUs | Main memory (M) | Channels |
|-----------|------|-----------------|----------|
| 4361 | 1 | 2-12 | 1-6 |
| 4381 | 1 | 4-32 | 6-18 |
| 3083 | 1 | 8-32 | 8-24 |
| 3081 | 2 | 16-64 | 16-24 |
| 3084 | 4 | 32-128 | 48 |
| 3090 | 1-6 | 64-256 | 32-128 |

Figure 1-3     Characteristics of IBM's current System/370-family processors

Contrary to what you might expect, I/O devices are not connected directly to channels. Instead, intermediate devices called *control units* are used. Each channel can attach to eight control units, each of which in turn can attach to one or more I/O devices. Depending on the processor and the I/O device, a control unit may be housed within the processor's cabinet, the I/O device's cabinet, or in its own cabinet. Just as channels relieve the CPU of some I/O processing functions, the control units remove some I/O processing functions from the channels. That way, the channels can handle even more work.

## Members of the System/360-370 family

To give you some perspective on the processing power of IBM processors, figure 1-3 lists several characteristics of the current System/370 processors that can be used under VM. For each processor, I've listed the amount of main storage, the number of channels, and the number of CPUs that can be configured in the processor. (The abbreviation *M* in the main memory column stands for *megabyte*; a megabyte is about one million *bytes*, or positions, of storage.) Most of these values are ranges of numbers because the processors come in a variety of models that offer various features.

Figure 1-3 lists only the processors that were current when I wrote this book. Naturally, IBM continues to develop new processors. As a result, by the time you read this, IBM may have bigger and better processors that make the ones listed in figure 1-3 obsolete. By the same token, most installations don't install new processors immediately after they're announced. So there are plenty of installations around that use older processors that aren't shown in figure 1-3, such as the smaller 4341 and 303X models. Nevertheless, I think figure 1-3 gives you a good overview of the capabilities of IBM's major processor families.

## Input/output devices

Input/output devices are the devices that connect to a processor to provide it with input, receive output, or provide secondary storage. The common types of I/O devices found on IBM mainframes are illustrated in figure 1-1: (1) unit record devices, such as printers; (2) magnetic tape devices; (3) direct access devices, such as disk drives; and (4) telecommunications devices, such as terminals. There are still other types of I/O devices, but I won't cover them because they're for specialized uses.

When I described processor channels, I mentioned that they are connected to I/O devices by control units. As I describe each class of I/O devices, then, I'll describe not only the individual I/O devices themselves, but also the control units that connect the I/O devices to processor channels.

### Unit record devices

*Unit record devices* include two types of devices: card devices and printers. The term "unit record device" implies that each record processed by the device is a physical unit. In the case of card devices, each record is a punched card. For printers, each record is a printed line. Unit record devices usually have built-in control units which attach directly to channels, so separate control units aren't required.

Card devices, which aren't commonly used anymore, come in three types: readers, punches, and reader/punches. A card reader is an input-only device; it can read data from punched cards, but can't punch data into blank cards. A card punch is just the opposite; it can punch data into cards, but can't read previously punched cards. A reader/punch combines the functions of a reader and punch, and serves both as an input and an output device. Although a reader/punch is housed in one cabinet, the reader and punch components are viewed by the system as separate devices.

Unlike card devices, printers are in widespread use today; they provide the primary form of permanent output from the computer. There are a variety of different types of printers, but the most commonly used printers fall into two categories: impact printers and non-impact printers.

*Impact printers* produce printed output by striking an image of characters to be printed against a ribbon, which in turn transfers ink to the paper. The most common type of impact printer uses a train of characters which spins at high speed; when the correct character passes a print position, a hammer strikes the character against a ribbon to produce the printed text. Most impact printers operate in the range of 600-2,000 lines per minute.

Currently, IBM manufactures one form of *non-impact printer* for its mainframes: the 3800 Printing Subsystem. This printer uses laser technology to print at rates up to 20,000 lines per minute. The actual speed of the 3800 printer depends on the size of each page and the number of lines per inch, because the 3800 transfers images to the paper an entire page at a time. For standard computer paper (11"x14") and normal print size (6 lines per inch), the 3800 prints 10,020 lines per minute. At that print rate, the 3800 can process more than a mile-and-a-half of paper each hour.

## Magnetic tape devices

A *tape drive*, or *magnetic tape drive*, reads and writes data on a *magnetic tape*. The tape is a continuous strip of plastic coated on one side with a metal oxide. Although most tape drives process tape that's wrapped around a *reel*, some of IBM's newer tape drives process tape that's sealed within a special *cartridge*. The concepts I'll present here apply to either type of storage.

How much data a reel or cartridge of tape can contain depends on the length of the tape and the *density* used to record the data. Density is a measurement of how many bytes are recorded in one inch of tape. Tape densities for standard reel tapes are usually 1600 or 6250 *bytes per inch* (*bpi*). Cartridge tape drives record data at a much higher density: 38,000 bpi.

Of course, meaningful data on a tape isn't a random collection of bytes. A number of bytes are strung together along the tape to form a *record*, which is a collection of related data much like a punched card or printed line. Between the records on a tape are spaces where no data is recorded. These spaces are called *inter-record gaps*, or *IRGs*.

When a technique called *blocking* is used, more than one record is stored between IRGs. Then, a group of records stored together is called a *block*, and the IRG is called an *IBG*, or *inter-block gap*. The number of records stored in each block is called the *blocking factor*. Because blocking reduces the number of gaps required for files, it can significantly reduce the amount of wasted space on a tape.

To attach a tape drive to a channel, a control unit is required. For some models, the control unit is inside one of the tape drives. For other models, it's in a separate cabinet. Depending on the model, the control unit can attach up to four or eight tape drives.

Tape processing has one serious drawback: it must be sequential. In other words, to read the 50,000th record on a tape, the preceding 49,999 records must be read first. As a result, tape is ill-suited for applications that require direct access to stored data. Instead, tape is most often used for off-line storage of large quantities of data. In particular, tape is frequently used to store data that serves as a backup for on-line data on direct access storage devices.

## Direct access storage devices

A *direct access storage device*, or *DASD*, makes it possible to access any record quickly. Because DASDs allow direct and rapid access to large quantities of data, they've become a key component of mainframe systems. They're used not only to store user programs and data, but also to store programs and data for system functions.

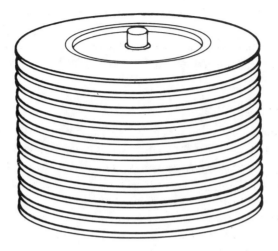

**Figure 1-4**          A disk pack

The most common type of DASD is the *disk drive*, a unit that reads and writes data on a *disk pack*, or *volume*. A disk pack, shown in figure 1-4, is a stack of metal platters coated with a metal oxide material. Data is recorded on both sides of the platters.

Most of IBM's older DASDs use removable disk packs, but with all of IBM's newer DASDs the pack is fixed in a permanent, sealed assembly inside the drive. Nonremovable disk packs have two advantages over removable packs: they're faster, and they're more reliable. Because speed and reliability are important requirements for typical mainframe applications, DASDs with nonremovable packs are well suited for today's mainframe systems.

*Tracks and cylinders*          Data is recorded on the usable surfaces of a disk pack in concentric circles called *tracks*, as figure 1-5 shows. The number of tracks per surface varies with each device type. For example, the surface in figure 1-5 has 808 tracks, numbered from 000 to 807; a disk pack with 19 usable surfaces, each with 808 tracks, has a total of 15,352 tracks. Although the tracks get smaller towards the center of the surface, each track holds the same amount of data.

Figure 1-6 shows a side view of an *access mechanism*, or *actuator*, the component that reads and writes data on the tracks of a disk pack. As you can see, the actuator has one read/write head for each recording surface. When the actuator moves, all of its heads move together so they're all positioned at the same track of each recording surface. As a result, the disk drive can access data on all of those tracks without moving the actuator.

The tracks that are positioned under the heads of the actuator at one time make up a *cylinder*. As a result, there are as many tracks in a cylinder as there are usable surfaces on the pack, and there are as many cylinders in a pack as there

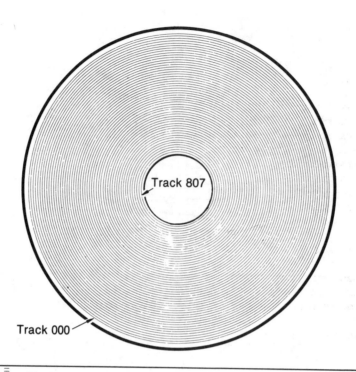

Track 807

Track 000

Figure 1-5      Tracks on a disk surface

are tracks on a surface. So a pack that has 19 surfaces, each with 808 tracks, has 808 cylinders, each with 19 tracks.

Incidentally, some DASD models provide a small amount of *fixed-head storage*. In that case, certain tracks on the disk pack have their own assemblies of read/write heads. Access to data on those tracks is faster than when a movable actuator is used because the fixed heads never move away from those tracks. Because fixed-head storage is expensive, however, it's reserved for uses where speed is especially critical.

In addition, some newer IBM DASD models have two actuators, each of which accesses half of the cylinders on the device. Each actuator is treated as a separate device, so when two actuators are used, two volumes share a single set of recording surfaces.

***Device capacity and data format***      Figure 1-7 presents some characteristics of the various IBM DASD units supported by VM systems. Frankly, many operating characteristics of DASD units, such as how fast the disk pack rotates or how fast data is transferred, just aren't significant to most programmers.

What is relevant is the capacity of each device: the maximum number of bytes per track, the number of tracks per cylinder, the number of cylinders per drive, and the total capacity of the drive. That's the information shown in figure 1-7.

Read/write heads

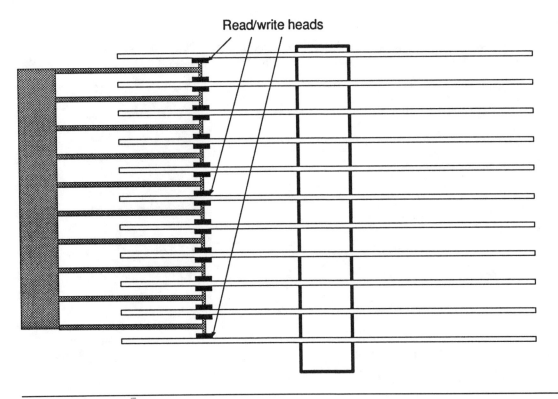

**Figure 1-6**    Side view of a DASD actuator

To understand the information in figure 1-7, you need to know a little about the format in which data is stored. IBM manufactures two basic types of disk drives which store their data in different formats. The drives listed in the top section of figure 1-7 are *count-key-data* (*CKD*) devices, which store data in variable-length blocks. The other type of devices, called *fixed-block architecture* (*FBA*) devices, store data in fixed-length blocks of 512 bytes each. The FBA DASDs supported by VM are listed in the bottom section of figure 1-7.

Figure 1-8 shows how data is stored on a CKD device. Here, each data block is preceded by a *count area* and a *key area*. (The count area is required; the key area is optional.) Because the disk revolves counterclockwise, the read/write head encounters the count and key areas before the data area. The count area contains the information the disk needs to locate the appropriate data record using the key and data areas.

One of the problems with CKD devices is that the data capacity of each track depends on the size of the blocks used to store the data. That's partly because gaps are required to separate the count, key, and data areas, just as gaps are required on magnetic tape. When smaller data areas are used, more blocks of data can

**CKD DASD**

| Device | Fixed/ removable | Maximum bytes per track | Tracks per cylinder | Cylinders per volume | Total capacity per volume (M) |
|---|---|---|---|---|---|
| 3330-1 | Removable | 13,030 | 19 | 404 | 100 |
| 3330-11 | Removable | 13,030 | 19 | 808 | 200 |
| 3340-35 | Removable | 8,368 | 12 | 348 | 35 |
| 3340-70 | Removable | 8,368 | 12 | 696 | 70 |
| 3350 | Fixed | 19,069 | 30 | 555 | 317 |
| 3375 | Fixed | 35,616 | 12 | 1,918 | 819 |
| 3380 | Fixed | 47,476 | 15 | 885 | 630 |
| 3380-E | Fixed | 47,476 | 15 | 1,770 | 1,260 |

**FBA DASD**

| Device | Fixed/ removable | 512-byte blocks per volume | Total capacity per volume (M) |
|---|---|---|---|
| 3310 | Removable | 126,016 | 65 |
| 3370 | Removable | 558,000 | 286 |

Figure 1-7    Capacities of IBM DASD units supported by VM

be stored on each track. But when more blocks are stored, more space is used for gaps and count/key information, so the usable capacity of the track is reduced.

The total capacity for each CKD drive shown in figure 1-7 is the maximum capacity for the device. That assumes that all of the data in each track is stored in a single block; if more than one block is stored per track (and that's usually the case), the capacity is reduced because of the additional gaps required to separate the blocks.

In contrast, the capacities shown for the two FBA models is the same regardless of the blocking factors used. With FBA units, records are grouped or split as necessary to fit into the machine's fixed 512-byte blocks. Fortunately, that's transparent to the user.

*Control units*    Up to four or eight DASD units, depending on the model, can be connected to a common control unit, called a *string controller*, which is housed within one of the DASD units' cabinets. The DASD units connected to

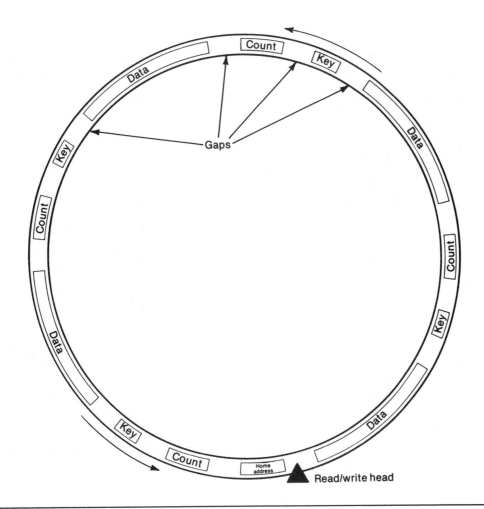

**Figure 1-8**   Count-key-data format

the string controller make up a *string*; all of the devices in a string must be of the same type.

A string controller can be connected to a channel in one of two ways: directly or indirectly via an intermediate control unit called a *storage control*, which in turn is connected to a channel. The most common type of storage control is the 3880, which is available in various models that attach four or eight strings of various DASD types.

### Data communications devices

*Data communications devices* let an installation create a *data communications network* (or *communications network* or just *network*) through which users at *local terminals* (terminals at the computer site) and *remote terminals* (terminals that aren't at the computer site) access a computer system. Now, I'll briefly describe the components of a data communications network, with emphasis on the most common type of terminal system used on IBM mainframe networks: the 3270 Information Display System.

*Elements of a data communications network*     Figure 1-9 shows the five basic components that make up a data communications network: (1) a host system, (2) a communications controller, (3) modems, (4) communications lines, and (5) terminal systems.

At the center of the network is the host system, a System/370 processor. The control unit which attaches to the host system's channels is called a *communications controller*; it manages the communications functions necessary to connect remote terminal systems via modems and communications lines. A *modem* is a device that translates digital signals from the computer equipment at the sending end (either the host or remote system) into audio signals that are transmitted over the *communications line*, which can be a telephone line, a satellite link, or some other type of connection. At the receiving end of the line, another modem converts those audio signals back into digital signals.

Although the terminal systems in figure 1-9 are connected remotely via communications lines and modems, that's not a requirement. If the terminal system is located close enough to the host system, the modems and communications lines can be eliminated.

Whether attached locally or remotely, the most commonly used terminal system on IBM mainframes is the *3270 Information Display System*. Because you're likely to use a 3270 terminal as you work with VM, it's important that you have a basic understanding of the 3270 system's components and how they work together.

*The 3270 Information Display System*     The 3270 Information Display System is not a single terminal, but rather a subsystem of terminals, printers, and controllers. A typical 3270 controller (such as a 3274) controls up to 32 terminals and printers. 3270 terminals are available in a variety of configurations, offering screen displays of anywhere from 12 lines of 40 characters each to 43 lines of 80 characters, with one model that displays 27 lines of 132 characters. Recent additions to the 3270 family are the 3178 and 3191, low-cost terminals that provide 24 lines of 80 characters each, the standard screen size for most 3270 display stations.

In addition to display stations, printers can be attached to a 3270 system. Many 3270 systems have a *local-print feature* that allows the data on the screen of a display station to be transferred to the controller and then printed by one of its printers. Since this operation doesn't involve transmission of data between the 3270 system and the host processor, it's an efficient way to print small quantities of data. In general, though, the printers attached to a 3270 controller are used for a lower volume of output than the high-speed printers attached directly to the processor.

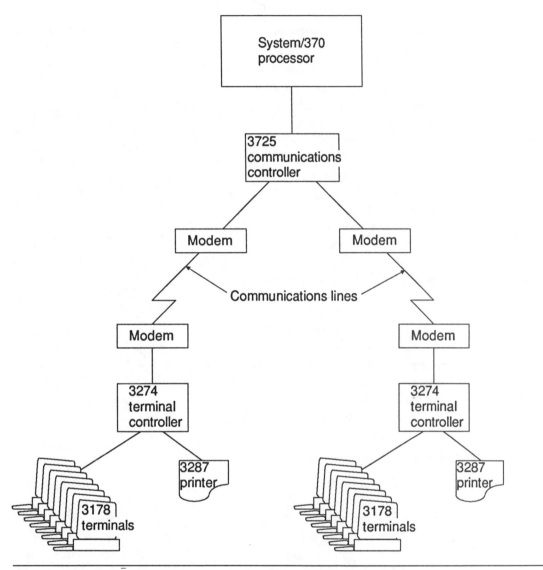

**Figure 1-9**    Components of a data communications network

## Two typical mainframe configurations

With such variety in the types of IBM mainframe processors and I/O devices, the number of possible system configurations is endless. As a result, one IBM mainframe configuration is likely to be different from another, even though the two systems might be used for similar purposes. Now, I'll present two typical, though hypothetical, mainframe configurations. By studying these configurations, you'll get a better understanding of how the various hardware components I've already described might be used together in an actual computer system.

## A medium-sized configuration

Figure 1-10 represents a medium-sized computer system built around a 4381 processor. Before I describe the individual components of this system, I want to be sure you realize that the term "medium-sized" is relative. When compared with a microcomputer system, a minicomputer system, or even a 9370 mainframe system, this configuration is large. But when compared with the largest of mainframe configurations, the system in figure 1-10 seems small.

For direct access storage, the configuration in figure 1-10 uses three strings of 3350s, each containing eight drives. Since each of these twenty-four 3350s has a capacity of 317M, the total DASD capacity of this system is about 7.6 billion bytes.

The 3350s are fixed-media DASDs; their disk packs cannot be removed. To provide a way to create backup copies of data on the 3350s, tape drives are used. The configuration in figure 1-10 contains four 3420 tape drives which are used almost exclusively for that purpose.

The 3279 operator console lets system operators control the system. (The 3279 is a type of 3270 terminal that uses a color display.)

A local 3270 system, directly attached to the 4381 processor, provides 15 terminals and one printer. Its terminals are used by the programming and operations staffs, who are based in the same building that houses the computer. The three modems connect to three remote 3270 systems via telephone lines. The terminals attached to the remote systems, which aren't shown in figure 1-10, are used by data-entry clerks and other end users.

## A small configuration

Figure 1-11 presents a second system configuration. As you can see, this one is smaller than the example in figure 1-10. I'm presenting it after the medium-sized configuration in figure 1-10 because I want to discuss it in more detail.

The basic components in the smaller system configuration are the same as the ones in the larger configuration. However, there are fewer of them. The system is built around a 4331 processor, which dates from the late 1970s. The processor is a small one; it's configured with just one megabyte of real storage.

Secondary storage on this system is provided by five 3310 fixed-block architecture DASDs. Because the capacity of each 3310 unit is 65 megabytes, the total secondary storage available on this system is just 325 megabytes.

The operator interacts with the system through the 3278-2A console. Commands to manage the 8809 magnetic tape drive and the 3262 system printer (a medium-speed impact printer) are entered through the console.

The terminal system in this configuration is also small. Because it's a local system, neither telecommunication lines nor modems are required. The three 3178 display stations and the one 3287 terminal printer are all attached by coaxial cable to a special adapter that's part of the processor.

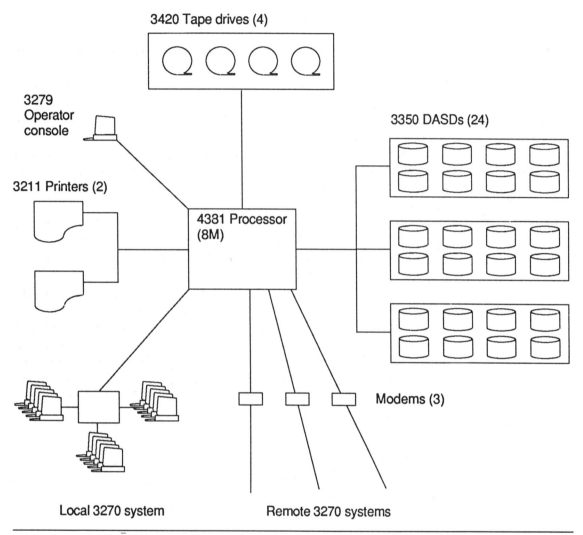

3420 Tape drives (4)

3279
Operator
console

3350 DASDs (24)

3211 Printers (2)

4381 Processor
(8M)

Modems (3)

Local 3270 system         Remote 3270 systems

**Figure 1-10**    A medium-sized mainframe configuration

There are two technical details I want you to notice in figure 1-11. The first is that a special name (like DOSRES, SYSWK1, and VMSRES) is associated with each of the disk drives. The names are called *volume serial numbers*, or just *volsers*. They make it easy for system users to refer to the particular disk drives that contain data they need.

The other detail I want you to notice is that each I/O device in the configuration is identified by a unique three-character code. For example, the system console is identified by the code 01F. These codes are called *device addresses*, or just *addresses*. A device address is actually a combination of three hexadecimal values that identify the channel, control unit, and physical device for each machine.

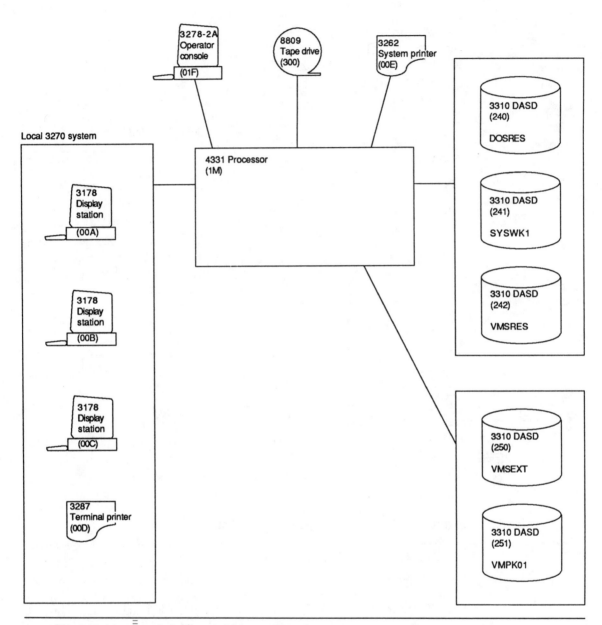

**Figure 1-11**      A small mainframe configuration

For example, all five DASDs in figure 1-11 have addresses that begin with the number 2. That means they're all attached to the processor through channel 2. The second character of a device address identifies the control unit. So the first three DASDs in the configuration (addresses 240, 241, and 242) are all attached through the same control unit, while the other two (addresses 250 and 251) are attached through another. The last character in a device address is used to identify uniquely each individual device attached to a particular control unit.

Unless you're a systems programmer, you probably don't need to know the addresses of *all* the I/O devices on your system. However, for some functions, it is necessary to know some device addresses. You can find out the device addresses you need to know from your supervisor or a co-worker.

## IBM mainframe operating systems

Now that you're familiar with the hardware components that make up an IBM mainframe system, I'll introduce you to the *system software* that manages its resources. The heart of system software is the *operating system*, a set of programs that directly controls the operation of the computer. As you can imagine, the operating system for a mainframe computer system is extremely complicated. For its System/370 processors and their related I/O devices, IBM currently supports three families of operating systems: OS, DOS, and VM.

### The batch operating systems

The first two families of IBM mainframe operating systems, OS and DOS, date from the first System/360 processors and have a batch orientation. With *batch processing*, work is collected in a *batch*, which is then submitted to the computer system in a unit of work called a *job*. On the first System/360 and System/370 models, batch input was provided through a card reader. As a result, even though the heyday of card processing ended years ago, both OS and DOS have a strong card orientation in their design and operation. That's true even in spite of the fact that they have been enhanced and supplemented over the years so that they now support interactive terminal users.

Although this book is about VM, not OS or DOS, you should still understand these batch operating systems. That's because many shops use one or the other along with VM. Because the batch operating systems have such a long history on IBM mainframes, many shops have large investments in OS or DOS software that they simply cannot abandon. Therefore, much of the program development work that's done under VM is for one of the older batch operating systems. (If you'd like to know more about DOS or OS than what follows, I recommend my book, *DOS/VSE JCL*, or *MVS JCL* by Doug Lowe; both are available from Mike Murach and Associates, Inc.)

***VSE and the DOS family***     The first disk-based operating system for the System/360 was called, logically, *Disk Operating System*, or just *DOS*. DOS has been enhanced repeatedly since the 1960s. During its evolution, its name has been DOS, DOS/VS, DOS/VSE, VSE/AF, and, today, VSE/SP. You don't need to know what all these acronyms stand for, but when you see them, you should recognize that they're all DOS-family operating systems. Today, you're as likely to see *VSE* used as the name of the current release as you are to see DOS.

In general, VSE is used on small to medium-sized mainframe systems. Although VSE is a powerful operating system, it's generally not appropriate for large mainframe systems. On larger configurations, the OS family of operating systems is more likely to be used.

*MVS and the OS family*        *OS*, which stands for *Operating System*, was introduced after DOS, but still very early in the life of the System/360-370 family of processors. Originally, OS was intended to replace DOS. Instead, the two operating systems developed along parallel yet separate paths. As a result, today OS- and DOS-family operating systems are incompatible with one another.

Like DOS, OS has had several names during its development: OS, OS/MFT, OS/MVT, OS/VS1, OS/VS2, MVS, MVS/SP, and MVS/XA; the last two are the versions that are current today. As a result, you'll frequently see current versions of OS called simply *MVS*.

The larger an IBM mainframe system is, the more likely it is to use MVS instead of VSE. However, that's just a general rule. Some small mainframe systems use MVS, while some large systems run under VSE.

## VM/SP

The third family of IBM mainframe operating systems is *VM*; its most recent members are the various releases of *VM/SP*, which stands for *Virtual Machine/System Product*. VM uses a different approach to managing computer system hardware than do DOS and OS. Basically, it simulates multiple computer systems on a single hardware configuration. Each of the simulated systems is called a *virtual machine*. Under VM, many virtual machines are likely to be active at the same time, all running on the same real system.

Each virtual machine, like a real machine, needs an operating system. One option is to use an OS- or a DOS-family operating system. When that's the case, jobs and programs developed for one of the batch operating systems can be used just as if DOS or OS "owned" a real system. When an OS or DOS operating system is used in a virtual machine, it's called a *guest operating system*.

Another option is to use a special operating system supplied with VM called the *Conversational Monitor System*, or just *CMS*. CMS is a single-user, interactive operating system. In other words, a CMS user has complete control over her virtual machine's resources; she communicates with the virtual machine directly through her terminal. When a CMS user signs on to use VM, the first thing that happens is that a virtual machine is dynamically created for her. Then, the CMS operating system is typically loaded into her virtual machine automatically. Once CMS is running, the user can interact with it to perform a variety of data processing functions.

In addition, VM provides facilities that let users communicate with other virtual machines. For example, suppose a CMS user wants to use the facilities of another virtual machine that's running the VSE operating system. The CMS user can create and store a VSE job using CMS facilities, then have VM transfer the job to the VSE virtual machine, where it's scheduled and executed.

## Discussion

Quite frankly, this chapter has oversimplified the characteristics of the hardware and software of a typical IBM mainframe system configuration. Still, the information I presented here is all you need to know to begin learning how to use VM effectively. So, as long as you understand the basic ideas this chapter presents, you're ready to move on to the next chapter where you'll learn about the basics of VM.

### Terminology

mainframe computer system
mainframe
processor
input/output device
I/O device
System/360-370 family
central processing unit
CPU
main storage
main memory
multiprocessor system
multiprocessing
channel
channel command
control unit
M
megabyte
unit record device
impact printer
non-impact printer
tape drive
magnetic tape drive
magnetic tape
reel
cartridge
density

bytes per inch
bpi
record
inter-record gap
IRG
blocking
block
IBG
inter-block gap
blocking factor
direct access storage device
DASD
disk drive
disk pack
volume
track
access mechanism
actuator
cylinder
fixed-head storage
count-key-data
CKD
fixed-block architecture
FBA
count area
key area

string controller
string
storage control
data communications devices
data communications network
communications network
network
local terminal
remote terminal
communications controller
modem
communications line
3270 Information Display System
local-print feature
volume serial number
volser
device address
address

system software
operating system
batch processing
batch
job
Disk Operating System
DOS
VSE
OS
Operating System
MVS
VM
VM/SP
Virtual Machine/System Product
virtual machine
guest operating system
Conversational Monitor System
CMS

## Objectives

1. List the three basic components of a System/360-370 processor.

2. List the four main groups of input/output devices.

3. Describe how blocking can improve I/O efficiency for tape and DASD data.

4. Describe the differences in how data is stored on CKD and FBA DASDs.

5. Describe how controllers are used to connect DASD units to processor channels.

6. List the elements of a data communications network.

7. Differentiate between IBM's batch operating systems for mainframe computers and VM.

Chapter 2

# An introduction to VM environments and commands

This chapter begins to lay the foundation for your VM training. It introduces you to VM by describing its Control Program and the commands you can enter to request the Control Program's services. This is vital information that you'll use throughout the rest of your VM training and afterward. As a result, I encourage you to take the time you need to master this material.

## The CMS and CP environments

The central component of VM, the *Control Program*, or just *CP*, manages the resources of the real system and makes them available to many users. In that sense, VM is much like other computer operating systems. However, VM differs in the way it makes the system's resources available to users.

For each user, CP provides a *virtual machine*, a simulation of a real computer system. A virtual machine has virtual components that correspond to the real devices on the real system. All virtual machines are configured with a processor, a console, DASDs, and unit record devices (printers and card devices). In the next chapter, I'll describe how VM provides for all these devices, and I'll show you how they're used.

A single virtual machine seems to its user to be a separate, independent, and complete computer system. As a result, a user can treat his virtual machine as if he owned it, even though the real system is shared by many users. The user can activate and deactivate his virtual machine, change its configuration, and run programs in it as he pleases without worrying about how those actions might affect other users on the system.

**23**

In addition to providing each user with a virtual machine, CP also provides a set of facilities that let virtual machines communicate with each other and share real devices. The result is that under VM the system is more available to users and easier for them to use than with IBM's other mainframe operating systems.

To use VM, you must be aware that two levels of operating system software, each with its own set of commands, are involved. At the higher level, the VM Control Program manages the real system and supports all the active virtual machines on the system. At the lower level, operating systems run in individual virtual machines to manage their resources to provide support for end-user applications.

To understand these two operating system environments, consider figure 2-1. It represents a real computer system running under VM's Control Program. Subordinate to the Control Program in this example are three virtual machines. CMS (the single-user, interactive operating system for virtual machines that's supplied as a part of VM) is being used as the operating system in the first two virtual machines, while the third doesn't have an operating system.

### The CMS environment

Because the first two virtual machines in figure 2-1 are running under the control of CMS, they're said to be in the *CMS environment*. This is the typical situation for a VM user; most of your VM use will be through CMS. As you'll learn in chapter 4 and throughout this book, VM provides many functions you can invoke in your virtual machine with *CMS commands*. You can only issue CMS commands from the CMS environment (that is, when CMS is loaded into your virtual machine). In the first virtual machine in figure 2-1, the terminal user has issued a CMS command, which is processed by CMS running in the virtual machine.

However, don't forget that above CMS (or, for that matter, above a guest operating system like DOS or OS), the VM Control Program is running to support your virtual machine and relate it to the real system. So in addition to requesting CMS services with CMS commands in your virtual machine, you can also request CP services with VM's *CP commands*. When you issue CP commands from the CMS environment, they're passed through CMS to the Control Program. That's what the second virtual machine in figure 2-1 illustrates.

### The CP environment

Because the Control Program is always active on a functioning VM system, you can issue CP commands whether or not you've loaded an operating system into your virtual machine. If your virtual machine is not running under the control of its own operating system, it's said to be in the *CP environment*; that's the case with the third virtual machine in figure 2-1.

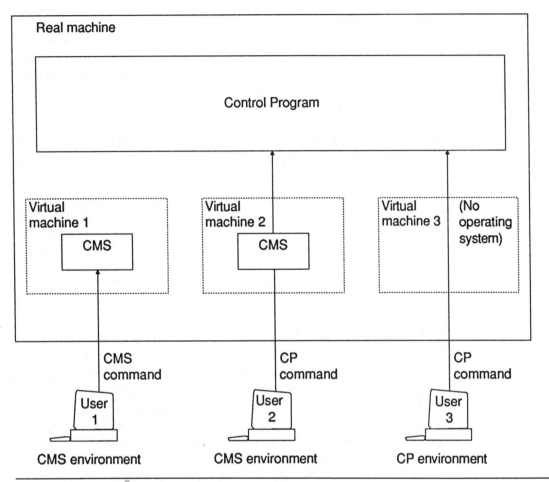

**Figure 2-1**          Virtual machines in the CMS and CP environments

Frankly, your virtual machine is nearly useless in the CP environment; to do any productive work, you must load an operating system in it. However, there are some basic functions that you can perform in the CP environment. For example, requesting CP to load an operating system in your virtual machine is an essential function that can be performed in the CP environment. As a general rule, CP commands, whether they're issued from the CMS or the CP environment, affect the configuration of your virtual machine or its relationship to the real hardware on the system.

As you read on, don't forget the two operating system levels that are in effect as you use VM. In this chapter and the next, I'll focus on basic functions that are provided by CP. Specifically, you'll learn how to access the system and activate your virtual machine in this chapter, and you'll see how your virtual machine is configured and supported by CP in chapter 3. Then, in chapter 4, you'll learn some of the functions provided by CMS.

## Basic CP commands

In this section, I'll describe four basic CP commands you can use. You use two of them, LOGON and LOGOFF, to control your access to the VM system. The other two, MESSAGE and QUERY, you won't use as often, but they provide functions you need to understand.

### How to use the LOGON and LOGOFF commands to control your access to the VM system

This section describes the steps you go through to use the VM system. For the most part, it describes how to issue the LOGON command to identify yourself to VM. In addition, it shows you how to end a terminal session with the LOGOFF command. However, before you can even issue the LOGON command to start a terminal session, you have to be sure your terminal is properly set up.

*Preparing your terminal to start a session*     Although VM supports a variety of real terminal types, those in the 3270 Information Display System family (such as 3278, 3279, 3178, 3179, 3193, and 3194 models) are by far the most commonly used. As a result, the description I provide here will focus on 3270-type terminals. All operate in essentially the same way.

The procedure you have to follow to access VM on your terminal depends on a variety of factors, such as whether your terminal is local or remote, whether it's attached via a leased or dial-up line, and whether VTAM is in use as your system's telecommunications access method. (VTAM is an IBM mainframe system software product that's widely used to manage TC networks.) In some instances, all you have to do is turn your terminal on to be able to use it.

However, if you're a remote terminal user whose terminal system is attached to the host via dial-up lines, you may have to establish the telecommunications connection by dialing the host system. (If your terminal subsystem is attached to the host via a leased line, this step isn't required.) And if your shop uses VTAM to manage telecommunications, you may have to go through a preliminary logon to be able to access VM. In any case, you should find out what you have to do to prepare your terminal for a session from your supervisor.

After your 3270-type terminal has been prepared for a session, you'll see the VM logo on your screen. Part 1 of figure 2-2 shows what it might look like. The exact format of the logo varies from one release of VM to another and also depends on the way your terminal is attached to the host. In any event, though, it's easy to recognize. To start a logon from this screen, you press either the enter key or the clear key, as the prompt at the top of the screen indicates; that signals to the Control Program that you're ready to start a session. (On some networks, you may press only the enter key from the logo screen; that depends on the communications software that's used to manage the network.)

*The LOGON command starts your VM terminal session*    After you indicate to VM that you want to start a session, the VM Control Program removes the logo from your terminal screen and prompts you to enter one of four commands (LOGON, DIAL, MSG, or LOGOFF), as part 2 of figure 2-2 shows. For now, I want to discuss two of these commands: LOGON and LOGOFF. The command you're almost certain to want to enter from this screen is LOGON. The LOGOFF command is provided as an option on the screen in part 2 of figure 2-2 to let you cancel the logon process if you need to.

The *cursor*, the mark on the screen that indicates where the next character you enter will appear, is near the bottom left corner of the screen in part 2 of figure 2-2. (It's shown here as an underline.) This lower lefthand screen position is where you'll key in most VM commands, including the LOGON command.

In part 3 of figure 2-2, I've keyed in the command

```
LOGON STEVE ECKOLS NOIPL
```

to start my terminal session. When I press the enter key, CP processes the LOGON command and responds with the logon time and date message, as you can see in part 4 of the figure.

The LOGON command, like all other VM commands, has a specific *syntax*, the way the command's components have to be put together for it to work properly. Throughout this book, you'll see figures that illustrate the syntax of a variety of VM commands. Figure 2-3 shows the syntax for LOGON.

In syntax figures like the one for LOGON, I use a notational convention that you'll see in many manuals. Entries in capital letters are literals or keywords; you key them in just as they appear in the syntax, although sometimes they can be abbreviated. Entries in lowercase letters are variables. For them, you key in the particular value that's relevant to the operation you want to perform. Usually, some length and format restrictions apply to the values you can supply for command variables.

For example, in the LOGON command I just showed you, I keyed in the command name just as it appears in the syntax figure. The first variable value I supplied on the command was my *user identification*, called *user-id* for short. Notice that for this variable item, I keyed in not the characters "user-id," which appear in the command syntax, but rather the actual value for my user identification (STEVE).

Another term you should be familiar with is *operand*. An operand is a value you supply on a command in addition to the command name itself. So in this LOGON command, the first operand value is STEVE.

Whenever you issue the LOGON command, you must supply your user-id. VM uses it to verify that you're authorized to use the system. In addition, VM uses the user-id to retrieve the configuration for your virtual machine. (In other words, each virtual machine is tied to a specific user-id.) User-ids can be up to eight characters long. Although they're assigned by the system administrator, you might be able to request a particular one.

The VM logo display shows the terminal has been prepared for a VM session

```
VM/370 ONLINE--PRESS ENTER OR CLEAR KEY TO BEGIN SESSION


                        VV        VV    MM          MM
                        VV        VV    MMM        MMM
                        VV        VV    MMMM      MMMM
                        VV        VV    MM MM    MM MM
         3333333333     777777777777MMMM  00000000
         333333333333   77777777777  MM  00000000000
         33      VV33   77VV    77      00MM        00
                 V33    VV     77M      00MM        00
                 33     VV     77MM     00MM        00
              3333VV  VV      77 MM     00MM        00
              3333 VVVV       77 MM     00MM        00
                33 VV         77 MM     00MM        00
                33            77        00          00
         33      33           77        00          00
         333333333333         77         0000000000
           3333333333         77          00000000

  -
                                                   RUNNING
  Ia                                          □─□04
```

**Figure 2-2**    Logging on to a VM system (part 1 of 4)

When you press the enter or clear key, CP prompts you to enter one of four commands

```
ENTER ONE OF THE FOLLOWING COMMANDS:

    LOGON USERID          (EXAMPLE:  LOGON VMUSER1)
    DIAL USERID           (EXAMPLE:  DIAL VMUSER2)
    MSG USERID MESSAGE    (EXAMPLE:  MSG VMUSER2 GOOD MORNING)
    LOGOFF












  -
                                                   CP READ
  Ia                                          □─□04
```

**Figure 2-2**    Logging on to a VM system (part 2 of 4)

The LOGON command lets you start a terminal session

```
ENTER ONE OF THE FOLLOWING COMMANDS:

    LOGON USERID           (EXAMPLE:  LOGON VMUSER1)
    DIAL USERID            (EXAMPLE:  DIAL VMUSER2)
    MSG USERID MESSAGE     (EXAMPLE:  MSG VMUSER2 GOOD MORNING)
    LOGOFF








LOGON STEVE ECKOLS NOIPL_
                                                          CP READ
  Iª                                                      ▢—▢04
```

**Figure 2-2**   Logging on to a VM system (part 3 of 4)

When you press the enter key, CP processes the LOGON command and displays the logon time and date

```
ENTER ONE OF THE FOLLOWING COMMANDS:

    LOGON USERID           (EXAMPLE:  LOGON VMUSER1)
    DIAL USERID            (EXAMPLE:  DIAL VMUSER2)
    MSG USERID MESSAGE     (EXAMPLE:  MSG VMUSER2 GOOD MORNING)
    LOGOFF

LOGON STEVE ECKOLS NOIPL
LOGON AT 09:36:20 PDT TUESDAY 04/07/87




-
                                                          CP READ
  Iª                                                      ▢—▢04
```

**Figure 2-2**   Logging on to a VM system (part 4 of 4)

**The LOGON command**

```
LOGON user-id [password [NOIPL]]
```

**Explanation**

| | |
|---|---|
| user-id | The one- to eight-character user identification assigned to you by your system administrator. Always required. |
| password | The one- to eight-character password assigned to you by the system administrator. If you don't enter it on the LOGON command, VM prompts you for it. |
| NOIPL | Specifies that automatic IPL of an operating system in your virtual machine should not be performed. May be abbreviated as N. |

---

**Figure 2-3**     The LOGON command

---

The second item I keyed in for my LOGON command, ECKOLS, is my *password*. You have to supply it too before VM will let you access the system. Like the user-id, a password can be up to eight characters long and is also assigned by the system administrator. Because the purpose of a password is to keep unauthorized users off the system, you should keep your password (and for that matter, your user-id) a secret.

Although I included my password on the LOGON command line, you don't have to supply it that way. In fact, a more typical way to logon is to enter just your user-id on the LOGON command. For example, if I entered the command

```
LOGON STEVE
```

VM would prompt me for my password with this message:

```
ENTER PASSWORD   (IT WILL NOT APPEAR WHEN TYPED):
```

Then, I'd key in my password in the command entry area at the bottom of the screen. As the message indicates, the characters you key in for your password are not displayed on the screen as you enter them. This affords an extra measure of security by making it harder for others to learn your password. When an operand is optional, it appears in a command's syntax between square brackets. That's the case with the password operand in figure 2-3.

The third value I supplied on my original LOGON command, NOIPL, specifies that no operating system should be loaded into my virtual machine automatically as a part of my logon process. As a general rule, CMS is automatically loaded when a user accesses the system. However, in this chapter I want to show you how to issue CP commands in the CP environment, so I don't want to activate CMS. When you logon, you probably will want to load CMS, so you won't include NOIPL.

**The LOGOFF command**

```
LOGOFF [HOLD]
```

**Explanation**

HOLD    Specifies that your dial-up line should remain connected in anticipation of a subsequent logon. May be abbreviated as H.

Figure 2-4    The LOGOFF command

As the brackets that surround it in figure 2-3 indicate, the NOIPL operand is optional. Notice in figure 2-3 that the NOIPL operand is contained within the brackets that surround the password operand. That means that to be able to use NOIPL, you must supply a password on the command. That's because VM always interprets the second operand of a LOGON command as a password; if you code NOIPL right after your user-id, VM considers it to be your password. Operands like LOGON's password and NOIPL are called *positional operands* because they must appear in specific positions, or VM won't interpret them correctly.

*The LOGON command activates a virtual machine for you*     When you logon to a VM system, the Control Program activates your virtual machine. As I mentioned at the start of this chapter, a virtual machine has components that correspond to the real devices on the real system. For now, I want you to realize that all users who access VM the way I just described have their own, independent virtual machines. That means that at any one time a system might have dozens or even hundreds of active virtual machines.

*The LOGOFF command deactivates your virtual machine and ends your VM terminal session*     To end a VM session, all you do is key in the command

```
LOGOFF
```

Then, VM deactivates your virtual machine and releases the system resources it required. Issuing the LOGOFF command in a virtual machine is equivalent to powering down the components of a real machine.

The syntax of the LOGOFF command, illustrated in figure 2-4, is simpler than that of the LOGON command. Only one operand is available, and it's optional. If you access VM through a switched (dial-up) line, the line is normally disconnected when you logoff. Then, you must redial the host system to use the terminal again. However, if you want to maintain the connection (perhaps because another user is going to logon at the terminal immediately), you can specify the HOLD operand on the LOGOFF command.

## Other basic CP commands

LOGON and LOGOFF are just two of more than 80 CP commands VM provides. However, you don't need to know most of them. In fact, most of them are for system operators who are responsible for managing the hardware of the real system and probably aren't available to you at all. And of the CP commands which are available to all terminal users, only a few are genuinely useful. For now, I want to describe just two of them: MESSAGE and QUERY.

*The MESSAGE command*        You can use the MESSAGE command (which you can abbreviate as MSG or just M) to send a message to a specified virtual machine. Figure 2-5 gives the syntax of the MESSAGE command. Its basic form is

```
MESSAGE user-id text
```

where *user-id* is the user identification associated with the virtual machine to which you want to send the message, and *text* is the message text itself.

For example, I could enter

```
MSG TAPEOPR IS A TAPE UNIT AVAILABLE?
```

to send the text "IS A TAPE UNIT AVAILABLE?" to the virtual machine associated with the user-id TAPEOPR. At that user's terminal, this is what the message looks like:

```
MSG FROM STEVE   : IS A TAPE UNIT AVAILABLE?
```

Notice that VM includes the identification of the user who sent the message along with the text itself.

Figure 2-5 shows two other ways you can specify the destination of the message text. (They're enclosed between braces; when braces appear in a command's syntax, they mean you should select one of the items they contain.) If you enter OPERATOR (or just OP) as the user-id, your message is routed to the main system operator, regardless of the actual user-id associated with his virtual machine.

The other way you can specify a message's destination is to code an asterisk (*) in place of the user-id. That causes the message text to be routed back to your terminal. Frankly, this particular form of the MESSAGE command isn't very useful. In fact, the only reason I'm presenting it now is to illustrate a feature common to many CP commands. In general, an asterisk in a CP command refers to the user of the virtual machine that entered the command.

The only time during typical operations that you might want to send a message to yourself is when a VM terminal has been left unattended, and you want to know what user-id is associated with it. Because the output of the command indicates the user-id of the sender, routing a message to the sending terminal displays the user-id of the currently active virtual machine. This is an awkward way

**The MESSAGE command**

MESSAGE $\begin{Bmatrix} \text{user-id} \\ \text{OPERATOR} \\ * \end{Bmatrix}$ text

**Explanation**

MESSAGE          The command name may be abbreviated as MSG or M.

user-id           The user-id associated with the virtual machine to which the message is to be sent.

OPERATOR        Specifies that the message text is to be sent to the system operator. May be abbreviated as OP.

*                Specifies that the message is to be sent back to the originating terminal; can be useful to determine the user-id associated with a particular terminal.

text             The text of the message to be sent.

---

Figure 2-5          The MESSAGE command

---

to get a simple piece of information. Another way, one that's easier and more sensible, is to use the CP QUERY command.

*The QUERY command*          The QUERY command (which you can abbreviate as Q) lets you ask VM for a variety of status information regarding your virtual machine and the real system. Because the command can provide lots of information, it's complicated; its description in the VM manual runs for 26 pages, and that's just for the subset of the command's functions that is available to all users. In this chapter, I'll present just a few of the ways you can use the QUERY command. In later chapters, I'll show you other options of the command.

Figure 2-6 presents the operands of the QUERY command this chapter covers. The first, the USERID operand, requests the Control Program to display the user-id for the virtual machine that's running at the terminal from which the command is entered. For example, if I enter

    QUERY USERID

VM's reply is simply

    STEVE

I think you'll agree that this is a more sensible way to find out what user-id is associated with an unattended terminal than entering a MESSAGE command that's routed back to yourself.

**The QUERY command**

```
         ⎛ USERID                                      ⎞
         ⎜                                             ⎟
         ⎜ TIME                                        ⎟
         ⎜        ⎡ ⎛ CHANNELS          ⎞ ⎤ ⎟
QUERY    ⎨        ⎢ ⎜ GRAF              ⎟ ⎥ ⎬
         ⎜        ⎢ ⎜ CONSOLE           ⎟ ⎥ ⎟
         ⎜ VIRTUAL⎢ ⎨ DASD              ⎬ ⎥ ⎟
         ⎜        ⎢ ⎜ TAPES             ⎟ ⎥ ⎟
         ⎜        ⎢ ⎜ UR                ⎟ ⎥ ⎟
         ⎜        ⎢ ⎜ STORAGE           ⎟ ⎥ ⎟
         ⎝        ⎣ ⎝ address[-address] ⎠ ⎦ ⎠
```

**Explanation**

| | |
|---|---|
| QUERY | The command name may be abbreviated as Q. |
| USERID | Specifies that the user-id associated with the currently active virtual machine should be displayed. |
| TIME | Specifies that the current date and time and time counts for the current terminal session should be displayed. May be abbreviated as T. |
| VIRTUAL | Specifies that elements of the virtual machine's configuration should be displayed. May be abbreviated as V. |
| CHANNELS | Specifies that the channels of the virtual machine's configuration should be displayed. May be abbreviated as CHAN. |
| GRAF | Specifies that the graphic devices (terminals) that are part of the virtual machine's configuration should be displayed. May be abbreviated as GR. |
| CONSOLE | Specifies that the characteristics of the virtual machine's console should be displayed. May be abbreviated as CON. |
| DASD | Specifies that the status and location of each of the virtual machine's minidisks should be displayed. May be abbreviated as DA. |
| TAPES | Specifies that tape drives that are part of the virtual machine's configuration should be displayed. May be abbreviated as TA. |
| UR | Specifies that the characteristics of the virtual machine's unit record devices should be displayed. |
| STORAGE | Specifies that the amount of storage available on the virtual machine should be displayed. May be abbreviated as STOR. |
| address | Specifies a hexadecimal virtual address whose associated device characteristics should be displayed. You may specify a single address or a range of addresses in the format *address-address*. |

Figure 2-6    Basic operands of the CP QUERY command

Another QUERY command function you may want to use is TIME. If you enter

```
QUERY TIME
```

or the abbreviated form

```
Q  T
```

VM displays a reply like

```
TIME IS 09:54:13 PDT FRIDAY 05/08/87
CONNECT= 00:00:18 VIRTCPU= 000:01.35 TOTCPU= 000:08.78
```

Here, the first line contains the current time and date.

The second line contains time statistics for the current terminal session. The first item is how long you've been logged on in hours, minutes, and seconds. In this example, I've been logged on for just 18 seconds. Obviously, I entered the Q T command right after I completed my logon process. The second item, VIRTCPU, is the amount of virtual processor time my virtual machine has used in minutes, seconds, and hundredths of seconds. And the third item, TOTCPU, is the total amount of processor time I've used (both for the virtual machine and for CP overhead needed to operate the virtual machine), also in minutes, seconds, and hundredths of seconds.

The third QUERY command function you can invoke with the operands in figure 2-6 lets you display the configuration of your virtual machine. If you enter

```
QUERY VIRTUAL
```

or just

```
Q  V
```

VM displays the complete configuration of your virtual machine. The other values you can specify on the command let you request information about specific elements of your virtual machine's configuration. I'll illustrate the output some of these values provide as I describe the components of a virtual machine in the next chapter.

## Discussion

With all of the talk about virtual machines in this chapter, you're probably wondering just what they are. Frankly, the virtual machine concept is one of the most confusing concepts for new VM users. So in the next chapter, you'll learn how virtual machines are defined, what their configurations can be, and how they relate to the devices of the real computer system.

## Terminology

Control Program
CP
virtual machine
CMS environment
CMS command
CP command
CP environment
cursor
syntax
user identification
user-id
operand
password
positional operand

## Objectives

1. Distinguish between the CP and CMS environments.
2. Use the LOGON command to access the VM system through a 3270 terminal.
3. Use the LOGOFF command to end a VM terminal session.
4. Use the MESSAGE command to send a message to another terminal user or to the system operator.
5. Use the QUERY command to get the user-id associated with a terminal, the current time, and the amount of time used by both the virtual and real processors.

# Chapter 3

## An introduction to virtual machines

This chapter presents the details you need to know about virtual machines to use your VM system effectively. As a result, you should be prepared to spend whatever time you need to get a good grasp of the information presented here.

As I've said before, a virtual machine has components that correspond to the real devices on the real system. All virtual machines are configured with a virtual processor that has a *virtual address space* of between 512K and 16M of storage (one *K*, or *kilobyte*, is 1024 bytes of storage) and a *virtual console* through which the user communicates with the virtual machine. In addition, virtual machines have *virtual unit record devices* (at least one *virtual card reader*, one *virtual card punch*, and one *virtual printer*) and *virtual DASDs*. In this chapter, you'll learn how CP provides for all these components and how they're used.

### How the configuration of a virtual machine is defined

The configuration of your virtual machine is defined in a system file called the *VM system directory*. When the system administrator authorizes you to use the system, she codes several control statements that specify, among other things, your user-id and password and the components of the virtual machine that will be activated when you logon.

Figure 3-1 shows the statements in my system's directory that identify me as a VM user and define my virtual machine's configuration. By the time you've finished this book, you'll understand all of the elements in these statements. In this chapter, I just want to point out a few details.

```
USER STEVE ECKOLS 1M 3M ABCDEG
 IPL CMS
 CONSOLE 009 3215
 SPOOL 00C 2540 READER *
 SPOOL 00D 2540 PUNCH A
 SPOOL 00E 1403 A
 LINK MAINT 190 190 RR
 LINK MAINT 19D 19D RR
 LINK MAINT 19E 19E RR
 LINK DOSVSE 240 240 RR
 LINK DOSVSE 241 241 RR
 MDISK 191 FB-512 041218 003262 VMSRES MW ALL
 MDISK 192 FB-512 000016 001984 VMSEXT MW ALL
```

Figure 3-1    A sample VM directory entry

The USER statement, the first statement in the directory entry, supplies my user-id (STEVE) and my password (ECKOLS). In a sense, the user-id is the "key" to my directory entry. When a user logs on, VM uses the user-id he specifies to look up his directory entry. Then, VM verifies the password the user enters with the one coded in the directory entry. If they match, the rest of the information in the directory entry is used to create that user's virtual machine.

After the IPL statement, which I'll explain later in this chapter, the rest of the statements in my directory entry define the devices that will make up my virtual machine's configuration. Figure 3-2 shows them in relation to the components of one of the real system configurations I presented in chapter 1; the virtual machine, except for the virtual console, is shown on the left, and the real machine is shown on the right. Now, I'll describe each of the components of the virtual machine.

## Virtual address space

The next items after the password in the USER statement in figure 3-1 specify how much storage should be simulated for the processor of the virtual machine; this is the size of the machine's virtual address space. (You can call this virtual storage if you like, but that term is used in other ways that might be confusing to you.) Two values are coded. The first, 1M in figure 3-1, specifies the default address space size for the virtual machine. That means that my virtual machine is created to *appear* to have one megabyte of real storage. If you look to the processor in the virtual machine configuration in figure 3-2, you'll see that's what it has.

If you want to find out how much storage is provided on your virtual machine, you can use the QUERY command:

```
QUERY VIRTUAL STORAGE
```

or the abbreviated form

```
Q  V  STOR
```

When I enter this command,

```
STORAGE=01024K
```

is the reply the Control Program issues on my virtual machine (1024K is equal to one megabyte).

When a user logs on, a virtual machine is created with the default storage specification. If the user needs a larger virtual address space, he can issue a CP command (DEFINE) to request more storage, up to the maximum size specified in the user's directory entry. The maximum size is the second storage value in the USER statement. In figure 3-1, that's three megabytes (3M). The maximum virtual address space VM can provide for a single virtual machine is 16 megabytes.

### Virtual console

The third statement in my directory entry,

```
CONSOLE 009 3215
```

specifies that the virtual console of my virtual machine should be simulated as a model 3215 terminal. This is the typical device type that's specified, and it doesn't have much significance for you. All you really need to know is that the virtual console is the component of your virtual machine through which VM communicates with you.

The other value on the CONSOLE statement, 009, is the *virtual address* of the virtual machine's console. The virtual devices that make up a virtual machine are uniquely identified by virtual addresses. That's also true for real devices on a real system. Be aware, though, that there's not necessarily a correlation between a virtual address and a real address that are the same. For example, if you have a device at virtual address 009 on your virtual machine and there's a device with real address 009 on the real system, those addresses aren't the same at all, and they don't have to refer to the same type of device.

For some functions, you need to know both real and virtual addresses, so you should be aware of what's what. However, the virtual address of your virtual console is not one that you'll need to know. I'm describing it here just so you'll understand the specifications that appear in a directory entry.

You can issue the command

```
QUERY VIRTUAL CONSOLE
```

or the abbreviated form

```
Q  V  CONS
```

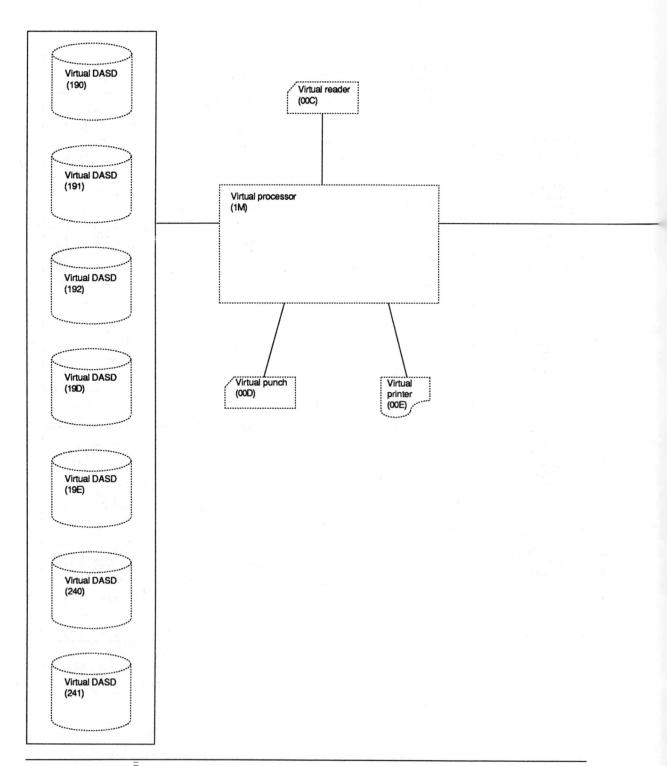

**Figure 3-2**    A virtual machine configuration

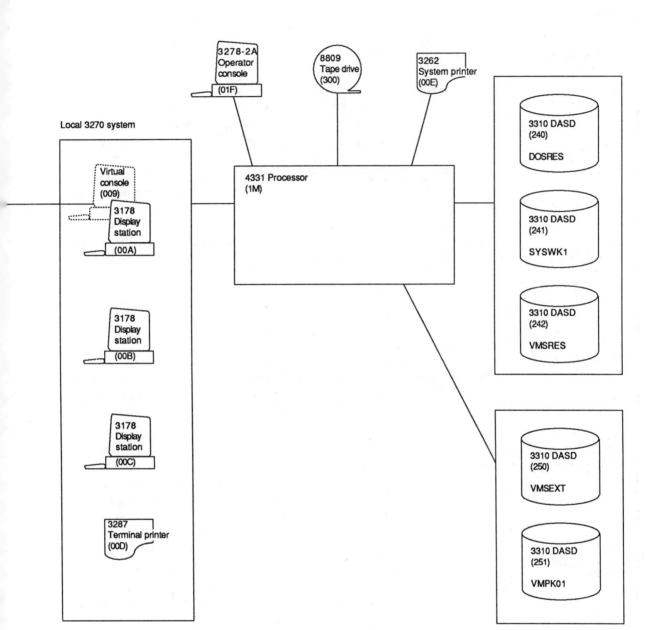

to get information about your virtual console. I'll show you what the output of this command looks like in a moment. For the most part, the information it provides is of limited use.

***How VM communicates with you***          The virtual console for most users is associated with the real terminal through which the user logged on. For me, my virtual console (virtual address 009) is associated with my real 3178 terminal (real address 00A). As a result, commands I enter at my 3178 are interpreted by my virtual machine as having come from the virtual console. And output from my virtual machine that's routed to virtual address 009 is displayed at my terminal. The Control Program maintains the relationship between my real terminal and my virtual machine's console.

***How to interpret terminal status messages***          If you look back to the four parts of figure 2-2, you'll see the message

    RUNNING

or

    CP READ

in the lower right corner of each screen image. These are called *terminal status messages*, and they always appear in that position of a 3270 display station's screen. Altogether, there are six different terminal status messages you might see; figure 3-3 lists them.

As you can see in figure 3-3, VM's terminal status messages fall into two groups: messages related to terminal input and messages related to terminal output. The RUNNING message indicates that you can enter a command. It's displayed when your virtual machine is idle or is busy running a program, but can still accept a command from you. When it does, the virtual machine buffers ("remembers") your entries until it has finished what it's doing.

The CP READ terminal status message means the Control Program is waiting to read input from your terminal. Usually, the CP READ message appears after you enter a CP command that interacts with you or after you signal to the Control Program that you want its attention. For example, when you initiate the logon procedure, you signal to CP that you want its attention by pressing the enter or clear key from the logo screen in part 1 of figure 2-2. Then, CP responds by providing you with the display in part 2 of the figure; the terminal status message is CP READ because CP expects you to make an entry.

The examples in figure 2-2 don't illustrate the other terminal status messages, although you'll see them often as you use VM. The message

    VM READ

indicates that a program running in a virtual machine, either an operating system

**Terminal status messages related to input**

| | |
|---|---|
| RUNNING | The Control Program or a program loaded in your virtual machine is running. You may enter a command, although VM may not process it immediately if your virtual machine is doing other work you requested earlier. |
| CP READ | The Control Program expects you to enter specific data at your terminal and is waiting to read your entry. |
| VM READ | A program running in your virtual machine (either your virtual machine's operating system or an application program) expects you to enter specific data at your terminal and is waiting to read your entry. |
| NOT ACCEPTED | VM wasn't able to handle the command or data you entered. Wait until the current operation finishes, then try again. |

**Terminal status messages related to output**

| | |
|---|---|
| MORE... | There is more output to be displayed at your terminal. Press PA2 to scroll to the next section, or press enter to disable automatic scrolling. |
| HOLDING | The output currently displayed is being held because you pressed the enter key when the terminal status was MORE. Press the PA2 key to return to normal output display mode. |

---

**Figure 3-3**    Terminal status messages

or an application program running under an operating system's control, is waiting to read a terminal entry you make. It corresponds to the CP READ condition, only at the virtual machine level.

The last of the four terminal status messages related to input is

    NOT ACCEPTED

It means VM wasn't ready to process the command or data you entered. For example, if several screens of output are being sent to your terminal and you try to enter a command from any of them except the last, you'll get the NOT ACCEPTED message. Usually, the reason for the message is clear. If it appears, complete the operation in progress, then try to enter the command again. If you still can't make it work, something may be wrong with the way your terminal environment is set up.

The other two terminal status messages,

    MORE...

and

    HOLDING

relate to output that's being sent back to your terminal. If output is displayed at your terminal and there isn't enough room for it on your screen, VM displays the MORE message. Then, to cause more of the output to display, you can press the PA2 key on your keyboard. If you don't press the PA2 key to scroll ahead immediately, VM will scroll automatically after one minute. Ten seconds before it scrolls automatically, the terminal beeps.

If you don't want the terminal output to be scrolled automatically, you can press the enter key instead of PA2. When you do, the terminal status changes to HOLDING, and the output that's currently displayed on the screen remains there until you press PA2. Then, the next screen of data is displayed.

To understand, consider figure 3-4. In part 1 of the figure, you can see that I've entered two commands (Q V STOR and Q V CONS), and VM's output has been displayed. The four lines of output produced in response to the Q V CONS command contain detailed information related to how data entered at the virtual machine console is recorded.

At the bottom of the screen in part 1, I've keyed in another variation of the QUERY command,

```
Q V UR
```

to display information on the unit record devices that are attached to my virtual machine. When I press the enter key, VM displays the screen in part 2 of the figure. Here, output from the command has filled the screen, but there is still more output to be displayed, as the terminal status message MORE indicates.

To keep the screen data in part 2 of the figure from being automatically scrolled after one minute, I press the enter key. As a result, the terminal status message changes to HOLDING, as you can see in part 3 of the figure.

After I finish reviewing the data displayed in part 3, I press PA2 to move ahead to see the rest of the command's output. Part 4 of the figure displays it. Because the remaining output doesn't use the entire screen, the terminal status here is CP READ again, indicating to me that I can enter another command. If I had tried to enter a command from the screen in part 2 or part 3 of the figure, VM would have displayed the NOT ACCEPTED message.

### Virtual unit record devices

Most of the interaction you do with your virtual machine will be through your terminal (that is, through your virtual machine's console). However, that's not the only way you can supply input to and receive output from your virtual machine. You can also use its virtual reader, punch, and printer.

If you examine the output of the Q V UR command in parts 3 and 4 of figure 3-4, you'll see that information for three virtual devices is provided: a reader (RDR) at virtual address 00C, a punch (PUN) at virtual address 00D, and a printer (PRT) at virtual address 00E. (Remember, these virtual addresses have nothing

The Q V UR command gives information about the unit record devices attached to the virtual machine

```
ENTER ONE OF THE FOLLOWING COMMANDS:

    LOGON USERID              (EXAMPLE:  LOGON VMUSER1)
    DIAL USERID               (EXAMPLE:  DIAL VMUSER2)
    MSG USERID MESSAGE        (EXAMPLE:  MSG VMUSER2 GOOD MORNING)
    LOGOFF

LOGON STEVE ECKOLS NOIPL
LOGON AT 09:36:20 PDT TUESDAY 04/07/87
Q V STOR
STORAGE = 01024K
Q V CONS
CONS 009 ON GRAF 00A    TERM STOP
     009 CL T  NOCONT NOHOLD COPY 001    READY FORM STANDARD
     009 FOR STEVE    DIST STEVE     FLASHC 000
     009 FLASH        CHAR       MDFY      0 FCB




Q V UR_
                                                       CP READ
I͏ᵃ                                                     ◻—◻04
```

Figure 3-4    Screen output showing the CP READ, MORE, and HOLDING terminal status messages (part 1 of 4)

The terminal status message MORE means there's more output to be displayed in response to the query

```
ENTER ONE OF THE FOLLOWING COMMANDS:

    LOGON USERID              (EXAMPLE:  LOGON VMUSER1)
    DIAL USERID               (EXAMPLE:  DIAL VMUSER2)
    MSG USERID MESSAGE        (EXAMPLE:  MSG VMUSER2 GOOD MORNING)
    LOGOFF

LOGON STEVE ECKOLS NOIPL
LOGON AT 09:36:20 PDT TUESDAY 04/07/87
Q V STOR
STORAGE = 01024K
Q V CONS
CONS 009 ON GRAF 00A    TERM STOP
     009 CL T  NOCONT NOHOLD COPY 001    READY FORM STANDARD
     009 FOR STEVE    DIST STEVE     FLASHC 000
     009 FLASH        CHAR       MDFY      0 FCB
Q V UR
RDR  00C CL *  NOCONT NOHOLD  EOF        READY
PUN  00D CL A  NOCONT NOHOLD COPY 001    READY FORM STANDARD
     00D FOR STEVE    DIST STEVE
PRT  00E CL A  NOCONT NOHOLD COPY 001    READY FORM STANDARD

—
                                                       MORE...
I͏ᵃ                                                     ◻—◻04
```

Figure 3-4    Screen output showing the CP READ, MORE, and HOLDING terminal status messages (part 2 of 4)

To keep the screen data from being scrolled after one minute, press the enter key, and the terminal status message HOLDING will appear

```
ENTER ONE OF THE FOLLOWING COMMANDS:

    LOGON USERID              (EXAMPLE:  LOGON VMUSER1)
    DIAL USERID               (EXAMPLE:  DIAL VMUSER2)
    MSG USERID MESSAGE        (EXAMPLE:  MSG VMUSER2 GOOD MORNING)
    LOGOFF

LOGON STEVE ECKOLS NOIPL
LOGON AT 09:36:20 PDT TUESDAY 04/07/87
Q V STOR
STORAGE = 01024K
Q V CONS
CONS 009 ON GRAF 00A     TERM STOP
     009 CL T  NOCONT NOHOLD COPY 001      READY FORM STANDARD
     009 FOR STEVE     DIST STEVE      FLASHC 000
     009 FLASH       CHAR       MDFY       0 FCB
Q V UR
RDR  00C CL *  NOCONT NOHOLD    EOF       READY
PUN  00D CL A  NOCONT NOHOLD COPY 001     READY FORM STANDARD
     00D FOR STEVE     DIST STEVE
PRT  00E CL A  NOCONT NOHOLD COPY 001     READY FORM STANDARD

-                                                            HOLDING
Iᵃ                                                      ▭–▭04
```

---

**Figure 3-4**   Screen output showing the CP READ, MORE, and HOLDING terminal status messages (part 3 of 4)

Press the PA2 key to display more of the output; when the last of the output has been displayed, the CP READ message appears, indicating that you can now enter another command

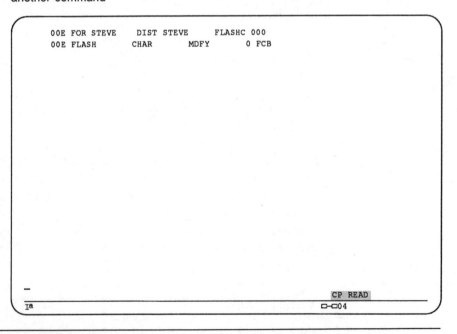

```
    00E FOR STEVE     DIST STEVE      FLASHC 000
    00E FLASH       CHAR       MDFY       0 FCB




















-                                                            CP READ
Iᵃ                                                      ▭–▭04
```

---

**Figure 3-4**   Screen output showing the CP READ, MORE, and HOLDING terminal status messages (part 4 of 4)

to do with the addresses for real unit record devices on the real system.) The rest of the information in the display is related to how data associated with those virtual devices is handled, and I'll describe it more fully in section 4 of this book.

For now, I want you to realize that it's not reasonable to provide you with exclusive use of real unit record devices. That's because the percentage of time you actually need to use real unit record devices is small. Dedicating them to you would mean others couldn't use them.

As a result, VM provides your virtual machine with facilities that simulate unit record devices. When you run programs that read card input or produce card or printer output, VM intercepts the I/O requests for those devices and satisfies them by reading data from or writing data to disk files instead. This process is called *spooling*, and those disk files are called *spool files*.

On a modern system, the chances are that the only real unit record device type you'll use is a printer. When you produce printer output from a virtual machine, VM stores that output temporarily on disk. Then, when an appropriate real printer is available, VM routes your output to it. CP manages that process independently of your virtual machine. If you need to produce a real deck of punched cards, the process is similar.

If you need to read a deck of real cards, they're first processed by the system card reader and stored by CP in a spool file that's associated with your virtual reader. Then, you can retrieve them from your virtual reader when you're ready to use them.

Keep in mind that real card devices are infrequently used on VM systems. In fact, many VM systems don't have card devices at all. However, that doesn't mean you won't use your virtual reader and punch.

For example, one way to send data from your virtual machine to another is to punch it on your virtual punch after you've issued the commands to insure that your punch output will be routed to the proper destination. Then, the destination virtual machine receives the data in its virtual reader. If your shop uses a guest operating system, you'll probably submit jobs to it by routing your virtual punch output to the virtual reader of the virtual machine on which the guest runs. CP takes care of transferring the data from one virtual machine to another, and it makes it appear to both virtual machines that they're working with cards. However, the entire data transfer is done through spool files VM maintains on disk.

The spool files VM uses are stored on DASD, but in areas that are reserved for the exclusive use of the Control Program. Spooling requests from all virtual machines are handled by VM using disk space in those areas. In addition, VM provides DASD storage for individual virtual machines in areas that are "owned" by them.

### Virtual DASDs

Each virtual machine configuration includes one or more virtual DASDs, also called *virtual disks*, that can be used to store data owned by that machine. For example, my virtual machine configuration includes two virtual DASDs that I use to store program source and object code, test data, text, and procedures I enter.

VM provides virtual DASDs by allocating *extents* (portions of the total storage available) on real DASDs to specific user-ids. For most users, these extents are less than the total capacity of the volume from which they're allocated. Because they're relatively small compared to the total capacity of a real volume, virtual DASDs are often called *minidisks*. A virtual machine views each minidisk as an individual DASD.

To illustrate, if you look at the directory entry that defines my virtual machine in figure 3-1, you'll see these two lines:

```
MDISK 191 FB-512 041218 003262 VMSRES MW ALL
MDISK 192 FB-512 000016 001984 VMSEXT MW ALL
```

These two MDISK statements define the two minidisks that my virtual machine owns; their virtual addresses are 191 and 192, and they're simulated as FBA DASDs (FB-512).

The first of these minidisks, the one with virtual address 191, is simulated on the real DASD with the volser VMSRES. The 3262 blocks of storage beginning at relative block 41218 on that volume are allocated to this minidisk. The second minidisk (virtual address 192) is simulated on the real DASD with the volser VMSEXT. It uses the 1984 blocks of real DASD storage that begin at relative block 16 on that unit. Don't worry for now about the last two values on each line (MW and ALL); I'll describe them later.

If you look back to figure 3-2, you'll see that the two real DASD units that contain my owned minidisks have the real addresses 242 (VMSRES) and 250 (VMSEXT). However, programs that run in my virtual machine need not be concerned with those real addresses. They view the minidisks as complete and separate FBA devices with 3262- and 1984-block capacities at addresses 191 and 192. The Control Program takes care of storing data that appears to be on the virtual DASDs on the real units; that's transparent to the virtual machine.

You should also notice in figure 3-2 that my virtual machine configuration includes not only the two minidisks it owns (virtual addresses 191 and 192), but five others as well (virtual addresses 190, 19D, 19E, 240, and 241). These are *shared minidisks*, virtual volumes that are owned by another virtual machine, but which I can access.

The LINK statements in my directory entry in figure 3-1 define these shared minidisks:

```
LINK MAINT 190 190 RR
LINK MAINT 19D 19D RR
LINK MAINT 19E 19E RR
LINK DOSVSE 240 240 RR
LINK DOSVSE 241 241 RR
```

It's easy to understand the LINK statement. For example, the first of these LINK statements says the minidisk defined for the MAINT user-id's virtual machine with virtual address 190 should be available to my virtual machine, also with the virtual address 190. The same is true for MAINT's 19D and 19E minidisks.

On my system, the MAINT user is the systems programmer who is responsible for maintaining the operating system files. (MAINT is the default user-id for this user; it may be different on your system.) The MAINT user's 190 minidisk contains all the files necessary to run CMS in a virtual machine. To avoid duplicating these files for all CMS users, it's more efficient for a single set to be shared; that's why my virtual machine is defined with link access to MAINT's 190 minidisk.

Similar access is provided for MAINT's 19D and 19E minidisks. The 19D minidisk contains help files that can be accessed for information during a terminal session. The 19E minidisk contains files for optional software products in use on the system, but which aren't an integral part of VM/SP.

These virtual addresses (190, 19D, and 19E) are the VM defaults specified for these minidisks. As a result, the chances are good that your virtual machine configuration contains specifications for linked minidisks that are similar to these.

The other two minidisks to which I have access (virtual addresses 240 and 241) are owned by the DOSVSE user. This is the user-id associated with a virtual machine that's used to run VSE as a guest operating system. I have access to them so I can use special CMS features which simulate DOS functions.

To find out what minidisks are part of your virtual machine's configuration, you can use still another variation of the QUERY command. If I enter the command

```
Q V DASD
```

VM responds by displaying

```
DASD 190 3310 VMSRES R/O   30000 BLK
DASD 191 3310 VMSRES R/W    3262 BLK
DASD 192 3310 VMSEXT R/W    1984 BLK
DASD 19D 3310 VMSRES R/O   20904 BLK
DASD 19E 3310 VMSEXT R/O    7210 BLK
DASD 240 3310 DOSRES R/O  126016 BLK
DASD 241 3310 SYSWK1 R/O   60000 BLK
```

Each of these lines identifies one minidisk. For example, the first line says my virtual DASD at address 190 is a 3310 unit on the real volume with the volume serial number VMSRES. I have read/only access (R/O, in contrast to R/W which means read/write access) to that minidisk, which has 30,000 blocks of storage. Note that three of the minidisks reside on a single real volume, VMSRES, two on another real volume, VMSEXT, and one each on the real volumes DOSRES and SYSWK1.

### Additional devices can be added to a virtual machine

A virtual machine isn't necessarily restricted to the configuration specified for it in the user's directory entry. It's possible to add other devices to a virtual machine when they're needed. For example, you'll learn later in this book how to add temporary minidisks to your virtual machine. That's a case of adding another virtual device to your virtual machine.

You can also add, or *attach*, real devices to your virtual machine. For example, if you need to use a tape drive (perhaps to make a backup copy of one of your minidisks), it can be attached to your virtual machine.

As a general rule, the system operator must attach real devices. That's because a central point of control is necessary to make sure single users don't monopolize system resources. At any rate, you can send a message to the system operator requesting a tape unit. When one becomes available, the operator attaches it to your machine. When a real device is attached to your machine, a message from CP is displayed at your terminal to tell you the virtual address you should use. For example,

    TAPE 181 ATTACHED

means the operator has attached a real tape unit to your virtual machine, and the virtual address you should use to access it is 181.

When you've finished using the device, you detach it from your virtual machine. Then, a message to that effect is displayed at the system console, and the operator is free to attach the device to another user's virtual machine. You'll learn how to perform these functions in sections 2 and 3 of this book.

## Loading an operating system into a virtual machine

As I've said before, to be able to use a virtual machine for productive work, you need to load an operating system into it. To start an operating system on either a virtual machine or a real machine, you have to load it through a process called an *initial program load*, or *IPL*. In an IPL, the program data required to start the operating system is read from an external device, usually a disk drive.

On a real system, after the processor and attached hardware have been readied (that is, have been turned on and have completed their power-up sequences), the system operator specifies a real device address to which the system should look for IPL data. In normal operations, that device is a disk drive that's been specially formatted with IPL data and that contains the data sets necessary to load the operating system. Because this is the disk where the operating system is stored, it's called the *system residence volume*. (Although IPLs are almost always performed from the system residence volume, they can be performed from units like tape drives; that's typical when loading an operating system onto new hardware for the first time.)

**The IPL command**

```
IPL {virtual-address  }
    {saved-system-name}
```

**Explanation**

virtual-address    The virtual address of the device from which IPL data is to be retrieved. This is usually the virtual address of a minidisk. The default CMS IPL volume's virtual address is 190.

saved-system-name  The name of a previously defined saved system. The default name of the CMS saved system is CMS.

---

Figure 3-5    The IPL command

The situation is similar in a virtual machine. After your virtual machine has been started (that is, after your logon process is complete), it needs an operating system to function. Typically, one of the minidisks in the configuration of the virtual machine is the *CMS system residence volume*, the minidisk that contains the programs required to load CMS into the virtual machine. That's almost always one of the linked minidisks that's owned by the system administrator, and its usual virtual address is 190.

Instead of requesting the hardware to perform an IPL, as a system operator does on a real system, you issue a CP command, IPL, to start the IPL process. Figure 3-5 presents the format of the IPL command. As the figure shows, there are two ways you can perform an IPL: from a virtual device address or from a saved system.

### IPLing an operating system from a virtual device address

The first way to perform an IPL is to specify the virtual address of the device that contains the required operating system files. Almost always, this will be your CMS system residence volume. The usual virtual address for the CMS system residence minidisk is 190. So if you entered

```
IPL 190
```

CP would look to the device at virtual address 190 to retrieve the necessary data to load CMS into your virtual machine.

This IPL technique isn't limited to CMS. Suppose, for example, that you're starting a virtual machine in which you want to run VSE, not CMS. To start VSE, you specify the address of the minidisk that's the VSE system residence volume, not the CMS system residence volume. Because a typical VSE system residence volume address is 240,

```
IPL 240
```

would tell CP to look to the minidisk at virtual address 240 for IPL data. And because the IPL data to be found there is for VSE, it's VSE that's loaded into the virtual machine.

### IPLing a saved system

The second way to use the IPL command is to specify the name of a *saved system*. A saved system is an image of the memory used by an operating system after it has been loaded. When you specify a saved system on the IPL command, that image is loaded directly into your virtual machine's address space. This eliminates the overhead of preparing the storage that would be required for a more typical IPL from a device address, so system performance is improved.

When CMS is configured as a saved system, as it almost always is, you can IPL by entering

```
IPL CMS
```

instead of specifying a virtual address.

### Automatic IPL

Because a virtual machine is nearly useless without an operating system, it's typical for users to want to perform an IPL immediately after logging on. And for individual terminal users, CMS is almost always the operating system that's to be IPLed. To make this easier, the system administrator can specify an automatic IPL for a virtual machine by coding the IPL statement in the VM system directory entry that defines the virtual machine.

For example, if you look back to figure 3-1 to the system directory entry statements that define my virtual machine, you'll see the statement

```
IPL CMS
```

This tells CP to load the saved CMS system automatically when I logon. (However, this can be overriden with the NOIPL parameter of the LOGON command, as I illustrated when I showed you how to logon in figure 2-2.)

### Discussion

Now you understand the basic services that VM provides for you through its Control Program. Although you must have this background to use VM effectively, most of the work you do will not be through the CP commands you've learned so far. Instead, you'll depend on CMS facilities, which you invoke through CMS commands. So in the next chapter, I'll introduce the CMS concepts you have to be familiar with, and I'll present the basic CMS commands you'll use frequently.

## Terminology

virtual address space
K
kilobyte
virtual console
virtual unit record devices
virtual card reader
virtual card punch
virtual printer
virtual DASD
VM system directory
virtual address
terminal status message
spooling
spool file
virtual disk
extent
minidisk
shared minidisk
attach
initial program load
IPL
system residence volume
CMS system residence volume
saved system

## Objectives

1. Describe how the configuration of a virtual machine is defined.

2. List the components of a virtual machine.

3. Describe the function of a virtual machine's virtual console.

4. Given any terminal status message on your virtual console, respond appropriately to it.

5. Describe how virtual unit record devices are typically used.

6. Describe how VM provides disk space for virtual machines.

7. Describe how real devices other than those named in a VM system directory entry can be added to a virtual machine's configuration.

8. Use the QUERY command to get information about your virtual machine's configuration.

# Chapter 4

## An introduction to VM's Conversational Monitor System (CMS)

As you learned in chapter 1, CMS, the Conversational Monitor System, is an interactive, single-user operating system that's supplied as a part of VM for use on virtual machines. Whether you use VM to develop programs, run user-written applications, or run IBM program products (like SQL/DS or PROFS), you'll be working with CMS. As a result, you need to understand CMS concepts and commands.

This chapter has four topics. The first teaches you how to access CMS and how to issue commands in the CMS environment. After you've mastered those basic skills, you need to know how CMS views minidisks; that's the subject of topic 2. Next, topic 3 presents the commands and concepts you need to know to manage the CMS files you store on your minidisks. Finally, topic 4 teaches you how to create and change files using the XEDIT command.

An introduction to VM's Conversational Monitor System (CMS)

| Topic one |

## How to access CMS and issue commands in the CMS environment

In the last chapter, you learned how to start CMS in a virtual machine by explicitly issuing the IPL command. That's fine, but it's easier—and more common—to start CMS using the automatic IPL feature I described at the end of the last chapter. So the first part of this topic shows you how to logon when CMS is automatically IPLed. Then, the second part of the topic shows you how to issue commands after you've entered the CMS environment.

### How to logon when CMS is automatically IPLed

To learn how to logon when CMS IPLs automatically, consider figure 4-1. In part 1 of figure 4-1, I entered the command

```
LOGON MAINT
```

to request that the virtual machine for the MAINT user-id be activated. (Remember that the MAINT user-id is the default for the system administrator.) After I pressed the enter key, I was prompted for the password for the MAINT user, which I entered in part 2 of the figure. (The password text was not displayed, but the cursor did advance one position for each character of the password I entered.)

After I keyed in the password, my virtual machine was activated. In part 3 of the figure, you can see that CP advised me that four of the minidisks in my virtual machine's configuration were in use by other virtual machines. I had read/write access (R/W) to all four; three of them were available for read/only access (R/O) to two other users. (The minidisk at virtual address 190 is the CMS system residence volume. All CMS users on my system have read/only access to it, but only the MAINT user, the system administrator, has read and write authority for it.) Notice also that one of the linked minidisks (virtual address 126) was in use for read and write operations by another virtual machine, the one associated with the user-id DOSVSE.

This information about linked minidisks is displayed to show you who else is using the minidisks you'll be able to access during your terminal session. After the disk-use messages are displayed, CP displays the logon-complete message you saw in chapter 2.

Next is a new message:

```
VM/SP REL 4 08/25/86 12:01
```

which comes not from CP, but from CMS. This message really isn't important.

The LOGON command says to activate the virtual machine for user-id MAINT

```
ENTER ONE OF THE FOLLOWING COMMANDS:

    LOGON USERID            (EXAMPLE:   LOGON VMUSER1)
    DIAL USERID             (EXAMPLE:   DIAL VMUSER2)
    MSG USERID MESSAGE      (EXAMPLE:   MSG VMUSER2 GOOD MORNING)
    LOGOFF








LOGON MAINT_
                                                           CP READ
  Iᵃ                                                     ▭—▭04
```

**Figure 4-1**   A typical logon sequence with automatic CMS IPL (part 1 of 4)

The prompt asks for the MAINT user's password (the password's not displayed as it's keyed in, but the cursor moves one position for each character)

```
ENTER ONE OF THE FOLLOWING COMMANDS:

    LOGON USERID            (EXAMPLE:   LOGON VMUSER1)
    DIAL USERID             (EXAMPLE:   DIAL VMUSER2)
    MSG USERID MESSAGE      (EXAMPLE:   MSG VMUSER2 GOOD MORNING)
    LOGOFF

LOGON MAINT
ENTER PASSWORD  (IT WILL NOT APPEAR WHEN TYPED):






                                                           CP READ
  Iᵃ                                                     ▭—▭04
```

**Figure 4-1**   A typical logon sequence with automatic CMS IPL (part 2 of 4)

After several informational messages are displayed (including one that tells you what release of VM you're using), the terminal status changes to VM READ; press the enter key if you don't want to override any CMS defaults during the IPL process

```
ENTER ONE OF THE FOLLOWING COMMANDS:

   LOGON USERID            (EXAMPLE:  LOGON VMUSER1)
   DIAL USERID             (EXAMPLE:  DIAL VMUSER2)
   MSG USERID MESSAGE      (EXAMPLE:  MSG VMUSER2 GOOD MORNING)
   LOGOFF

LOGON MAINT
ENTER PASSWORD  (IT WILL NOT APPEAR WHEN TYPED):

DASD 19E LINKED R/W; R/O BY 002 USERS
DASD 126 LINKED R/W; R/W BY DOSVSE
DASD 190 LINKED R/W; R/O BY 002 USERS
DASD 19D LINKED R/W; R/O BY 002 USERS
LOGON AT 10:25:49 PDT WEDNESDAY 04/29/87
VM/SP REL 4 08/25/86 12:01




-
                                                                 VM READ
IA                                                            □-□04
```

**Figure 4-1**    A typical logon sequence with automatic CMS IPL (part 3 of 4)

Once the IPL process is complete, CMS displays a ready message

```
ENTER ONE OF THE FOLLOWING COMMANDS:

   LOGON USERID            (EXAMPLE:  LOGON VMUSER1)
   DIAL USERID             (EXAMPLE:  DIAL VMUSER2)
   MSG USERID MESSAGE      (EXAMPLE:  MSG VMUSER2 GOOD MORNING)
   LOGOFF

LOGON MAINT
ENTER PASSWORD  (IT WILL NOT APPEAR WHEN TYPED):

DASD 19E LINKED R/W; R/O BY 002 USERS
DASD 126 LINKED R/W; R/W BY DOSVSE
DASD 190 LINKED R/W; R/O BY 002 USERS
DASD 19D LINKED R/W; R/O BY 002 USERS
LOGON AT 10:25:49 PDT WEDNESDAY 04/29/87
VM/SP REL 4 08/25/86 12:01

'19E' REPLACES ' Y (19E) '
Y (19E) R/O
SHARED YSTAT NOT AVAILABLE.
R; T=0.01/0.06 10:26:24


-
                                                                 RUNNING
IA                                                            □-□04
```

**Figure 4-1**    A typical logon sequence with automatic CMS IPL (part 4 of 4)

It tells you which release of Virtual Machine/System Package (VM/SP) you're using; here, it's release 4. Also, the message shows you the date and time the current operating system was generated in your shop. (Don't make the mistake of thinking that these are the current date and time.)

When CMS displays this message, the terminal status message changes to

```
VM READ
```

This message means that a program running in a virtual machine (here, the CMS operating system) is waiting for you to enter data. During the IPL process, CMS lets you enter specifications to override some CMS defaults. Generally, all you do during CMS IPL is press the enter key to send a null (blank) line. That tells CMS that you don't want to supply any overrides. If you don't press the enter key, CMS waits indefinitely. (This is the default; it's possible that your system administrator set up your virtual machine so you don't have to press the enter key to go on.)

After you respond, the IPL process finishes. You might see several other messages, depending on how your CMS environment is defined. If there are so many additional messages that your screen is filled, you'll see the MORE terminal status message, and you'll have to press the PA2 key to proceed.

Additional messages that appear at this point are produced as a result of commands stored in your *user profile*. The user profile contains commands that are automatically executed each time you start a CMS session. Although you can include a wide range of commands in your user profile, commands to prepare your minidisks for use by CMS are most common.

When the IPL process is complete, the CMS ready message appears. In part 4 of figure 4-1, it's

```
R; T=0.01/0.06 10:26:24
```

The R; indicates the ready message. The other data is time information. On the far right of the ready message is the current time; the other time values represent the amount of virtual and real processor time the previous CMS operation took. You might also see simply

```
R;
```

as the ready message. Which message format appears depends on the options that are in effect for your virtual machine. You can switch between the long and short forms of the ready message by entering either

```
SET RDYMSG SMSG
```

for the short version or

```
SET RDYMSG LMSG
```

for the long version. These are just two examples of CMS commands; the next section presents the information you need to know to use both CP and CMS commands in the CMS environment.

### How to issue commands in the CMS environment

After the CMS IPL is complete, you can issue CMS as well as CP commands. You issue a CMS command just like a CP command: You type the complete command (or an acceptable abbreviation) at the bottom of the screen along with any operands required for the command to perform the function you request.

While there are only a few CP commands you're likely to use, you'll probably use many CMS commands for a broad range of functions. As with the CP commands you're likely to use, I'll present the CMS commands you need to know as I describe how to use VM facilities. In this chapter, you'll learn only a few; the chapters that follow present more.

*A typical CMS command: QUERY*    CMS provides a QUERY command, which is similar to the CP QUERY command. Like the CP QUERY command, the CMS QUERY command can be abbreviated simply as Q , and it has a variety of operands you can specify to request many functions. You'll see examples of how to use the CMS QUERY command throughout this book.

In this chapter, I'll describe just two of the functions of the CMS QUERY command: SEARCH and DISK. Figure 4-2 illustrates their syntax elements. You use both the SEARCH and DISK functions to get information about your virtual machine's minidisks. For example, if you enter

```
QUERY SEARCH
```

or the abbreviated form

```
Q SEARCH
```

CMS displays the sequence in which it searches your minidisks for files. You'll learn how to use this information, as well as the information the DISK operand causes to be displayed, in the next topic.

*How to issue a CP command from CMS: The #CP prefix*    Because CMS is running in a virtual machine that's actually managed by VM's Control Program, it makes sense that you ought to be able to issue commands to either CP or CMS from CMS, and you can. Although a variety of option settings can affect the way commands are interpreted, it's typical for CMS to evaluate a command you enter and, if it recognizes it as one of its commands, to process it. On the other hand, if it doesn't recognize it, it passes it to CP for handling. In either case, display output that results from the command is sent to your terminal. For example, you can enter the CP command

```
LOGOFF
```

**The CMS QUERY command**

```
         (SEARCH                           )
         {        [ [ *              ] ]    }
QUERY    {        | { filemode-letter| |    }
         | DISK   | { R/W            | |    |
         (        [ [ MAX            ] ]    )
```

**Explanation**

| | |
|---|---|
| QUERY | The command name may be abbreviated as Q. |
| SEARCH | Specifies that the filemode letters currently in use should be displayed along with the minidisk virtual addresses associated with them. CMS searches your minidisks for files in this order. |
| DISK | Specifies that identification and usage data for all accessed minidisks should be displayed. |
| * | Used with DISK; specifies that information for all accessed minidisks should be displayed. |
| filemode-letter | Used with DISK; specifies that information should be displayed only for the accessed minidisk associated with the indicated letter. |
| R/W | Used with DISK; specifies that information should be displayed only for minidisks accessed for read/write processing. |
| MAX | Used with DISK; specifies that information should be displayed for the accessed minidisk with the largest amount of free space. |

**Figure 4-2**  Basic operands of the CMS QUERY command

from the CMS environment, even though LOGOFF isn't a CMS command. In fact, to end a CMS session, that's all you have to do; there's no need to issue any special commands to stop CMS before you deactivate your virtual machine.

There may be times when you want to force a command through CMS to CP. If a command is meaningful to both CMS and CP, and you want to execute the CP version, you need to tell CMS to ignore the command. To do that, all you have to do is use a special prefix (#CP) on the CP command.

For example, suppose your system has a virtual machine with the user-id SEARCH. If you enter the CMS command

```
Q SEARCH
```

you'll get information about the sequence in which your minidisks are searched for files. If you want to find out if the SEARCH user's virtual machine is active, you have to force the command to CP by entering

```
#CP Q SEARCH
```

Then, the output you get is what you want.

### Terminology

user profile

### Objectives

1. Assuming your VM system directory entry is set up so CMS is automatically IPLed, logon and reach the CMS ready message.

2. Issue both CP and CMS commands from the CMS environment.

# Topic two

# An introduction to CMS minidisks

As you should remember from the last chapter, DASD storage for virtual machines is provided through the VM minidisk facility. A minidisk is typically an extent (that is, a portion) of a real DASD unit. However, VM makes it appear to the virtual machine that its minidisks are complete, separate devices.

Most of your CMS work will involve handling data stored on minidisks. As a result, to use CMS effectively, you must understand how CMS views your virtual machine's minidisks and the files stored on them. That's what you'll learn in this topic.

Rather than focus on the physical organization of CMS minidisks in this topic, I want to describe two concepts you need to keep in mind as you use minidisks. First, you need to understand that minidisks that are part of your virtual machine's configuration can be owned either by you or by others. And second, you need to know how to identify minidisks that are part of your virtual machine's configuration.

## Minidisk ownership

As I showed you in the last chapter, your VM system directory entry specifies the minidisks that are part of your virtual machine's configuration. To refresh your memory, these are the statements that define the minidisks that are part of my virtual machine's configuration:

```
LINK MAINT 190 190 RR
LINK MAINT 19D 19D RR
LINK MAINT 19E 19E RR
LINK DOSVSE 240 240 RR
LINK DOSVSE 241 241 RR
MDISK 191 FB-512 041218 003262 VMSRES MW ALL
MDISK 192 FB-512 000016 001984 VMSEXT MW ALL
```

First, consider the two MDISK statements. They define two minidisks that belong to my virtual machine; they're called *owned minidisks*. The MDISK statement specifies the physical location of the real disk extent that will be used for a virtual DASD.

For example, the minidisk that will have virtual address 191 on my virtual machine will be a simulated FBA DASD (FB-512) and will use the 3262 blocks of real DASD space that begin at block 41218 on the real unit with the volser VMSRES. The MW in each of these statements means that I have write access to these minidisks, and that other users can access them, also with write access.

ALL is a password other users need to supply to access these minidisks. (You'll learn more about access modes and passwords in chapter 6.)

The LINK statements in my directory entry give me access to five minidisks owned by two other user-ids. Three are owned by MAINT, and two are owned by DOSVSE. These are called *shared minidisks*.

The first of these LINK statements specifies that the MAINT user's minidisk with virtual address 190 should be accessed by my virtual machine, which will also use virtual address 190 to refer to it. (Remember, the minidisk with virtual address 190 is typically the CMS system residence volume.) The RR means that I can access the minidisk only to read it; I cannot write data on it. The directory entry for the MAINT user's virtual machine contains MDISK statements that define not only its 190 minidisk, but also its 19D and 19E minidisks, and the entry for the DOSVSE user's virtual machine includes MDISK statements for its 240 and 241 minidisks. Notice that the LINK statements don't give the DASD locations of the minidisk extents. That information is supplied in the MDISK statements that define the minidisks in the owners' directory entries.

Within a single virtual machine, device addresses must be unique. For example, your virtual machine can't have two minidisks that both have the address 191. However, the same virtual addresses can be used on different virtual machines. Obviously, the MAINT user has a 190 minidisk, and so do I. It's typical for all users to have their primary minidisk, the one where they store their active data, defined with an MDISK statement that assigns it the virtual address 191. However, because each MDISK statement specifies a unique physical DASD extent for a minidisk and because CP keeps the operations of one virtual machine separate from the operation of others, that doesn't present a problem.

### Filemode letters

Although minidisks are identified with virtual device addresses, you don't identify them that way for typical CMS data management operations. Instead, you identify each minidisk with a *filemode letter*, which can be from A to Z; as a result, a virtual machine can have access to up to 26 minidisks at any one time. It's typical to refer to minidisks by their filemode letters. For instance, because the minidisk at virtual address 191 is usually assigned the filemode letter A, you're as likely to refer to it as "the A-disk" as you are to call it "the 191 disk."

*Default assignments*    If there aren't any specifications to the contrary in your user profile, some of your minidisks are automatically associated with particular filemode letters when you IPL CMS. Figure 4-3 lists them. As you can see, the minidisk at virtual address 190 (the CMS system residence volume) is automatically associated with filemode letter S. If your virtual machine's configuration includes a minidisk with virtual address 19E, it's automatically associated with filemode letter Y. This is an extension of the system residence volume. (I'll describe

| Address | Filemode letter | Function |
|---------|-----------------|----------|
| 190 | S | CMS system residence minidisk |
| 191 | A | Primary user data minidisk |
| 192 | D | Secondary user data minidisk |
| 19E | Y | CMS system residence extension minidisk |

**Figure 4-3**    Default filemode letter assignments

filemode extensions in chapter 6.) Both the S-disk and the Y-disk are typically owned by the VM system administrator and shared by all other CMS users.

Two owned minidisks can also be associated automatically with filemode letters when CMS is IPLed. Your minidisk at virtual address 191 is associated with filemode letter A. And if your virtual machine's configuration includes a minidisk at 192, it's associated with filemode letter D. Your A-disk is your primary data minidisk; if you have a D-disk, it's your secondary data disk by default.

***How to find out what the current filemode letter assignments are***    Filemode letters do more than just identify particular minidisks in your system configuration. They also determine the order in which CMS searches your minidisks for files. The CMS search sequence is alphabetical. So if CMS has to look for a file, it looks first on your A-disk, then on your B-disk (if one is accessed), and so on.

You can find out what filemode letters are associated with the minidisks in your virtual machine's configuration (and, therefore, the file search sequence that's in effect) by issuing the command I introduced in the last topic:

```
QUERY SEARCH
```

Figure 4-4 shows the output of this command on my virtual machine. The second column of the output gives the virtual device addresses of my minidisks, and the third column gives the filemode letter (or letters) associated with each. Note here that I did *not* use the default filemode letter for my 192 disk. The first column shows the volume serial number assigned to the minidisk when it was formatted. The fourth column indicates whether I have read/write access (R/W) or read/only access (R/O) to each minidisk. Finally, the fifth column indicates whether the minidisk is formatted for DOS, OS, or CMS. (If the fifth column is blank for a particular minidisk, it's a CMS minidisk.)

You can also find out what filemode letters are associated with your minidisks by issuing the command

```
QUERY DISK
```

```
Q SEARCH
STEVE1   191   A     R/W
MNT19D   19D   D     R/O
MNT190   190   S     R/O
STE192   192   V     R/W - DOS
DOSEXT   241   X     R/O - DOS
MAINTY   19E   Y/S   R/O
DOSVSE   240   Z     R/O - DOS
R; T=0.08/0.24 11:23:16




                                          RUNNING
                                          ▭-▭04
```

**Figure 4-4**  Screen output of the CMS QUERY command with the SEARCH operand

Figure 4-5 presents its output for my virtual machine. As you can see, it includes not only the information in the QUERY SEARCH output, but also information about the size and usage of each minidisk.

***How to manage filemode letter assignments: The ACCESS and RELEASE commands***  Although the minidisks that are commonly used by CMS virtual machines are automatically associated with filemode letters during CMS IPL, your virtual machine configuration may contain other minidisks. If your virtual machine's configuration includes virtual DASDs with addresses other than 190, 191, 192, and 19E, you must explicitly associate filemode letters with them. The same is true if you want to use filemode letters other than S, A, D, and Y with the minidisks at addresses 190, 191, 192, and 19E.

To manage filemode letter assignments, you use the CMS ACCESS and RELEASE commands. Figures 4-6 and 4-7 present their formats.

Suppose your virtual machine configuration includes a minidisk with virtual address 193. To be able to access this virtual disk, you have to use the ACCESS command to associate a filemode letter with it. For example, you'd enter

```
ACCESS 193 B
```

if you wanted to access that minidisk as your B-disk.

If you want to change the filemode letter associated with a virtual disk, you can simply enter another ACCESS command. However, if you want to disable

```
Q DISK
LABEL  CUU M  STAT  CYL TYPE BLKSIZE  FILES  BLKS USED-(%) BLKS LEFT BLK TOTAL
STEVE1 191 A  R/W   FB 3310 1024        53        936-57       695       1631
MNT19D 19D D  R/O   FB 3310 1024      2505       6389-61      4063      10452
MNT190 190 S  R/O   FB 3310 1024       190       9754-73      3686      13440
STE192 192 V  R/W   FB 3310            DOS
DOSEXT 241 X  R/O   FB 3310            DOS
MAINTY 19E Y/S R/O  FB 3310 1024        72       1975-55      1630       3605
DOSVSE 240 Z  R/O   FB 3310            DOS
R; T=0.08/0.24 11:24:42




-
                                                            RUNNING
  Iª                                           ▭─▭04
```

**Figure 4-5**   Screen output of the CMS QUERY command with the DISK operand

access to a virtual DASD, you have to use the RELEASE command. So if your minidisk at address 193 is accessed as your B-disk, you could enter either

**RELEASE B**

or

**RELEASE 193**

to remove it from your virtual machine. After you release a minidisk, you can reaccess it by issuing another ACCESS command.

Frankly, you're likely to use RELEASE only for disks you've accessed temporarily. You'll learn how to do that in chapter 6. Usually, there's no reason to release minidisks that are a permanent part of your virtual machine's configuration.

Like CP commands, CMS commands often allow for options you can code when you issue a command. For the ACCESS command, you can use the option in figure 4-6: NOPROF. (There are other options for the ACCESS command, but NOPROF if the only one I think you'll ever need to use.)

Whenever the syntax for a command indicates that you can supply options, you include them on the command line after the basic operands and, as figure 4-6 indicates, separate them from the basic operands by a left parenthesis. Actually, options can be bracketed by paired parentheses, but the right (closing) parenthesis is optional. Because it's easier to code just the left parenthesis, that's all I've shown in the syntax figures in this book.

### The ACCESS command

```
ACCESS [virtual-address filemode-letter] [(NOPROF]
```

**Explanation**

virtual-address    The virtual address of the minidisk to be accessed. If you omit the virtual address, 191 is used as the default.

filemode-letter    The letter to be associated with the accessed minidisk. If you omit filemode-letter, A is used as the default.

NOPROF    Specifies that your user profile should be bypassed; this option is valid only when you issue the ACCESS command immediately after you IPL CMS.

Figure 4-6    The ACCESS command

### The RELEASE command

```
RELEASE  {virtual-address}
         {filemode-letter}
```

**Explanation**

virtual-address    The virtual address of the minidisk to be released.

filemode-letter    The filemode letter associated with the minidisk to be released.

Figure 4-7    The RELEASE command

NOPROF lets you override the specifications in your user profile. Remember, CMS pauses during IPL and waits for you to enter overrides. Usually, you just press the enter key, which means your user profile is processed. However, if you enter

```
ACCESS (NOPROF
```

CMS does not access your user profile, but does assign the default filemode letters to your minidisks that figure 4-3 presents.

### Discussion

Although the information in this topic is enough to get you started using CMS minidisks, there's plenty more to know. For example, you will probably want to learn how to access other user's minidisks dynamically during a terminal session. Or, you might want to use the temporary minidisk facility VM provides.

Chapter 6 presents these advanced minidisk management features and others. But before you learn them, you need to know how to manage the CMS files stored on your minidisks. That's what the next topic and chapter 5 present.

### Terminology

owned minidisk
shared minidisk
filemode letter

### Objectives

1. Use the CMS QUERY command to display your current minidisk search order and information about the minidisks in your virtual machine's configuration.

2. Distinguish between an owned minidisk and a shared minidisk.

3. Use the ACCESS and RELEASE commands to manage the filemode letters associated with your minidisks.

| Topic three | ## An introduction to CMS files, file management commands, and procedures |
|---|---|

The data you store on the system as a CMS user is stored in CMS files. A *CMS file* is simply a uniquely identified collection of records on a CMS disk. In this topic, I'll show you how to identify CMS files, then I'll describe what their characteristics can be. Finally, I'll introduce the essential CMS commands you can issue to manage your files. (Chapter 5 presents CMS file management commands in more detail.)

### How CMS files are identified

The complete identification of a CMS file has three parts: (1) the *filename*, (2) the *filetype*, and (3) the *filemode*. Figure 4-8 presents the formats for these parts of a file's identification. As you can see, they can be abbreviated as fn, ft, and fm; you'll see these abbreviations in representations of CMS command syntax in this book and in IBM's reference manuals. Together, all three parts are called the *file identifier*.

You can use whatever values you like for both the filename and filetype to identify a file (as long as the values aren't more than eight characters long, as described in figure 4-8). In practice, though, you should use a filetype value that indicates what the contents of a file are. For instance, a file that contains COBOL source statements should have the filetype COBOL.

In fact, when you issue the CMS commands to compile a COBOL program, CMS expects the COBOL source code to be in a file with filetype COBOL. *COBOL* is one of a set of special-purpose filetypes called *reserved filetypes*; figure 4-9 lists the most common ones. When you use reserved filetypes, CMS will make some assumptions that can save you work. For example, when you create a file with filetype COBOL with the CMS editor, it will automatically be created with 80-byte records, which is what you want. Although you probably should use the reserved filetypes only when they're appropriate, nothing stops you from doing otherwise. For instance, you could use the filetype COBOL for a file that contains assembler language statements, even though it doesn't make much sense.

You have the most naming flexibility when you assign a filename. The filename provides unique identification for a file of a particular type on a particular minidisk. To illustrate,

```
ORD1100  COBOL  B
ORD1110  COBOL  B
ORD1120  COBOL  A
ORD1130  COBOL  B
```

**Format of a CMS file identifier**

```
fn ft fm
```

**Explanation**

| | |
|---|---|
| fn | Filename of the CMS file. The filename must be from one to eight characters long, consisting of the letters A-Z and a-z, the numerals 0-9, and the special characters @, #, $, +, :, – (the hyphen), or _ (the underscore). You may use uppercase and lowercase letters interchangeably. |
| ft | Filetype of the CMS file. The filetype must be from one to eight characters long, consisting of the same characters that are valid for filenames. Often, you'll use reserved filetypes to identify the kind of data a file contains; figure 4-9 presents commonly used reserved filetypes. |
| fm | Filemode of the CMS file. The filemode has two parts: the filemode letter and the filemode number. The filemode letter is the one-letter value associated with the currently accessed minidisk on which the file resides. The filemode number is for special purposes, as figure 4-10 specifies; you seldom need to specify it. |

---

Figure 4-8    Format of a CMS file identifier

---

are typical names. These files contain COBOL source code for four programs, named ORD1100, ORD1110, ORD1120, and ORD1130. All of the files reside on the currently accessed B-drive, except the third (ORD1120), which resides on the currently accessed A-drive.

You're already familiar with the filemode. Most often, it's just the filemode letter of an accessed minidisk. Because different filemode letters can be assigned to the same minidisk at different times, the filemode letter associated with files on a given minidisk can vary depending on how the virtual machine is set up.

In addition to the filemode letter, the filemode can have a second part, the *filemode number*, which can be a single digit from 0 to 6. Each filemode number has a particular meaning, as you can see in figure 4-10.

Filemode number 1 means the file can be read and written; it's used as the default if you don't specify a filemode number. So the complete file identifiers of the four files I showed you a moment ago are

```
ORD1100 COBOL B1
ORD1110 COBOL B1
ORD1120 COBOL A1
ORD1130 COBOL B1
```

I want to stress that most of the files you'll access will have filemode number 1. As a result, you won't need to worry about filemode numbers most of the time when you issue file handling commands. Filemode numbers 2 and 5 are

| If the filetype is | The file contains |
|---|---|
| AMSERV | VSAM Access Method Services control statements |
| ASSEMBLE | Assembler language source code |
| BASIC | BASIC source code |
| COBOL | COBOL source code |
| EXEC | A VM procedure |
| FREEFORT | FREEFORM FORTRAN source code |
| FORTRAN | FORTRAN source code |
| LISTING | Print output |
| LOADLIB | Multiple executable program modules |
| MACLIB | Multiple macro definitions or copy books |
| MACRO | A macro definition |
| MEMO | Text |
| MODULE | An executable program |
| PLI | PL/I source code |
| PLIOPT | PL/I source code |
| SCRIPT | Text to be processed by SCRIPT |
| TEXT | An object program |
| TXTLIB | Multiple object programs |
| VSBASIC | VS BASIC source code |

**Figure 4-9**    Reserved filetypes

essentially the same as filemode number 1, but are provided to make it possible for you to group related files.

The other filemode numbers (0, 3, 4, and 6) are for more specialized functions. If you create a file with filemode number 0, it's a *private file*. In other words, users who access the minidisk where that file resides with read/only privileges (as is typical) won't be able to access the file. (You'll learn more about access privileges in chapter 6.)

| Filemode number | Description |
|---|---|
| 0 | Used for private files. Only users with read and write access to the minidisk may view this file. Users who access the minidisk with read/only access may not view it. |
| 1 | Makes a file eligible for read and write access. The default filemode number. |
| 2 | Makes a file eligible for read and write access; essentially the same as filemode number 1. |
| 3 | Temporary file; deleted after it is read. |
| 4 | A simulated OS-format data set. |
| 5 | Makes a file eligible for read and write access; essentially the same as filemode number 1. |
| 6 | The file may be updated in place. |

**Figure 4-10**    Filemode numbers

A file with filemode number 3 is a *temporary file*. It's automatically deleted after it has been read. For example, a program might create a listing file with filemode number 3. Then, after the listing has been printed, the file is deleted automatically.

A file with filemode number 4 is a simulated OS-format data set. Such files are commonly used by programmers who develop applications under CMS that will eventually be used on OS production systems.

Finally, a file with filemode number 6 is one that can be updated in place. In other words, as records are read then rewritten to the file, they're stored in their original locations rather than elsewhere. This feature is available only to specially written CMS applications.

## Characteristics of CMS files

The way data is physically stored under the CMS file system and the way it appears to you are different. For now, suffice it to say that data in a CMS file is stored in fixed-length blocks in the extent allocated to a minidisk, regardless of the characteristics of the file's records. Perhaps the most important thing you need to know about CMS files as they're viewed by you and the programs you use is that they're sequential. In other words, records processed by the CMS file system are read from a file in the same order that they were written. That means that random access, such as through an indexing scheme, is not available under CMS. As a general rule, that doesn't present a problem because for most uses of CMS files, sequential access is appropriate.

The records that make up a CMS file can be of either fixed or variable length. Most of the time, you don't need to worry about which is used. When you create a CMS file, the filetype you specify for it is used by CMS to determine whether the file should be created with fixed-length or variable-length records.

The filetype you specify for a new file also determines the record size used. As I mentioned above, the record length for a file created with the filetype COBOL is 80 characters, the standard card-image format used for high-level language source programs. Again, for most CMS functions, you don't need to worry about record size. (If you create a file with the CMS editor whose filetype is not reserved, the file will have fixed-length, 80-byte records.)

## Essential CMS file management commands

To get information about the files on your CMS minidisks and to manage those files, CMS provides a full set of file processing commands. The remainder of this chapter introduces the most important ones so you can use them right away. Then, the chapters in section 2 cover CMS's file management commands in greater detail.

For now, then, I'll introduce you to the first six commands listed in figure 4-11: LISTFILE, TYPE, PRINT, RENAME, COPYFILE, and ERASE. (I'll present XEDIT by itself in topic 4.) Then, I'll describe how you can group sequences of commands you use often into executable files called procedures.

***The LISTFILE command***     To find out if a file exists on a minidisk, or to find out its characteristics, you can use the LISTFILE command (abbreviated L). To find out if a file exists, enter the command in this format:

```
L fn ft fm
```

For instance, you'd enter

```
L ORD2400 COBOL A
```

to find out if you have a COBOL source file named ORD2400 on your A-disk.

You can omit the filemode from the file identifier if you like. When you do, CMS uses A as the default. As a result,

```
L ORD2400 COBOL
```

is equivalent to the command I just showed you.

Also, in place of any or all parts of the file identifier, you can enter an asterisk (called a *wild-card character*). The wild-card character indicates that you want to display all files regardless of the value represented by the wild-card. For instance, to display all COBOL source files on your A-disk, you'd enter

```
L * COBOL A
```

**To display file identifiers and attributes**

```
LISTFILE [fn ft [fm]] [(LABEL]
```

**To display the contents of a file**

```
TYPE fn ft [fm]
```

**To print the contents of a file**

```
PRINT fn ft [fm]
```

**To change the name of a file**

```
RENAME fn1 ft1 fm1 fn2 ft2 fm2 [(TYPE]
```

**To make a copy of a file**

```
COPYFILE fn1 ft1 fm1 fn2 ft2 fm2 [(TYPE]
```

**To delete a file**

```
ERASE fn ft [fm] [(TYPE]
```

**To create a new file or change the contents of an existing file**

```
XEDIT fn ft [fm]
```

---

Figure 4-11       Basic CMS file management commands

Or, to see all of your COBOL source files on all minidisks, you'd enter

```
L * COBOL *
```

Finally, to see all of your files on all of your minidisks, you could enter

```
L * * *
```

(You should realize that this form of the command will give you much more information than you need or can use. For example, on my system, the output of this command returns over 100 screens of file identifiers.)

To see more than just file identifiers, you can include the LABEL option on any LISTFILE command you issue. When you do, the command's output

**Sample output of the LISTFILE command without the LABEL option**

```
L * ASSEMBLE *
RENUM     ASSEMBLE A1
EUDXASM   ASSEMBLE Y2
EUDXTRAN  ASSEMBLE Y2
```

**Sample output of the LISTFILE command with the LABEL option**

```
L * ASSEMBLE * (LABEL
FILENAME FILETYPE FM FORMAT LRECL     RECS     BLOCKS    DATE      TIME    LABEL
RENUM    ASSEMBLE A1 F        80        71        ·6    3/10/87 14:17:58 STEVE1
EUDXASM  ASSEMBLE Y2 F        80       364        29    8/18/83 11:44:02 MAINT1
EUDXTRAN ASSEMBLE Y2 F        80        23         2    4/23/86  9:22:27 MAINT1
```

| Figure 4-12 | Sample output of the LISTFILE command with and without the LABEL option |
|---|---|

includes not only the identifiers of the files that meet the criteria you specified, but also the format of the records in each file (fixed-length or variable-length), their logical record length, the number of records in each file, the number of physical blocks the file uses, the date and time the file was created, and the CMS volume serial number for the minidisk where the file resides.

For example, to display complete information for all the files on my accessed disks that contain assembler language source code, I'd enter

```
L * ASSEMBLE * (LABEL
```

Figure 4-12 compares the output of this command with and without the LABEL option.

The LISTFILE command includes other options and advanced features. However, you're not likely to use them. That's because the CMS FILELIST facility is easier to use and more powerful. You'll learn about it in the first topic of the next chapter.

***The TYPE command***    To display the contents of a CMS file, you issue the TYPE command. For instance, to display the records in the file ORD2400 COBOL on my A-disk, I'd enter

```
TYPE ORD2400 COBOL A
```

You can omit the filemode letter from the file identifier if you like, and CMS will use A as the default.

If you're not sure which minidisk contains the file you want to view, you can enter an asterisk for the filemode. Then, CMS searches through your accessed disks in alphabetical sequence by filemode letter until it finds a file with the filename and filetype you specified.

In topic 2 of the next chapter, I'll describe advanced functions of the TYPE command. For now, though, you might like to know that if you want to terminate a type operation, you can key in

```
HT
```

at the bottom of your terminal screen at any point in the output process and press enter. HT is an *immediate command* that stands for "Halt Typing." (As the name indicates, a CMS immediate command is processed immediately when it is received; normally, CMS commands are stacked and processed in queued fashion.) After you've entered HT, press PA2 to reply to the MORE terminal status message. Then, your terminal will redisplay the CMS ready message. Topic 2 of the next chapter presents a figure that illustrates how to use the HT immediate command.

***The PRINT command*** If you want a printed copy of a file, you can issue the PRINT command. For example, the command

```
PRINT ORD2400 COBOL A
```

causes the contents of the named file to be copied to the printer. In section 4 of this book, I'll describe print (along with card) operations in much more detail. For now, this is enough to let you print copies of files you need.

***The RENAME command*** To change the name of a file, you use the RENAME command. On it, you specify the complete old identifier and the complete new identifier. For instance,

```
RENAME ORD2400 COBOL A ORD2410 COBOL A
```

changes the filename of a COBOL source file on your A-disk from ORD2400 to ORD2410. With the RENAME command, you can enter an equal sign in place of a new filename, filetype, or filemode if you want it to be the same as for the old file. So

```
RENAME ORD2400 COBOL A ORD2410 = =
```

is the same as the command I just showed you.

If you need to rename several related files, you can use the asterisk as a wild-card character. For instance,

```
RENAME * COBOL A = OLDCOBOL =
```

changes the filetype of all COBOL source files on my A-disk from COBOL to OLDCOBOL. When you use a wild-card character, you might also want to specify the TYPE option. It causes all the new names to be displayed on your terminal screen as the command executes.

When you rename a file with the RENAME command, you cannot move it from one minidisk to another by changing its filemode letter. However, you can change its filemode number. For example, to make a file a private file, you could enter a command like

```
RENAME ORD1100 COBOL A1 = = A0
```

To copy a file from one minidisk to another, you use another command: COPYFILE.

**The COPYFILE command**    To make copies of CMS files, you use the COPY-FILE command, which can be abbreviated as COPY. Its basic syntax is much like that of the RENAME command. For example,

```
COPY ORD1100 COBOL A ORD1100 COBOL B
```

makes a copy on my B-disk of the file ORD1100 COBOL on my A-disk.

You can also process multiple files with a single command by using the asterisk and the equal sign, just as with the RENAME command. And you don't have to use the input file filename(s) and filetype(s) for the output file(s). The command

```
COPY * COBOL A = CPY B
```

copies all the COBOL source files on my A-disk to my B-disk and gives the copies the filetype CPY. COPYFILE is a powerful command with several options; topic 3 of the next chapter describes it in detail.

**The ERASE command**    To delete one or more CMS files, you use the ERASE command. Its syntax follows the pattern you've already seen. In its simplest form, you just supply the file identifier on the command. For instance,

```
ERASE ORD1100 COBOL B
```

deletes the file ORD1100 COBOL on my B-disk.

You can also delete multiple files with one command. The command

```
ERASE * CPY B
```

deletes all the files with the filetype CPY on my B disk, while

```
ERASE * CPY *
```

deletes files with that filetype from *all* of my accessed minidisks. If you omit file-mode, A is assumed. If you specify the TYPE option for a multiple-file ERASE operation, the file identifier of each file deleted is displayed as the command executes.

*How to group commands in EXEC files*   As you use CMS, you'll probably find that there are some sequences of commands you issue over and over. If you like, you can store those commands in a file; then, to execute them, all you have to do is identify the file that contains them. This can save you time, make using the system less tedious, and eliminate keying errors.

A file that contains a sequence of commands that will be executed as a group should have the filetype EXEC. EXEC files are often called *EXECs*, *EXEC procedures*, or just *procedures*. The name EXEC comes from the CMS command that processes procedures. One way to run a procedure is to invoke the EXEC command and supply as an operand the identifier of the EXEC procedure file.

For example, if you've stored a series of commands in a file you've named CLG EXEC on your A-disk, you could execute those commands by entering

```
EXEC CLG EXEC A
```

Here, I specified the complete file identifier for my procedure file. The CMS EXEC command uses A as the default filemode and EXEC as the default filetype. As a result,

```
EXEC CLG
```

also runs the procedure.

Frankly, it can be cumbersome to issue the EXEC command each time you want to run a procedure. Because the only reason you group commands into an EXEC file is so they can be executed, it makes sense that you should be able to execute them directly, without having to invoke the EXEC command explicitly. And you can, as long as the CMS *implied execution option*, also called *impex*, is in effect. When that's the case, as it almost always is, all you have to do is key in the filename of the EXEC file, and CMS will automatically invoke the EXEC command to process the commands it contains. So if the impex option is in effect,

```
CLG
```

is all you need to enter to execute the procedure stored in the file CLG EXEC A.

To find out if the implied execution option is in effect for your virtual machine, you can use the CMS QUERY command:

```
Q IMPEX
```

If the reply indicates the option is off, you can enter

```
SET IMPEX ON
```

to activate it.

As VM has evolved, its procedure processing facilities have been enhanced. Originally, VM procedure processing was handled by the *CMS EXEC Facility*. Later, a more advanced facility, the *EXEC2 Processor* was added. And still later, the most sophisticated of VM's procedure processing facilities was introduced: the *System Product Interpreter*, also called the *Restructured Extended Executor*, or just *REXX*. In addition to handling sequences of commands, REXX includes features that let you communicate with a terminal user, store and process data in CMS disk files, use variables and control structures, and perform string and numeric manipulations. In short, it's a sort of programming language all its own.

If you intend to develop sophisticated "procedure programs," you should learn and use REXX; it has superseded both the EXEC and EXEC2 facilities. However, EXEC and EXEC2 procedures still work. And for simple procedures that are nothing more than a sequence of CP or CMS commands—the kind of procedures you're likely to write right now—you should probably use the CMS EXEC Facility. That's because the extra features of the more sophisticated procedure processors make them harder to use.

When you invoke a procedure, VM selects the EXEC, EXEC2, or REXX facility to process it based on the data in the first record of the procedure file. If that record is

```
&TRACE
```

EXEC2 is used. If it's a REXX comment (any text string that begins with a slash and an asterisk and ends with an asterisk and a slash), REXX is used. If it's anything else, the CMS EXEC Facility is used. So as a rule of thumb, make sure that the first record in an EXEC file you create does not begin with an ampersand or a slash. If you do, the CMS EXEC Facility will always be used to process it.

Writing procedures isn't as complicated as it might sound. For example, suppose you maintain multiple copies of a single file for backup purposes. Each time you work on the file, you save the current copy, then rename the older ones so you can easily tell which is which. Since four copies seems like enough, you delete the oldest one when you have five copies of the file. Here's a series of commands to perform this sort of operation:

```
RENAME LISTMAST SAVE3 A = SAVE4 =
RENAME LISTMAST SAVE2 A = SAVE3 =
RENAME LISTMAST SAVE1 A = SAVE2 =
COPY LISTMAST COBOL A = SAVE1 =
ERASE LISTMAST SAVE4 A
```

It would be tedious to enter these commands each time you wanted to cycle through the backup process. However, if you stored them exactly as they appear above in a file with the filetype EXEC, you could invoke them as a single procedure. For example, if you store them in a file called BACKUPLM EXEC on your A-disk, all you have to enter to execute them is

```
BACKUPLM
```

Basic procedures are just that simple.

## Discussion

Much of the rest of this book develops skills this topic has introduced. As you should be able to tell from the amount of space I've dedicated to CMS file management, it's important. Almost all of the CMS work you'll do will involve file handling in one way or another. As a result, you must thoroughly understand the concepts, terms, and commands this topic has introduced. If you don't feel comfortable with them, by all means go back and review.

There's one other file handling command, though, that you'll need to know before you can do much productive work under CMS—the XEDIT command. It invokes XEDIT, a powerful CMS text editor that offers you many options for creating files and manipulating their contents. In the next topic, I'll present the XEDIT features you'll use most.

## Terminology

| | |
|---|---|
| CMS file | EXEC |
| filename | EXEC procedure |
| filetype | procedure |
| filemode | implied execution option |
| file identifier | impex option |
| reserved filetype | CMS EXEC Facility |
| filemode number | EXEC2 Processor |
| private file | System Product Interpreter |
| temporary file | Restructured Extended Executor |
| wild-card character | REXX |
| immediate command | |

## Objectives

1. Describe the format and purpose of each of the three parts of a CMS file identifier.
2. Use the LISTFILE command to display information about the files on your minidisks.
3. Use the TYPE command to display the contents of any file on your minidisks.
4. Use the PRINT command to produce a hard copy of any file on your minidisks.
5. Use the RENAME command to change the name of any file to which you have read and write access.
6. Use the COPYFILE command to make a duplicate of any file on your minidisks.
7. Use the ERASE command to delete any file to which you have read and write access.
8. Write and execute a CMS EXEC Facility procedure to manage your CMS files.

**Topic four**

# How to use the XEDIT command

To create a CMS file that contains text, you're likely to use the CMS editor. Its full name is the *VM/SP System Product Editor*, but it's most often called *XEDIT*, and XEDIT is the name of the CMS command you use to invoke it. (There's another CMS editor, called *EDIT*, but it's seldom used because it isn't as powerful or as easy to use as the newer, eXtended EDITor, XEDIT.)

This topic teaches you how to use XEDIT to key in and save text. Although XEDIT is a powerful program product with a large set of features, you only need to know a few of them to use it for most of the work you'll do. Those are the features you'll learn here.

## How to start XEDIT

To start XEDIT, you key in the command name XEDIT (or the abbreviation X) followed by the name of a file. So if you want to edit a COBOL source file called LISTMAST that resides on your A-disk, you can invoke XEDIT with the command

```
X LISTMAST COBOL A
```

Whenever you want to edit a file on your A-disk, you can omit the filemode, so

```
X LISTMAST COBOL
```

is the same as the first command I showed you.

You must supply a file identifier when you invoke XEDIT. If you want to create a new file, supply the filename and filetype you want it to have. Then, when you save the file from XEDIT, it's stored with the identifier you specified. The characteristics of the new file are determined by XEDIT based on the filetype you provided in the file identifier.

## The XEDIT screen

When you use XEDIT, you work on a full-screen display, like the one shown in figure 4-13. This is the screen XEDIT displayed after I invoked it to edit the COBOL source file LISTMAST. The format of the XEDIT screen can vary depending on how particular options are set, so yours might look different from the one in figure 4-13. However, the functions I'll describe work the same way regardless of how the screen appears.

The XEDIT screen has several parts; they're labeled in figure 4-13. At the top of the screen is the *file identification line*. It gives the complete identifier for the file (here, LISTMAST COBOL A1) plus its characteristics. In this example,

File
identification
line

Prefix
area

Scale
line

Command
line

File
area

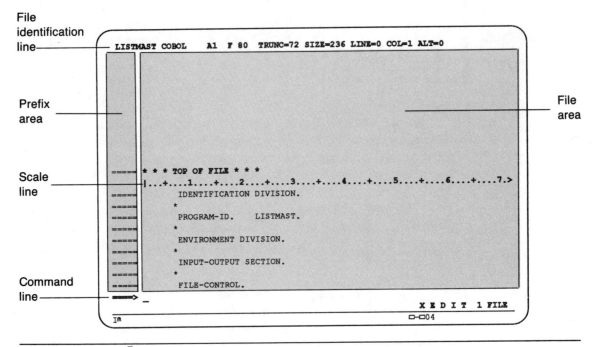

```
LISTMAST COBOL      A1  F 80   TRUNC=72 SIZE=236 LINE=0 COL=1 ALT=0




                    * * * TOP OF FILE * * *
              ====  |...+....1....+....2....+....3....+....4....+....5....+....6....+....7.>
              ====       IDENTIFICATION DIVISION.
              ====       *
              ====       PROGRAM-ID.    LISTMAST.
              ====       *
              ====       ENVIRONMENT DIVISION.
              ====       *
              ====       INPUT-OUTPUT SECTION.
              ====       *
              ====       FILE-CONTROL.
              ===>  _
                                                            X E D I T  1 FILE
              Iª                                   □-□04
```

**Figure 4-13**     Parts of the XEDIT screen

F 80 means the file has fixed-length, 80-byte records. TRUNC means data entered after column 72 will be truncated; data in column 73 and beyond is truncated in the display. SIZE tells me that the file contains 236 records. LINE and COL values indicate where in the file the cursor is positioned, and ALT indicates the number of changes made to the file during the editing session.

The line in the middle of the screen that seems to be a ruler is just that; it's called the *scale line*. The scale line helps you identify column positions.

The line at the bottom of the screen that begins with

    ====>

is the *command line*. This is where you can enter a variety of commands to control XEDIT operations. For example, if you want to save a copy of the file you're working on during an edit session, you can enter

    ====> SAVE

on the command line. I'll show you some other commands you can enter in this line later in this topic.

To mark the start and end of the file you're editing, XEDIT displays identifying lines. In figure 4-13, you can see the line that marks the start of the file:

    * * * TOP OF FILE * * *

This is not part of the data in the file; it's displayed by XEDIT as an aid for you. XEDIT displays a similar line at the end of the file.

The blank lines above the scale line and the lines below it where the top of the COBOL program appears are called the *file area*. It's here that the text you're editing is displayed, and you can change text anywhere in this area by simply typing over it. This is in contrast to the way you enter CP and CMS commands, where only the bottom line of the screen is active for data entry.

Within the file area, one line is displayed in bright characters. (In the screen images in this book, bright characters appear in boldface type.) That line is the *current line*, and some XEDIT functions operate based on it. In figure 4-13, the top of file indicator is shown as the current line; that means the current position in the file is before the first record.

The area at the left side of the screen that contains equal signs is called the *prefix area*. One row of equal signs appears in the prefix area next to each line in the file area. You can key in *prefix commands* in the prefix area; I'll show you several of them in a moment.

## How to use the basic XEDIT PF key assignments

To control XEDIT, you issue commands, either in the command line or in the prefix area. However, a few commands are so heavily used that they're automatically associated with PF (program function) keys to make it easier for you to use XEDIT. The most important of them let you scroll the text you're editing and end your editing session.

Even though you can use the entire 3270 screen when you edit a file with XEDIT, that's usually not enough space to see the entire file. As a result, you need to be able to move the text so you can see different parts of it. This process is called *scrolling*.

You can issue commands like UP and DOWN in the command line to scroll, but it's usually easier to use the PF keys with preassigned values for this purpose. If you press the PF8 key, the screen display is advanced almost one full screen ahead. For example, if I press the PF8 key when the data in figure 4-13 is displayed, XEDIT scrolls toward the bottom of the file (down) and displays the screen in figure 4-14. (Notice in figure 4-14 that the entire file area is now in use.) As you can see, the line that was at the bottom of the display in figure 4-13 is at the top of the display in figure 4-14. Also, notice that the current line is now the one that contains the text

```
LABEL RECORDS ARE STANDARD
```

PF7 works the same way, only it moves the display toward the top of the document (up).

Although it's usually easier to use PF7 and PF8 to scroll while you're editing, you'll sometimes need to scroll a large number of lines. For example, if you

```
 LISTMAST COBOL    A1  F 80  TRUNC=72 SIZE=236 LINE=18 COL=1 ALT=0

 =====          FILE-CONTROL.
 =====              SELECT INVMAST ASSIGN TO SYS020-AS-INVMAST.
 =====              SELECT INVLIST ASSIGN TO SYS006-UR-1403-S.
 =====          *
 =====          DATA DIVISION.
 =====          *
 =====          FILE SECTION.
 =====          *
 =====          FD  INVMAST
 =====              LABEL RECORDS ARE STANDARD
      |...+....1....+....2....+....3....+....4....+....5....+....6....+....7.>
 =====              RECORD CONTAINS 128 CHARACTERS.
 =====          *
 =====          01  INVENTORY-MASTER        PIC X(128).
 =====          *
 =====          FD  INVLIST
 =====              LABEL RECORDS ARE OMITTED
 =====              RECORD CONTAINS 132 CHARACTERS.
 =====          *
 =====          01  PRINT-AREA              PIC X(132).
 ====>  _
                                              X E D I T  1 FILE
  IA                                         □─□04
```

Figure 4-14          An XEDIT screen with the entire file area in use

want to scroll down 600 lines, it's easier and quicker to key in

    ====> DOWN 600

in the command line than to press the PF8 key repeatedly (about 30 times). Similarly, you can use the UP command to scroll upward.

    There is one trick that you should know about scrolling with PF7 and PF8. When you're at the top of a file and you press PF7, XEDIT takes you to the end of the file, and when you're at the end and you press PF8, XEDIT takes you to the top. This wraparound scrolling feature can be useful, but it can also confuse you if you don't understand what's happening.

    The other preassigned PF key you should know about is the PF3 key. You press it to end an XEDIT session. It's the same as entering the QUIT command in the command line. (I'll describe the QUIT command in a moment.)

### How to use XEDIT prefix commands

Aside from simply keying in text in the file area of the XEDIT screen, you need to be able to perform some basic operations like opening new lines for text entry or moving, copying, or deleting existing lines. You can use prefix commands, which you enter in the prefix area, to accomplish these tasks.

    Figure 4-15 lists the prefix commands you should know. They fall into four groups: commands to add, delete, duplicate, and copy or move lines.

**Add blank lines**

A or I                         Add one blank line at the indicated position.

An, nA,                        Add *n* blank lines at the indicated position.
In or nI

**Delete lines**

D                              Delete the indicated line.

Dn or nD                       Delete *n* lines from the indicated position.

DD                             Marks the beginning and end of a group of lines to be deleted.

**Duplicate lines**

"                              Duplicate the indicated line one time.

"n or n"                       Duplicate the indicated line *n* times.

""                             Marks the beginning and end of a group of lines to be duplicated one time.

""n                            Marks the beginning and end of a group of lines to be duplicated *n* times.

**Copy or move lines**

F                              Insert the copied or moved lines following the indicated line.

P                              Insert the copied or moved lines prior to the indicated line.

C                              Copy the indicated line.

Cn or nC                       Copy *n* lines beginning with the indicated line.

CC                             Marks the beginning and end of a group of lines to be copied.

M                              Move the indicated line.

Mn or nM                       Move *n* lines beginning with the indicated line.

MM                             Marks the beginning and end of a group of lines to be moved.

---

Figure 4-15    XEDIT prefix commands

You can issue prefix commands in two ways. First, you can enter a single command and specify how many lines it should affect. For example, to add seven blank lines into which you can key new data, you can enter

17

or

    7 I

in the prefix area of the line immediately before the position where the new lines are to be added. (By the way, you could also enter A7 or 7A; the I and A prefix commands have the same function.) When you press the enter key, the blank lines are added.

If you only want to process a single line with a prefix command, you can omit the number of lines from the command. As a result, you can enter simply

    D

to delete one line.

The other way to use a prefix command is as a *block command*. When you do that, you mark the beginning and end of a group of lines to be processed by the command. For example, to delete a block of lines, you'd enter

    D D

at the first line of the group to be deleted and at the last line of the group.

It's often desirable to use block commands when you want to operate on a group of lines that spans more than one screen. And even if a group of lines fits entirely on one screen, you're less likely to make a mistake if you use a block command instead of a regular prefix command; that's because you don't have to count the number of lines to be processed when you use a block command.

The prefix commands to add blank lines and delete existing lines are easy to understand. The commands to duplicate, copy, and move lines are just a little more complicated. I want to be sure you understand the difference between the duplicate and copy functions. Duplicate makes copies of the indicated line or lines immediately after the indicated lines. For instance, if you enter

    " 4

the indicated line is copied four times; the result is that the indicated line appears five times in succession in the file after the command is processed.

In contrast, when you use the copy command, you must use another prefix command (either F or P) to indicate where the copied lines will be inserted. F means the copied lines should be inserted following the indicated line; P means the copied lines should be inserted previous to the indicated line. The move command also requires that you specify F or P along with it. (In the simple XEDIT session I'll show you in a moment, you'll see how this works.)

You don't have to enter all of these commands on the same screen. In fact, you're likely to have to scroll the screen to position the commands properly to specify the range of lines to be processed and the target position where they should be inserted. If you enter one of these commands, it's said to be "pending" until you've supplied the other commands necessary to complete the operation or you remove the first block command.

### How to save a file you've edited and end your XEDIT session

Unless some special options are in effect, the editing work you do isn't immediately recorded in the file. Instead, your changes are recorded in a temporary XEDIT work file. As a result, before you end an XEDIT session, you'll probably want to save your work in the original file you specified.

You should know about two XEDIT commands that cause the work you've done to be stored in the file you named when you invoked the editor: SAVE and FILE. You can issue the SAVE command anytime during your editing session to store your work. You issue the FILE command when you're ready to leave XEDIT. In addition to saving your work file, the FILE command ends the editor.

Actually, the FILE command combines the functions of the SAVE and QUIT commands. QUIT simply ends XEDIT. If you issue the QUIT command without saving your work, XEDIT displays a message to that effect and tells you to enter QQUIT if you really want to end the session without saving your file. That reduces the chances that you'll accidentally leave the editor and lose your work.

### A simple XEDIT session

Figure 4-16 presents a simple XEDIT terminal session that illustrates how to use the commands this topic has presented. In part 1 of the figure, I invoke the editor by keying in

```
X LISTMAST COBOL
```

The editor responds by displaying the screen in part 2. (This is the same screen you saw in figure 4-13.) The part of the file I want to edit is located farther down, so I press the PF8 key to scroll forward twice; the editor responses are shown in parts 3 and 4 of the figure. (Part 3 is the same as figure 4-14.)

The part of the file I want to work on is the section beginning with the line

```
01  PRINT-FIELDS    COMP-3.
```

(It's just coincidental that this line turns out to be the current line in the screen in part 4.) I want to move that block of COBOL code to another part of the program. So in part 5 of the figure, I key in two MM block commands to mark the beginning and end of the range of lines I want to move.

When I press the enter key, XEDIT recognizes the block commands, and informs me that an MM operation is pending; you can see that message in part 6 of the figure. At this point, XEDIT expects me to supply an F or P prefix command to identify where to insert the moved text.

Next, I scroll down one more screen by pressing PF8 to display the part of the file shown in part 7 of the figure. Notice that the message

`'MM' PENDING`

is still displayed, even though the lines I marked with the MM commands are no longer on the screen. In part 8, I key in an F prefix command to indicate where the text I marked with the MM commands should be inserted. (Remember that the F command means the block should be inserted following, or after, the indicated line, while the P command means the block should be inserted prior to, or before, the indicated line.)

When I press the enter key, the marked block is inserted where I specified, as you can see in part 9. Notice here that the PENDING message is no longer present. Finally, to end the XEDIT session, I key in the FILE command in part 10. When I press the enter key, XEDIT saves my work and returns me to the CMS command environment (part 11).

## Terminology

VM/SP System Product Editor
XEDIT
EDIT
file identification line
scale line
command line
file area
current line
prefix area
prefix command
scroll
block command

## Objectives

1. Invoke XEDIT to edit either a new file or an existing file.

2. Identify the five main parts of the XEDIT screen.

3. Use XEDIT's basic PF key assignments to scroll the text you're using and to end your editing session.

4. Use the XEDIT prefix commands to add blank lines to a file and to erase, copy, move, and duplicate existing lines in a file.

5. Use the XEDIT SAVE or FILE command to store your edited file on disk.

6. Use the XEDIT FILE, QUIT, or QQUIT command, as appropriate, to end an editing session.

The X command invokes the editor

```
R; T=6.57/13.95 13:29:02


















X LISTMAST COBOL_
                                                                    RUNNING
 Ia                                                           ⊡–⊡04
```

**Figure 4-16**   A simple XEDIT session (part 1 of 11)

The editor displays the beginning of the file

```
   LISTMAST COBOL     A1  F 80  TRUNC=72 SIZE=236 LINE=0 COL=1 ALT=0









===== * * * TOP OF FILE * * *
       |...+....1....+....2....+....3....+....4....+....5....+....6....+....7.>
=====          IDENTIFICATION DIVISION.
=====       *
=====          PROGRAM-ID.    LISTMAST.
=====       *
=====          ENVIRONMENT DIVISION.
=====       *
=====          INPUT-OUTPUT SECTION.
=====       *
=====          FILE-CONTROL.
====>  _
                                                        X E D I T  1 FILE
 Ia                                                           ⊡–⊡04
```

**Figure 4-16**   A simple XEDIT session (part 2 of 11)

Use the PF8 key to scroll forward...

```
 LISTMAST COBOL    A1  F 80  TRUNC=72 SIZE=236 LINE=18 COL=1 ALT=0

 =====          FILE-CONTROL.
 =====              SELECT INVMAST ASSIGN TO SYS020-AS-INVMAST.
 =====              SELECT INVLIST ASSIGN TO SYS006-UR-1403-S.
 =====          *
 =====          DATA DIVISION.
 =====          *
 =====          FILE SECTION.
 =====          *
 =====          FD  INVMAST
 =====              LABEL RECORDS ARE STANDARD
   |...+....1....+....2....+....3....+....4....+....5....+....6....+....7.>
 =====              RECORD CONTAINS 128 CHARACTERS.
 =====          *
 =====          01  INVENTORY-MASTER      PIC X(128).
 =====          *
 =====          FD  INVLIST
 =====              LABEL RECORDS ARE OMITTED
 =====              RECORD CONTAINS 132 CHARACTERS.
 =====          *
 =====          01  PRINT-AREA            PIC X(132).
 ====> _
                                                   X E D I T  1 FILE
 IA                                                  ⊡-⊡04
```

**Figure 4-16**    A simple XEDIT session (part 3 of 11)

...to the part of the file you want to work on

```
 LISTMAST COBOL    A1  F 80  TRUNC=72 SIZE=236 LINE=36 COL=1 ALT=0

 =====          01  PRINT-AREA            PIC X(132).
 =====          *
 =====          WORKING-STORAGE SECTION.
 =====          *
 =====          01  SWITCHES.
 =====          *
 =====              05  INVMAST-EOF-SW         PIC X        VALUE 'N'.
 =====                  88  INVMAST-EOF                     VALUE 'Y'.
 =====          *
 =====          01  PRINT-FIELDS          COMP-3.
   |...+....1....+....2....+....3....+....4....+....5....+....6....+....7.>
 =====          *
 =====              05  SPACE-CONTROL      PIC S(9).
 =====              05  LINES-ON-PAGE      PIC S999 VALUE +55.
 =====              05  LINE-COUNT         PIC S999 VALUE +99.
 =====              05  PAGE-COUNT         PIC S999 VALUE ZERO.
 =====          *
 =====          01  DATE-AND-TIME-FIELDS.
 =====          *
 =====              05  TODAYS-DATE        PIC  X(6).
 ====> _
                                                   X E D I T  1 FILE
 IA                                                  ⊡-⊡04
```

**Figure 4-16**    A simple XEDIT session (part 4 of 11)

The MM block commands mark the block of code to be moved

```
LISTMAST COBOL    A1  F 80  TRUNC=72 SIZE=236 LINE=36 COL=1 ALT=0

=====        01  PRINT-AREA               PIC X(132).
=====        *
=====        WORKING-STORAGE SECTION.
=====        *
=====          01  SWITCHES.
=====          *
=====              05  INVMAST-EOF-SW           PIC X        VALUE 'N'.
=====              88  INVMAST-EOF                           VALUE 'Y'.
=====          *
MM===          01  PRINT-FIELDS          COMP-3.
       |...+....1....+....2....+....3....+....4....+....5....+....6....+....7.>
=====          *
=====              05  SPACE-CONTROL     PIC S(9).
=====              05  LINES-ON-PAGE     PIC S999 VALUE +55.
=====              05  LINE-COUNT        PIC S999 VALUE +99.
=====              05  PAGE-COUNT        PIC S999 VALUE ZERO.
MM===          *
=====          01  DATE-AND-TIME-FIELDS.
=====          *
=====              05  TODAYS-DATE       PIC X(6).
====>  _
                                                      X E D I T  1 FILE
Iª                                          □—□04
```

**Figure 4-16**    A simple XEDIT session (part 5 of 11)

When you press the enter key, XEDIT displays a message to say the move is pending and waits for you to enter an F or P prefix command to show where the moved text should go

```
LISTMAST COBOL    A1  F 80  TRUNC=72 SIZE=236 LINE=36 COL=1 ALT=0

=====        01  PRINT-AREA               PIC X(132).
=====        *
=====        WORKING-STORAGE SECTION.
=====        *
=====          01  SWITCHES.
=====          *
=====              05  INVMAST-EOF-SW           PIC X        VALUE 'N'.
=====              88  INVMAST-EOF                           VALUE 'Y'.
=====          *
MM             01  PRINT-FIELDS          COMP-3.
       |...+....1....+....2....+....3....+....4....+....5....+....6....+....7.>
=====          *
=====              05  SPACE-CONTROL     PIC S(9).
=====              05  LINES-ON-PAGE     PIC S999 VALUE +55.
=====              05  LINE-COUNT        PIC S999 VALUE +99.
=====              05  PAGE-COUNT        PIC S999 VALUE ZERO.
MM             *
=====          01  DATE-AND-TIME-FIELDS.
=====          *
=====              05  TODAYS-DATE       PIC X(6).
====>  _
                                                  'MM' PENDING...
Iª                                          □—□04
```

**Figure 4-16**    A simple XEDIT session (part 6 of 11)

Use the PF8 key to scroll down to the appropriate place in the file

```
 LISTMAST COBOL    A1  F 80   TRUNC=72 SIZE=236 LINE=54 COL=1 ALT=0

 =====             05   TODAYS-DATE        PIC  X(6).
 =====             05   TODAYS-DATE-R REDEFINES TODAYS-DATE.
 =====                  10  TODAYS-YEAR    PIC XX.
 =====                  10  TODAYS-MONTH   PIC XX.
 =====                  10  TODAYS-DAY     PIC XX.
 =====             05   TODAYS-TIME        PIC X(8).
 =====             05   TODAYS-TIME-R REDEFINES TODAYS-TIME.
 =====                  10  TODAYS-HOURS   PIC S99.
 =====                  10  TODAYS-MINUTES PIC XX.
 =====                  10  FILLER         PIC X(4).
     |...+....1....+....2....+....3....+....4....+....5....+....6....+....7.>
 =====        *
 =====        01  COUNT-FIELDS            COMP-3.
 =====        *
 =====             05  RECORD-COUNT       PIC S9(3)     VALUE ZERO.
 =====        *
 =====        01  INVENTORY-MASTER-RECORD.
 =====        *
 =====             05  IM-STATUS          PIC X.
 =====                 88  IM-IN-PRINT    VALUE 'I'.
 ====>  _
                                                    'MM'  PENDING...
 Iª                                          □—□04
```

**Figure 4-16**    A simple XEDIT session (part 7 of 11)

The F prefix command shows where the text should be inserted (*following the line marked*)

```
 LISTMAST COBOL    A1  F 80   TRUNC=72 SIZE=236 LINE=54 COL=1 ALT=0

 =====             05   TODAYS-DATE        PIC  X(6).
 =====             05   TODAYS-DATE-R REDEFINES TODAYS-DATE.
 =====                  10  TODAYS-YEAR    PIC XX.
 =====                  10  TODAYS-MONTH   PIC XX.
 =====                  10  TODAYS-DAY     PIC XX.
 =====             05   TODAYS-TIME        PIC X(8).
 =====             05   TODAYS-TIME-R REDEFINES TODAYS-TIME.
 =====                  10  TODAYS-HOURS   PIC S99.
 =====                  10  TODAYS-MINUTES PIC XX.
 =====                  10  FILLER         PIC X(4).
     |...+....1....+....2....+....3....+....4....+....5....+....6....+....7.>
 =====        *
 =====        01  COUNT-FIELDS            COMP-3.
 =====        *
 =====             05  RECORD-COUNT       PIC S9(3)     VALUE ZERO.
 F====        *
 =====        01  INVENTORY-MASTER-RECORD.
 =====        *
 =====             05  IM-STATUS          PIC X.
 =====                 88  IM-IN-PRINT    VALUE 'I'.
 ====>  _
                                                    'MM'  PENDING...
 Iª                                          □—□04
```

**Figure 4-16**    A simple XEDIT session (part 8 of 11)

When you press the enter key, XEDIT moves the text

```
LISTMAST COBOL     A1  F 80   TRUNC=72 SIZE=236 LINE=54 COL=1 ALT=1

=====              05   TODAYS-DATE        PIC  X(6).
=====              05   TODAYS-DATE-R REDEFINES TODAYS-DATE.
=====              10   TODAYS-YEAR        PIC XX.
=====              10   TODAYS-MONTH       PIC XX.
=====              10   TODAYS-DAY         PIC XX.
=====              05   TODAYS-TIME        PIC X(8).
=====              05   TODAYS-TIME-R REDEFINES TODAYS-TIME.
=====              10   TODAYS-HOURS       PIC S99.
=====              10   TODAYS-MINUTES  PIC XX.
=====              10   FILLER             PIC X(4).
    |...+....1....+....2....+....3....+....4....+....5....+....6....+....7.>
=====        *
=====        01  COUNT-FIELDS            COMP-3.
=====        *
=====              05   RECORD-COUNT        PIC S9(3)     VALUE ZERO.
=====        *
=====   —    01  PRINT-FIELDS            COMP-3.
=====        *
=====              05   SPACE-CONTROL       PIC S9.
=====              05   LINES-ON-PAGE       PIC S999 VALUE +55.
====>
                                                    X E D I T   1 FILE
 IᵃA                                              ☐–☐04
```

**Figure 4-16**    A simple XEDIT session (part 9 of 11)

The FILE command says to end the editing session

```
LISTMAST COBOL     A1  F 80   TRUNC=72 SIZE=236 LINE=54 COL=1 ALT=1

=====              05   TODAYS-DATE        PIC  X(6).
=====              05   TODAYS-DATE-R REDEFINES TODAYS-DATE.
=====              10   TODAYS-YEAR        PIC XX.
=====              10   TODAYS-MONTH       PIC XX.
=====              10   TODAYS-DAY         PIC XX.
=====              05   TODAYS-TIME        PIC X(8).
=====              05   TODAYS-TIME-R REDEFINES TODAYS-TIME.
=====              10   TODAYS-HOURS       PIC S99.
=====              10   TODAYS-MINUTES  PIC XX.
=====              10   FILLER             PIC X(4).
    |...+....1....+....2....+....3....+....4....+....5....+....6....+....7.>
=====        *
=====        01  COUNT-FIELDS            COMP-3.
=====        *
=====              05   RECORD-COUNT        PIC S9(3)     VALUE ZERO.
=====        *
=====        01  PRINT-FIELDS            COMP-3.
=====        *
=====              05   SPACE-CONTROL       PIC S9.
=====              05   LINES-ON-PAGE       PIC S999 VALUE +55.
====> FILE_
                                                    X E D I T   1 FILE
 IᵃA                                              ☐–☐04
```

**Figure 4-16**    A simple XEDIT session (part 10 of 11)

When you press the enter key, XEDIT saves the edited file and returns to the CMS
command environment

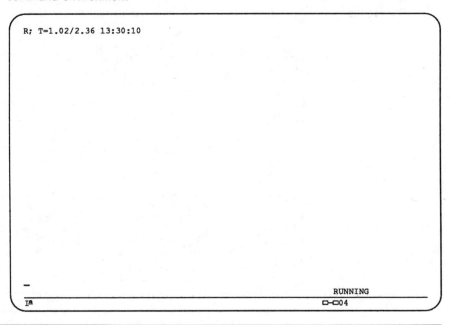

```
R; T=1.02/2.36 13:30:10
```

                                                                    RUNNING

**Figure 4-16**   A simple XEDIT session (part 11 of 11)

# Section 2

Disk file handling

Most of the CMS work you do will involve disk files. As a result, to use VM/CMS most effectively, you need to know more than the basic file-handling commands you learned in the last section. This section shows you how to use additional VM/CMS facilities to manage your disk data.

Chapter 5 expands your knowledge of some of the file-handling commands you learned in section 1, and it presents new commands that can enhance your ability to get the most from your system. In chapter 6, your attention will turn from managing individual files to managing your CMS minidisks. And in chapter 7, you'll learn how to use an optional software product that may be available on your system: VM's File Storage Facility.

Chapter 5

How to manage your
CMS disk files

The basic CMS commands you need to know to manage your CMS disk files are the ones I presented in the last chapter: LISTFILE, TYPE, PRINT, ERASE, RENAME, COPYFILE, and XEDIT. They're fundamental. As a result, if you're not confident in your ability to use their functions, I encourage you to go back to chapter 4 and review before you begin this chapter.

This chapter's four topics present additional functions that will make it easier for you to manage your files. Topic 1 shows you how to use the FILELIST command. It provides all the functions of LISTFILE, but does so in a format that can be easier to understand and use. Topics 2 and 3 present advanced functions of two of the basic commands that chapter 4 introduced: TYPE and COPYFILE. Finally, topic 4 covers two other CMS commands you'll probably need to use occasionally: COMPARE and SORT.

**Topic one**

# How to use the FILELIST command

The CMS FILELIST command provides a comprehensive file-management environment. FILELIST builds a list of files which it displays for you, then it lets you issue commands that affect those files from its display. For example, you can invoke XEDIT to edit a file directly from the FILELIST display. And you can copy, rename, and delete your files too. In this topic, I'll show you how to enter the FILELIST environment, how to interpret the FILELIST display, and how to issue commands from it. Then, I'll show you how to save the FILELIST data in a file for later use and how to add data incrementally to the FILELIST display.

Before you learn the syntax of the FILELIST command, I think it's useful for you to understand what it is and how it works. Actually, FILELIST is a procedure that's supplied with CMS; it's not user-written. FILELIST invokes the LIST-FILE command, which you learned how to use in the last chapter, to collect information about specified files. That information is stored in a file which the FILELIST procedure invokes XEDIT to manipulate. You can scroll up and down through the list and issue commands from the list to process the files. Those capabilities are provided through some advanced XEDIT functions.

## How to invoke FILELIST

Figure 5-1 presents the syntax of the FILELIST command. For now, I want you to ignore the options you can specify on the command; they're for the advanced functions I'll describe at the end of this topic. To invoke FILELIST for typical operations, you issue a command in this format:

```
FILELIST fn ft fm
```

Although the command lets you specify a single file, it's more likely that you'll use FILELIST to display information about groups of files.

The command defaults are set so it's easiest for you to get information about the group of files you're most likely to want to see: the ones on your A-disk. As figure 5-1 indicates, the default for the filemode letter is A, and the default for both filename and filetype is *. As you should recall from the last chapter, an asterisk in a CMS command operand means "all values." As a result, if you enter simply

```
FILELIST
```

or the abbreviation

```
FILEL
```

### The FILELIST command

```
FILELIST [fn [ft [fm]]] [({FILELIST|APPEND}]
```

### Explanation

FILELIST          The command may be abbreviated FILEL.

fn                Usually, the pattern mask for the filename component of the identifiers of the files
                  to be listed; may include the % or * characters. If you omit fn, all filenames are
                  accepted. If you specify the FILELIST option, fn is the filename of a saved list that
                  you want to access.

ft                Usually, the pattern mask for the filetype component of the identifiers of the files to
                  be listed; may include the % or * characters. If you omit ft, all filetypes are accepted.
                  If you specify the FILELIST option, ft is the filetype of a saved list that you want to
                  access.

fm                Usually, the pattern mask for the filemode component of the identifiers of the files
                  to be listed; may be the * to indicate all accessed minidisks. If you omit fm, A is
                  assumed. If you specify the FILELIST option, fm is the filemode for the saved list
                  that you want to access.

FILELIST          Specifies that a previously saved file containing FILELIST data should be accessed;
                  valid only when you invoke the FILELIST command from the CMS command environ-
                  ment. You may abbreviate the option as F.

APPEND            Specifies that the file data should be added to the currently displayed data; valid
                  only when you invoke the FILELIST command from the FILELIST display. You may
                  abbreviate the option as A.

---

Figure 5-1          The FILELIST command

your command is interpreted as

```
FILELIST * * A
```

Then, the FILELIST display will contain information for all of the files on your
A-disk.

    If you want to display a subset of the files on an accessed disk, that's easy.
For example, if you want the FILELIST display to include only the procedures
on your A-disk, you enter

```
FILEL * EXEC
```

Because the default for filemode is A, you don't need to key in a value for filemode on the command. However, if you want to display files on a disk other
than your A-disk, you must specify the filemode letter. For example,

```
FILEL * EXEC B
```

causes FILELIST to display all of the procedure files on your current B-disk. And if you want to display a set of files from all of your currently accessed disks, you specify an asterisk for filemode. For instance,

```
FILEL * EXEC *
```

causes FILELIST to display all of the procedure files on all of your currently accessed disks.

You can also use the asterisk within a component of the file identifier. For example, if you enter

```
FILEL D* EXEC *
```

all of the procedure files whose filenames begin with the letter D on all of your currently accessed minidisks will be displayed.

In addition to the asterisk, you can also use a percent sign (%) when you specify the file identifier pattern on the FILELIST command. In contrast with the asterisk, which means any characters in any number match the pattern, the percent sign means any *single* character in the indicated position matches the pattern. For instance,

```
FILEL D%%% EXEC *
```

tells FILELIST to display all procedure files on all accessed minidisks whose filenames begin with the letter D and are exactly five characters long. The command

```
FILEL D%%%% EXEC *
```

is similar, except it requests only files whose filenames are exactly six characters long. Although you might find some use for the percent sign when you invoke the FILELIST command, I suspect that you'll seldom need to use it.

When the file identifier contains an asterisk or a percent sign, it's called a *mask*. That simply means it's not the identifier for a single, specific file. Instead, it's a pattern that a file identifier has to match in order to be operated upon by the command.

## How to interpret the FILELIST display

Figure 5-2 shows a typical FILELIST display. The line at the top of the screen gives the name of the file that contains the displayed data (here, filename PAT, filetype FILELIST, and filemode A0). The other information on the first line is about the characteristics of the file and how it's viewed by XEDIT. The most useful item of information here is the SIZE value. It's the number of records in the file that contains the data being displayed by FILELIST; it indicates how many files met the selection criteria you specified when you invoked FILELIST.

Most of the screen is used to display file information. After a heading line, a single screen can display information for up to 17 files. If more than one screen

```
 PAT       FILELIST A0   V 108   TRUNC=108 SIZE=85 LINE=1 COL=1 ALT=0
 CMD      FILENAME FILETYPE FM FORMAT LRECL     RECORDS      BLOCKS    DATE      TIME
  _        SC2TAPE  ASCII    A1 F        80         8228         643   4/23/87  16:31:10
           RWCH4    LISTING  A1 F       121          279          33   4/20/87  17:35:59
           RWCH4    TEXT     A1 F        80          202          16   4/20/87  17:35:57
           RWCH4    COBOL    A1 F        80          256          33   4/20/87  17:34:55
           SYSDATE  TEXT     A1 F        80           32           3   4/20/87  16:01:19
           READSEQ  COPY     A1 F        80            5           1   1/05/87  11:42:45
           LISTTRAN TEXT     A1 F        80          109           9   1/05/87  11:02:35
           LISTTRAN COBOL    A1 F        80          227          18   1/05/87  11:01:53
           CREATMST COBOL    A1 F        80           95           8   1/05/87  10:58:45
           MAINTMST COBOL    A1 F        80          181          15   1/05/87  10:58:34
           LISTMAST COBOL    A1 F        80          237          19   1/05/87  10:58:23
           SYSTIME  TEXT     A1 F        80           38           3   1/05/87  10:55:27
           PHASELIB DOSLIB   A1 V      1024          764         716  12/19/86  14:59:56
           DEFRSDS  AMSERV   A1 F        80            7           1  12/19/86  14:28:44
           PRINT    AMSERV   A1 F        80            1           1  12/19/86  14:21:19
           DELETE   AMSERV   A1 F        80            4           1  12/19/86  13:40:59
           CASED4   MAP      A5 F       121           91          11  12/19/86  11:30:41
 1= HELP       2= REFRESH   3= QUIT    4= SORT(TYPE)  5= SORT(DATE)  6= SORT(SIZE)
 7= BACKWARD   8= FORWARD   9= FL /N  10=            11= XEDIT      12= CURSOR

 ====>

                                                        X E D I T   1 FILE
 Iª                                               □-□04
```

**Figure 5-2**    A typical FILELIST display

is necessary to display the file information you requested, you can scroll the list using the PF7 key (to scroll backward, or up) and the PF8 key (to scroll forward, or down). These are the same keys that you use to scroll during a typical XEDIT session.

You can also use function keys other than PF7 and PF8. At the bottom of the screen, the FILELIST display shows you the functions associated with the enabled PF keys. To leave the FILELIST screen and return to CMS, you press the PF3 key. In the next section, I'll describe the functions associated with other PF keys.

### How to enter commands from the FILELIST display

You can enter commands in three ways from the FILELIST display. First, you can press PF keys to request predefined command functions. Second, you can enter CMS file processing commands on the lines that identify the files to be affected. And third, you can key in some commands in the command line of the FILELIST display (the line at the bottom of the display that begins with ====>). In this section, I'll show you how to enter commands (1) to manipulate the FILELIST display and (2) to manipulate selected files.

*How to use commands to manipulate the FILELIST display*    I've already described how to use the PF7 and PF8 keys to scroll the FILELIST display and

```
 PAT          FILELIST A0   V 108   TRUNC=108 SIZE=85 LINE=1 COL=1 ALT=1
 CMD      FILENAME FILETYPE FM FORMAT LRECL      RECORDS      BLOCKS  DATE      TIME
         ALTER    AMSERV   A1 F        80           4            1 12/03/86 14:37:47
 __      ALTER2   AMSERV   A1 F        80           2            1 12/03/86 13:42:47
         BLDINDEX AMSERV   A1 F        80           3            1 12/03/86 13:25:38
         DEFAIX   AMSERV   A1 F        80          15            2 12/03/86 13:38:41
         DEFINE   AMSERV   A1 F        80           7            1 12/19/86 11:07:30
         DEFKSDS  AMSERV   A1 F        80           9            1 12/19/86 11:06:36
         DEFMCAT  AMSERV   A1 F        80           2            1  9/08/86  8:13:41
         DEFRSDS  AMSERV   A1 F        80           7            1 12/19/86 14:28:44
         DELCLUST AMSERV   A1 F        80           1            1 12/15/86 12:59:34
         DELETE   AMSERV   A1 F        80           4            1 12/19/86 13:40:59
         LISTCAT  AMSERV   A1 F        80           1            1 12/12/86 15:22:39
         PRINT    AMSERV   A1 F        80           1            1 12/19/86 14:21:19
         SC2TAPE  ASCII    A1 F        80        8228          643  4/23/87 16:31:10
         CASED1   COBOL    A1 F        80         430           34 11/24/86 11:14:44
         CREATMST COBOL    A1 F        80          95            8  1/05/87 10:58:45
         CUSTEXT  COBOL    A1 F        80         210           17 10/24/86 15:46:33
         DATEDITD COBOL    A1 F        80          69            6 12/12/86 15:21:39
 1= HELP        2= REFRESH    3= QUIT     4= SORT(TYPE) 5= SORT(DATE)  6= SORT(SIZE)
 7= BACKWARD    8= FORWARD    9= FL /N   10=           11= XEDIT      12= CURSOR

 ====>
                                                             X E D I T   1 FILE
  IA                                                        ▢–▢04
```

**Figure 5-3**     A FILELIST display with files sequenced by filetype

the PF3 key to return to CMS. As you can see in the bottom of figure 5-2, eight other PF keys also have predefined FILELIST functions.

PF1 invokes the CMS help facility for the FILELIST command. When you press PF1, a text file containing a summary of the information from the *CMS Command and Macro Reference* manual for the FILELIST command is displayed. You can scroll through it using PF7 and PF8 to review syntax and usage points, then press PF3 to return to the FILELIST display.

PF2, the refresh function, causes FILELIST to redisplay information for the specified files. As you'll see in a moment, as you issue file management commands from the FILELIST display, the display can become cluttered. The refresh function removes that clutter and presents an updated picture of your files.

PF4, PF5, and PF6 let you change the sequence in which information for the selected files is displayed. The default is for FILELIST to display file information in sequence by date of last modification. If you look at the DATE column in figure 5-2, you'll see that the files are ordered from most to least recent. That's useful because the files you worked on last are the ones you're most likely to be interested in, and they're displayed first on the list.

However, you may want to look at the files you've requested in another order. If you want to see the files grouped by filetype, all you have to do is press the PF4 key. When I press the PF4 key in figure 5-2, the screen in figure 5-3 is displayed. Notice here that the files in the display are sequenced by filetype and, in effect, grouped according to content. To restore the list to its original sequence

| Subcommand | Causes the selected files to be sorted by |
|---|---|
| SNAME | Filename, then filetype, then filemode. |
| SMODE | Filemode, then filename, then filetype. |
| SLREC | Logical record length, then size (in descending sequence). |
| SRECF | Record format (fixed or variable), then filename, then filetype, then filemode. |

**Figure 5-4**      FILELIST subcommands to sort the files displayed

(date), you can press the PF5 key. Or, to see the list in sequence by file size (that is, the amount of minidisk space the files use), you can press the PF6 key.

If you want to view the files in a sequence other than filetype, date, or size, you can use one of the special FILELIST subcommands in figure 5-4. Just key in the appropriate command in the command line at the bottom of the screen and press enter. For example, figure 5-5 shows how you can resequence the FILELIST display by filename using the SNAME subcommand. Of the subcommands available for resequencing the list, SNAME is the one I think you'll use most often. SMODE is useful if you display file information for all of your accessed minidisks.

PF9 lets you create a secondary FILELIST display that contains only files with a particular filename. To use this function, you position the cursor on the line of a particular file in the list. The filename of that file is the one that will be used for the operation. Any filetype and any filemode will satisfy the specification. As a result, all files with the indicated filename, regardless of their contents and the minidisk on which they reside, will be displayed.

Figure 5-6 illustrates how you can use PF9. In part 1 of the figure, I've moved the cursor to the line that contains the information for the file SYSTIME TEXT A. When I press PF9, FILELIST displays the screen in part 2 of the figure. Here, the display includes information for just three files, but they all have the filename SYSTIME. Notice that two of the files (SYSTIME SC1SRCE A1 and SYSTIME TEXT A1) reside on the minidisk that I queried with my original FILELIST command, but one (SYSTIME SC2SRCE B1) resides on another minidisk. To return to the original, complete FILELIST display, I press the PF3 key. The filename I used to create the secondary list is marked with an asterisk on the original screen, as you can see in part 3 of the figure.

*How to enter commands to manipulate selected files*      One of the advantages of using FILELIST is that you can enter commands to operate on individual files from its display. For example, PF11 lets you invoke XEDIT directly from the FILELIST environment. If you want to edit a file, just move the cursor to the line that contains the information for it and press PF11.

The SNAME subcommand causes the files to be sorted first by filename, then by filetype, then by filemode

```
PAT         FILELIST A0  V 108   TRUNC=108 SIZE=85 LINE=1 COL=1 ALT=2
CMD     FILENAME FILETYPE FM FORMAT LRECL    RECORDS     BLOCKS   DATE      TIME
        SC2TAPE  ASCII    A1 F       80        8228        643  4/23/87 16:31:10
        RWCH4    LISTING  A1 F      121         279         33  4/20/87 17:35:59
        RWCH4    TEXT     A1 F       80         202         16  4/20/87 17:35:57
        RWCH4    COBOL    A1 F       80         256         33  4/20/87 17:34:55
        SYSDATE  TEXT     A1 F       80          32          3  4/20/87 16:01:19
        READSEQ  COPY     A1 F       80           5          1  1/05/87 11:42:45
        LISTTRAN TEXT     A1 F       80         109          9  1/05/87 11:02:35
        LISTTRAN COBOL    A1 F       80         227         18  1/05/87 11:01:53
        CREATMST COBOL    A1 F       80          95          8  1/05/87 10:58:45
        MAINTMST COBOL    A1 F       80         181         15  1/05/87 10:58:34
        LISTMAST COBOL    A1 F       80         237         19  1/05/87 10:58:23
        SYSTIME  TEXT     A1 F       80          38          3  1/05/87 10:55:27
        PHASELIB DOSLIB   A1 V     1024         764        716 12/19/86 14:59:56
        DEFRSDS  AMSERV   A1 F       80           7          1 12/19/86 14:28:44
        PRINT    AMSERV   A1 F       80           1          1 12/19/86 14:21:19
        DELETE   AMSERV   A1 F       80           4          1 12/19/86 13:40:59
        CASED4   MAP      A5 F      121          91         11 12/19/86 11:30:41
1= HELP      2= REFRESH  3= QUIT    4= SORT(TYPE)  5= SORT(DATE)   6= SORT(SIZE)
7= BACKWARD  8= FORWARD  9= FL /N  10=            11= XEDIT      12= CURSOR

====> SNAME_
                                                         X E D I T   1 FILE
  Iª                                                      ⊡—⊡04
```

Figure 5-5    How the SNAME subcommand affects the FILELIST display (part 1 of 2)

The result of the SNAME sort

```
PAT         FILELIST A0  V 108   TRUNC=108 SIZE=85 LINE=1 COL=1 ALT=3
CMD     FILENAME FILETYPE FM FORMAT LRECL    RECORDS     BLOCKS   DATE      TIME
        ALTER    AMSERV   A1 F       80           4          1 12/03/86 14:37:47
        ALTER2   AMSERV   A1 F       80           2          1 12/03/86 13:42:47
        ARMAST   COPY     A1 F       80          28          3 11/20/86 11:37:37
        ARTRAN   COPY     A1 F       80          21          2 11/20/86 11:37:26
        ARTRANX  COPY     A1 F       80          26          3 11/20/86 11:36:52
        BACKUP   EXEC     A1 V       68          28          2 10/10/86  3:10:43
        BACKUP2  EXEC     A1 V       68          26          1 11/03/86 11:09:54
        BLDINDEX AMSERV   A1 F       80           3          1 12/03/86 13:25:38
        CASEC7T2 TEXT     A1 F       80          38          3 12/18/86 11:06:47
        CASED1   COBOL    A1 F       80         430         34 11/24/86 11:14:44
        CASED4   MAP      A5 F      121          91         11 12/19/86 11:30:41
        CASED4   TEXT     A1 F       80         172         14 12/19/86 11:29:57
        CLG      EXEC     A1 F       80          69          6  9/19/86 10:44:10
        CLG1     XEDIT    A1 F       80          11          1  9/19/86 10:44:26
        CLG2     EXEC     A1 V       72         104          4 12/16/86  9:08:15
        CLG2     XEDIT    A1 F       80           5          1  9/19/86 10:44:46
        CREATMST COBOL    A1 F       80          95          8  1/05/87 10:58:45
1= HELP      2= REFRESH  3= QUIT    4= SORT(TYPE)  5= SORT(DATE)   6= SORT(SIZE)
7= BACKWARD  8= FORWARD  9= FL /N  10=            11= XEDIT      12= CURSOR

====> _
                                                         X E D I T   1 FILE
  Iª                                                      ⊡—⊡04
```

Figure 5-5    How the SNAME subcommand affects the FILELIST display (part 2 of 2)

Position the cursor at the filename you want to have a listing for and press PF9 to invoke the FILELIST command

```
PAT          FILELIST A0   V 108    TRUNC=108 SIZE=85 LINE=1 COL=1 ALT=0
CMD     FILENAME FILETYPE FM FORMAT LRECL      RECORDS     BLOCKS     DATE       TIME
        SC2TAPE  ASCII    A1 F        80         8228        643    4/23/87  16:31:10
        RWCH4    LISTING  A1 F       121          279         33    4/20/87  17:35:59
        RWCH4    TEXT     A1 F        80          202         16    4/20/87  17:35:57
        RWCH4    COBOL    A1 F        80          256         33    4/20/87  17:34:55
        SYSDATE  TEXT     A1 F        80           32          3    4/20/87  16:01:19
        READSEQ  COPY     A1 F        80            5          1    1/05/87  11:42:45
        LISTTRAN TEXT     A1 F        80          109          9    1/05/87  11:02:35
        LISTTRAN COBOL    A1 F        80          227         18    1/05/87  11:01:53
        CREATMST COBOL    A1 F        80           95          8    1/05/87  10:58:45
        MAINTMST COBOL    A1 F        80          181         15    1/05/87  10:58:34
        LISTMAST COBOL    A1 F        80          237         19    1/05/87  10:58:23
_       SYSTIME  TEXT     A1 F        80           38          3    1/05/87  10:55:27
        PHASELIB DOSLIB   A1 V      1024          764        716   12/19/86  14:59:56
        DEFRSDS  AMSERV   A1 F        80            7          1   12/19/86  14:28:44
        PRINT    AMSERV   A1 F        80            1          1   12/19/86  14:21:19
        DELETE   AMSERV   A1 F        80            4          1   12/19/86  13:40:59
        CASED4   MAP      A5 F       121           91         11   12/19/86  11:30:41
1= HELP       2= REFRESH   3= QUIT      4= SORT(TYPE)  5= SORT(DATE)  6= SORT(SIZE)
7= BACKWARD   8= FORWARD   9= FL /N  10=             11= XEDIT       12= CURSOR

====>
                                                          X E D I T   1 FILE
 I͟ª                                          □─□04
```

Figure 5-6    Invoking FILELIST from within a FILELIST display with the PF9 key (part 1 of 3)

The FILELIST display now includes information for only the files named SYSTIME

```
PAT          FILELIST A0   V 108    TRUNC=108 SIZE=85 LINE=1 COL=1 ALT=0
CMD     FILENAME FILETYPE FM FORMAT LRECL      RECORDS     BLOCKS     DATE       TIME
_       SYSTIME  TEXT     A1 F        80           38          3    1/05/87  10:55:27
        SYSTIME  SC2SRCE  B1 F        80           61          5   12/18/86  11:04:12
        SYSTIME  SC1SRCE  A1 F        80           64          5   12/04/86   9:56:35




1= HELP       2= REFRESH   3= QUIT      4= SORT(TYPE)  5= SORT(DATE)  6= SORT(SIZE)
7= BACKWARD   8= FORWARD   9= FL /N  10=             11= XEDIT       12= CURSOR

====>
                                                          X E D I T   1 FILE
 I͟ª                                          □─□04
```

Figure 5-6    Invoking FILELIST from within a FILELIST display with the PF9 key (part 2 of 3)

Press PF3 to return to the original display; the selected filename is now marked with an asterisk

```
  PAT        FILELIST A0   V 108   TRUNC=108 SIZE=85 LINE=1 COL=1 ALT=2
  CMD      FILENAME FILETYPE FM FORMAT LRECL    RECORDS    BLOCKS    DATE      TIME
           SC2TAPE  ASCII    A1 F        80       8228       643   4/23/87  16:31:10
           RWCH4    LISTING  A1 F       121        279        33   4/20/87  17:35:59
           RWCH4    TEXT     A1 F        80        202        16   4/20/87  17:35:57
           RWCH4    COBOL    A1 F        80        256        33   4/20/87  17:34:55
           SYSDATE  TEXT     A1 F        80         32         3   4/20/87  16:01:19
           READSEQ  COPY     A1 F        80          5         1   1/05/87  11:42:45
           LISTTRAN TEXT     A1 F        80        109         9   1/05/87  11:02:35
           LISTTRAN COBOL    A1 F        80        227        18   1/05/87  11:01:53
           CREATMST COBOL    A1 F        80         95         8   1/05/87  10:58:45
           MAINTMST COBOL    A1 F        80        181        15   1/05/87  10:58:34
           LISTMAST COBOL    A1 F        80        237        19   1/05/87  10:58:23
   *       SYSTIME  TEXT     A1 F        80         38         3   1/05/87  10:55:27
           PHASELIB DOSLIB   A1 V      1024        764       716  12/19/86  14:59:56
           DEFRSDS  AMSERV   A1 F        80          7         1  12/19/86  14:28:44
           PRINT    AMSERV   A1 F        80          1         1  12/19/86  14:21:19
           DELETE   AMSERV   A1 F        80          4         1  12/19/86  13:40:59
           CASED4   MAP      A5 F       121         91        11  12/19/86  11:30:41
  1= HELP       2= REFRESH   3= QUIT      4= SORT(TYPE)  5= SORT(DATE)  6= SORT(SIZE)
  7= BACKWARD   8= FORWARD   9= FL /N  10=              11= XEDIT       12= CURSOR

  ====>
                                                              X E D I T  1 FILE
  1ª                                                   □─□04
```

**Figure 5-6**   Invoking FILELIST from within a FILELIST display with the PF9 key (part 3 of 3)

For example, to edit the file RWCH4 COBOL A, I'd move the cursor to its line in the display, as in part 1 of figure 5-7, then I'd press PF11. XEDIT is invoked, and the screen in part 2 of the figure appears. At this point, I can work on the file just as if I had invoked XEDIT from the CMS command environment. When I end the XEDIT session, the original FILELIST display reappears, as in part 3 of the figure.

As you can see in part 3, the file I edited is marked with an asterisk. Here, that means that the position of the file in the list might not be correct any more. If changes are made to a file, its date and time stamps will probably change, as will its size. To display updated information, I could press PF2 to refresh the screen.

To issue other file processing commands from the FILELIST display, all you do is type the command, starting in the column labelled CMD, right over the line for that file. (That's OK; only the data you key in is processed.) For example, to delete a file shown on the display, all you have to do is key in ERASE or DIS-CARD in the CMD column of the line for that file. (DISCARD is a special FILELIST subcommand that isn't available in the CMS command environment; it produces the same result as ERASE.)

You can issue commands for more than one file at the same time from the FILELIST display. To understand, consider the example in figure 5-8. Part 1 of the figure shows part of a FILELIST display. To delete the first four files in the list (with filenames LISTMAST and filetypes COBOL1, COBOL2, COBOL3,

Position the cursor at the file you want to edit, and press PF11 to invoke XEDIT

```
 PAT        FILELIST A0  V 108  TRUNC=108 SIZE=85 LINE=1 COL=1 ALT=0
 CMD    FILENAME FILETYPE FM FORMAT LRECL    RECORDS     BLOCKS   DATE      TIME
        SC2TAPE  ASCII    A1 F        80       8228        643 4/23/87  16:31:10
        RWCH4    LISTING  A1 F       121        279         33 4/20/87  17:35:59
        RWCH4    TEXT     A1 F        80        202         16 4/20/87  17:35:57
 __     RWCH4    COBOL    A1 F        80        256         33 4/20/87  17:34:55
        SYSDATE  TEXT     A1 F        80         32          3 4/20/87  16:01:19
        READSEQ  COPY     A1 F        80          5          1 1/05/87  11:42:45
        LISTTRAN TEXT     A1 F        80        109          9 1/05/87  11:02:35
        LISTTRAN COBOL    A1 F        80        227         18 1/05/87  11:01:53
        CREATMST COBOL    A1 F        80         95          8 1/05/87  10:58:45
        MAINTMST COBOL    A1 F        80        181         15 1/05/87  10:58:34
        LISTMAST COBOL    A1 F        80        237         19 1/05/87  10:58:23
        SYSTIME  TEXT     A1 F        80         38          3 1/05/87  10:55:27
        PHASELIB DOSLIB   A1 V      1024        764        716 12/19/86 14:59:56
        DEFRSDS  AMSERV   A1 F        80          7          1 12/19/86 14:28:44
        PRINT    AMSERV   A1 F        80          1          1 12/19/86 14:21:19
        DELETE   AMSERV   A1 F        80          4          1 12/19/86 13:40:59
        CASED4   MAP      A5 F       121         91         11 12/19/86 11:30:41
 1= HELP      2= REFRESH  3= QUIT    4= SORT(TYPE)   5= SORT(DATE)   6= SORT(SIZE)
 7= BACKWARD  8= FORWARD  9= FL /N  10=             11= XEDIT        12= CURSOR

 ====>
                                                       X E D I T  1 FILE
 Iᵃ                                              ⌑–⌑04
```

Figure 5-7     Invoking XEDIT from within the FILELIST display with the PF11 key (part 1 of 3)

The XEDIT session begins just as if it had been started from the CMS command environment

```
 RWCH4     COBOL    A1 F  80  TRUNC=72 SIZE=256 LINE=0 COL=1 ALT=0




 ===== * * * TOP OF FILE * * *
       |...+....1....+....2....+....3....+....4....+....5....+....6....+....7.>
 =====  CBL APOST
 ===== 000100 IDENTIFICATION DIVISION.
 ===== 000200*
 ===== 000300 PROGRAM-ID.          SLS1910.
 ===== 000400*AUTHOR.              STEVE ECKOLS.
 ===== 000500*
 ===== 000600 ENVIRONMENT DIVISION.
 ===== 000700*
 ===== 000800 INPUT-OUTPUT SECTION.
 ====> _
                                                       X E D I T  1 FILE
 Iᵃ                                              ⌑–⌑04
```

Figure 5-7     Invoking XEDIT from within the FILELIST display with the PF11 key (part 2 of 3)

When you end the XEDIT session, the original FILELIST display reappears, and the file you worked on is marked with an asterisk

```
 PAT         FILELIST A0   V 108    TRUNC=108 SIZE=85 LINE=1 COL=1 ALT=2
 CMD       FILENAME FILETYPE FM FORMAT LRECL    RECORDS       BLOCKS  DATE     TIME
           SC2TAPE  ASCII    A1 F        80       8228          643 4/23/87 16:31:10
           RWCH4    LISTING  A1 F       121        279           33 4/20/87 17:35:59
           RWCH4    TEXT     A1 F        80        202           16 4/20/87 17:35:57
   *       RWCH4    COBOL    A1 F        80        256           33 4/20/87 16:34:55
           SYSDATE  TEXT     A1 F        80         32            3 4/20/87 16:01:19
           READSEQ  COPY     A1 F        80          5            1 1/05/87 11:42:45
           LISTTRAN TEXT     A1 F        80        109            9 1/05/87 11:02:35
           LISTTRAN COBOL    A1 F        80        227           18 1/05/87 11:01:53
           CREATMST COBOL    A1 F        80         95            8 1/05/87 10:58:45
           MAINTMST COBOL    A1 F        80        181           15 1/05/87 10:58:34
           LISTMAST COBOL    A1 F        80        237           19 1/05/87 10:58:23
           SYSTIME  TEXT     A1 F        80         38            3 1/05/87 10:55:27
           PHASELIB DOSLIB   A1 V      1024        764          716 12/19/86 14:59:56
           DEFRSDS  AMSERV   A1 F        80          7            1 12/19/86 14:28:44
           PRINT    AMSERV   A1 F        80          1            1 12/19/86 14:21:19
           DELETE   AMSERV   A1 F        80          4            1 12/19/86 13:40:59
           CASED4   MAP      A5 F       121         91           11 12/19/86 11:30:41
 1= HELP        2= REFRESH   3= QUIT    4= SORT(TYPE)  5= SORT(DATE)  6= SORT(SIZE)
 7= BACKWARD    8= FORWARD   9= FL /N  10=            11= XEDIT      12= CURSOR

 ====>
                                                        X E D I T   1 FILE
 ⌐ᵃ                                               ▭▬▭04
```

Figure 5-7    Invoking XEDIT from within the FILELIST display with the PF11 key (part 3 of 3)

and COBOL4), I keyed in the commands in part 2. As I said, it's OK to enter a command that's longer than the CMD field. You can see in part 2 of figure 5-8 that the DISCARD command extends beyond the CMD field and covers part of the filename field.

When I pressed the enter key, the commands I entered were processed. Part 3 of figure 5-8 shows the messages displayed to confirm the operations. This screen image shows how cluttered the FILELIST display can become if you issue several commands from it. Although the first four files on the list have been deleted, their entries remain. To update the list, you can press the PF2 key. The refreshed FILELIST screen is shown in part 4 of the figure; as you can see, the files I deleted are no longer included in the list.

If you want to execute the same command for several of the files shown on the screen, you can enter the command for the first, then key in equal signs in the CMD fields of the lines for the files to be affected. So the commands in the screen in figure 5-9 are equivalent to those in part 2 of figure 5-8.

Other commands you can issue like DISCARD and ERASE are XEDIT, TYPE, and PRINT. Of course, it's easier to use the predefined function for PF11 to invoke XEDIT for a file. TYPE, as you should remember from the last chapter, displays the contents of a file on your terminal screen. PRINT causes the contents of the file to be routed to a real printer. (You'll learn more about the PRINT command in section 4 of this book).

The beginning FILELIST display

```
    STEVE      FILELIST A0   V 108   TRUNC=108 SIZE=61 LINE=1 COL=1 ALT=0
    CMD    FILENAME FILETYPE FM FORMAT LRECL    RECORDS      BLOCKS   DATE      TIME
    _      LISTMAST COBOL1   A1 F        80        236          19   5/27/87 13:07:05
           LISTMAST COBOL2   A1 F        80        236          19   5/27/87 13:06:56
           LISTMAST COBOL3   A1 F        80        236          19   5/27/87 13:06:36
           LISTMAST COBOL4   A1 F        80        236          19   5/27/87 13:06:26
           BCKUPCOB EXEC     A1 V        50         14           1   5/13/87 15:22:44
           LISTMAST COBOL    A1 F        80        236          19   5/12/87 11:41:31
           STEVE    NETLOG   A0 V       106          1           1   5/12/87 10:32:37
           POWEROFF JCL      A1 F        80          1           1   5/08/87 14:32:08
           LISTCAT  LISTING  A1 F       121         28           4   3/10/87 14:58:57
           RENUM    MODULE   A1 V       768          3           1   3/10/87 14:18:24
           RENUM    ASSEMBLE A1 F        80         71           6   3/10/87 14:17:58
           ASM      EXEC     A1 V        66         21           1   3/10/87 13:30:12
           PHASELIB DOSLIB   A1 V      1024         46          42   3/03/87 14:01:48
           CATPROC2 VSEJCL   A1 F        80        159          13  12/15/86 11:25:51
           LISTCAT  AMSERV   A1 F        80          1           1  12/12/86 14:58:11
           TEMP     VSBASIC  A1 F        80        102           8   9/23/86 10:00:32
           RN       XEDIT    A1 V        22         15           1   9/23/86  9:58:42
    1= HELP      2= REFRESH  3= QUIT     4= SORT(TYPE)  5= SORT(DATE)  6= SORT(SIZE)
    7= BACKWARD  8= FORWARD  9= FL /N  10=             11= XEDIT      12= CURSOR

    ====>
                                                              X E D I T   1 FILE
    Iª                                                        □-□04
```

**Figure 5-8**  Entering multiple commands on the FILELIST display (part 1 of 4)

The ERASE and DISCARD commands say to delete the first four files

```
    STEVE      FILELIST A0   V 108   TRUNC=108 SIZE=61 LINE=1 COL=1 ALT=0
    CMD    FILENAME FILETYPE FM FORMAT LRECL    RECORDS      BLOCKS   DATE      TIME
    ERASE  LISTMAST COBOL1   A1 F        80        236          19   5/27/87 13:07:05
    ERASE  LISTMAST COBOL2   A1 F        80        236          19   5/27/87 13:06:56
    DISCARDISTMAST COBOL3    A1 F        80        236          19   5/27/87 13:06:36
    DISCARDISTMAST COBOL4    A1 F        80        236          19   5/27/87 13:06:26
           BCKUPCOB EXEC     A1 V        50         14           1   5/13/87 15:22:44
           LISTMAST COBOL    A1 F        80        236          19   5/12/87 11:41:31
           STEVE    NETLOG   A0 V       106          1           1   5/12/87 10:32:37
           POWEROFF JCL      A1 F        80          1           1   5/08/87 14:32:08
           LISTCAT  LISTING  A1 F       121         28           4   3/10/87 14:58:57
           RENUM    MODULE   A1 V       768          3           1   3/10/87 14:18:24
           RENUM    ASSEMBLE A1 F        80         71           6   3/10/87 14:17:58
           ASM      EXEC     A1 V        66         21           1   3/10/87 13:30:12
           PHASELIB DOSLIB   A1 V      1024         46          42   3/03/87 14:01:48
           CATPROC2 VSEJCL   A1 F        80        159          13  12/15/86 11:25:51
           LISTCAT  AMSERV   A1 F        80          1           1  12/12/86 14:58:11
           TEMP     VSBASIC  A1 F        80        102           8   9/23/86 10:00:32
           RN       XEDIT    A1 V        22         15           1   9/23/86  9:58:42
    1= HELP      2= REFRESH  3= QUIT     4= SORT(TYPE)  5= SORT(DATE)  6= SORT(SIZE)
    7= BACKWARD  8= FORWARD  9= FL /N  10=             11= XEDIT      12= CURSOR

    ====>
                                                              X E D I T   1 FILE
    Iª                                                        □-□04
```

**Figure 5-8**  Entering multiple commands on the FILELIST display (part 2 of 4)

When you press the enter key, the files are deleted; to update the listing so it won't be so cluttered, press PF2

```
   STEVE      FILELIST A0   V 108   TRUNC=108 SIZE=61 LINE=1 COL=1 ALT=14
   CMD     FILENAME FILETYPE FM FORMAT LRECL      RECORDS      BLOCKS   DATE      TIME
    *      LISTMAST COBOL1   A1 ** DISCARDED OR RENAMED **
    *      LISTMAST COBOL2   A1 ** DISCARDED OR RENAMED **
    *      LISTMAST COBOL3   A1 HAS BEEN DISCARDED.
    *      LISTMAST COBOL4   A1 HAS BEEN DISCARDED.
           BCKUPCOB EXEC     A1 V       50        14            1  5/13/87 15:22:44
           LISTMAST COBOL    A1 F       80        236          19  5/12/87 11:41:31
           STEVE    NETLOG   A0 V      106         1            1  5/12/87 10:32:37
           POWEROFF JCL      A1 F       80         1            1  5/08/87 14:32:08
           LISTCAT  LISTING  A1 F      121        28            4  3/10/87 14:58:57
           RENUM    MODULE   A1 V      768         3            1  3/10/87 14:18:24
           RENUM    ASSEMBLE A1 F       80        71            6  3/10/87 14:17:58
           ASM      EXEC     A1 V       66        21            1  3/10/87 13:30:12
           PHASELIB DOSLIB   A1 V     1024        46           42  3/03/87 14:01:48
           CATPROC2 VSEJCL   A1 F       80       159           13 12/15/86 11:25:51
           LISTCAT  AMSERV   A1 F       80         1            1 12/12/86 14:58:11
           TEMP     VSBASIC  A1 F       80       102            8  9/23/86 10:00:32
           RN       XEDIT    A1 V       22        15            1  9/23/86  9:58:42
   1= HELP         2= REFRESH   3= QUIT    4= SORT(TYPE)  5= SORT(DATE)  6= SORT(SIZE)
   7= BACKWARD     8= FORWARD   9= FL /N  10=           11= XEDIT       12= CURSOR

   ====>
                                                             X E D I T   1 FILE
   TA                                                  □-□04
```

**Figure 5-8**   Entering multiple commands on the FILELIST display (part 3 of 4)

The updated FILELIST display

```
   STEVE      FILELIST A0   V 108   TRUNC=108 SIZE=57 LINE=1 COL=1 ALT=73
   CMD     FILENAME FILETYPE FM FORMAT LRECL      RECORDS      BLOCKS   DATE      TIME
    _      BCKUPCOB EXEC     A1 V       50        14            1  5/13/87 15:22:44
           LISTMAST COBOL    A1 F       80        236          19  5/12/87 11:41:31
           STEVE    NETLOG   A0 V      106         1            1  5/12/87 10:32:37
           POWEROFF JCL      A1 F       80         1            1  5/08/87 14:32:08
           LISTCAT  LISTING  A1 F      121        28            4  3/10/87 14:58:57
           RENUM    MODULE   A1 V      768         3            1  3/10/87 14:18:24
           RENUM    ASSEMBLE A1 F       80        71            6  3/10/87 14:17:58
           ASM      EXEC     A1 V       66        21            1  3/10/87 13:30:12
           PHASELIB DOSLIB   A1 V     1024        46           42  3/03/87 14:01:48
           CATPROC2 VSEJCL   A1 F       80       159           13 12/15/86 11:25:51
           LISTCAT  AMSERV   A1 F       80         1            1 12/12/86 14:58:11
           TEMP     VSBASIC  A1 F       80       102            8  9/23/86 10:00:32
           RN       XEDIT    A1 V       22        15            1  9/23/86  9:58:42
           CLG      EXEC     A1 V       72        69            3  9/19/86 10:37:15
           PROFILE  EXEC     A1 V       58        16            1  9/19/86 10:16:01
           CLG1     XEDIT    A1 V       30        11            1  9/19/86  9:19:39
           CLG2     XEDIT    A1 V       24         5            1  9/19/86  9:09:44
   1= HELP         2= REFRESH   3= QUIT    4= SORT(TYPE)  5= SORT(DATE)  6= SORT(SIZE)
   7= BACKWARD     8= FORWARD   9= FL /N  10=           11= XEDIT       12= CURSOR

   ====>
                                                             X E D I T   1 FILE
   TA                                                  □-□04
```

**Figure 5-8**   Entering multiple commands on the FILELIST display (part 4 of 4)

```
 STEVE      FILELIST A0  V 108   TRUNC=108 SIZE=61 LINE=1 COL=1 ALT=0
 CMD     FILENAME FILETYPE FM FORMAT LRECL     RECORDS      BLOCKS    DATE      TIME
 ERASE LISTMAST COBOL1   A1 F        80         236          19    5/27/87 13:07:05
 =     LISTMAST COBOL2   A1 F        80         236          19    5/27/87 13:06:56
 =     LISTMAST COBOL3   A1 F        80         236          19    5/27/87 13:06:36
 =     LISTMAST COBOL4   A1 F        80         236          19    5/27/87 13:06:26
       BCKUPCOB EXEC     A1 V        50          14           1    5/13/87 15:22:44
       LISTMAST COBOL    A1 F        80         236          19    5/12/87 11:41:31
       STEVE    NETLOG   A0 V       106           1           1    5/12/87 10:32:37
       POWEROFF JCL      A1 F        80           1           1    5/08/87 14:32:08
       LISTCAT  LISTING  A1 F       121          28           4    3/10/87 14:58:57
       RENUM    MODULE   A1 V       768           3           1    3/10/87 14:18:24
       RENUM    ASSEMBLE A1 F        80          71           6    3/10/87 14:17:58
       ASM      EXEC     A1 V        66          21           1    3/10/87 13:30:12
       PHASELIB DOSLIB   A1 V      1024          46          42    3/03/87 14:01:48
       CATPROC2 VSEJCL   A1 F        80         159          13   12/15/86 11:25:51
       LISTCAT  AMSERV   A1 F        80           1           1   12/12/86 14:58:11
       TEMP     VSBASIC  A1 F        80         102           8    9/23/86 10:00:32
       RN       XEDIT    A1 V        22          15           1    9/23/86  9:58:42
 1= HELP      2= REFRESH   3= QUIT    4= SORT(TYPE)  5= SORT(DATE)  6= SORT(SIZE)
 7= BACKWARD  8= FORWARD   9= FL /N  10=            11= XEDIT      12= CURSOR

 ====>
                                                        X E D I T  1 FILE
 Iª                                              □─□04
```

**Figure 5-9**     Using equal signs to duplicate a command on the FILELIST display

What these commands have in common is that they don't require any operands or options other than the name of the file to be accessed. In contrast, other commands you can issue from the FILELIST display, like COPYFILE and RENAME, require additional information, and they're a little more complicated to issue.

When you invoke the COPYFILE or RENAME command, you have to specify two complete file identifiers (filename, filetype, and filemode). For COPYFILE, you have to identify the input file and supply a complete identifier for the new output file. For RENAME, you have to supply the old and new identifiers for the file. For cases like these, you use a slash (/) in the command for the first file identifier.

To understand, consider figure 5-10. Here, I want to change the name of the file PROF XEDIT A to PROFILE XEDIT A. Parts 1 and 2 of the figure show the screen before and after I keyed in the command, and part 3 shows the screen displayed after the command had been processed. Next, I refreshed the screen (PF2), resorted it by filetype (PF4), and scrolled to the end of the list (PF8). The final display in part 4 of the figure shows that the name of the file was properly changed.

When they're appropriate, you can also use the special characters that are valid in commands you issue from the CMS command environment. For example, the equal sign can save you a lot of keystrokes when you use the RENAME and COPYFILE commands. In part 2 of figure 5-10, I could have entered

```
RENAME / PROFILE = =
```

The beginning FILELIST display

```
 STEVE      FILELIST A0  V 108  TRUNC=108 SIZE=57 LINE=49 COL=1 ALT=4
 CMD    FILENAME FILETYPE FM FORMAT LRECL      RECORDS     BLOCKS    DATE      TIME
        LVTOCD   VSEJCL   A1 F        80         10          1   8/29/86  9:22:14
        PAUSEBG  VSEJCL   A1 F        80          5          1   8/27/86 14:05:22
        PAUSEF1  VSEJCL   A1 F        80          5          1   8/27/86 14:05:49
        PRINTLOG VSEJCL   A1 F        80          5          1   8/27/86 14:07:19
        VSEUTIL  VSEJCL   A1 F        80        253         20   8/27/86 14:24:27
        CLG1     XEDIT    A1 V        30         11          1   9/19/86  9:19:39
        CLG2     XEDIT    A1 V        24          5          1   9/19/86  9:09:44
        PROF     XEDIT    A1 V        26          5          1   9/18/86 12:02:55
        RN       XEDIT    A1 V        22         15          1   9/23/86  9:58:42




 1= HELP     2= REFRESH   3= QUIT    4= SORT(TYPE)  5= SORT(DATE)  6= SORT(SIZE)
 7= BACKWARD 8= FORWARD   9= FL /N  10=            11= XEDIT      12= CURSOR

 ====>  _
                                                        X E D I T  1 FILE
 ]a                                                        ▢–▢04
```

**Figure 5-10**  Using the slash to indicate a file identifier in a command entered on the FILELIST display (part 1 of 4)

The RENAME command contains a slash to indicate the current file identifier and then gives the new file identifier

```
 STEVE      FILELIST A0  V 108  TRUNC=108 SIZE=57 LINE=49 COL=1 ALT=4
 CMD    FILENAME FILETYPE FM FORMAT LRECL      RECORDS     BLOCKS    DATE      TIME
        LVTOCD   VSEJCL   A1 F        80         10          1   8/29/86  9:22:14
        PAUSEBG  VSEJCL   A1 F        80          5          1   8/27/86 14:05:22
        PAUSEF1  VSEJCL   A1 F        80          5          1   8/27/86 14:05:49
        PRINTLOG VSEJCL   A1 F        80          5          1   8/27/86 14:07:19
        VSEUTIL  VSEJCL   A1 F        80        253         20   8/27/86 14:24:27
        CLG1     XEDIT    A1 V        30         11          1   9/19/86  9:19:39
        CLG2     XEDIT    A1 V        24          5          1   9/19/86  9:09:44
 RENAME / PROFILE XEDIT AA1 V        26          5          1   9/18/86 12:02:55
        RN       XEDIT    A1 V        22         15          1   9/23/86  9:58:42




 1= HELP     2= REFRESH   3= QUIT    4= SORT(TYPE)  5= SORT(DATE)  6= SORT(SIZE)
 7= BACKWARD 8= FORWARD   9= FL /N  10=            11= XEDIT      12= CURSOR

 ====>
                                                        X E D I T  1 FILE
 ]a                                                        ▢–▢04
```

**Figure 5-10**  Using the slash to indicate a file identifier in a command entered on the FILELIST display (part 2 of 4)

When you press the enter key, the file is renamed

```
  STEVE      FILELIST A0  V 108   TRUNC=108 SIZE=57 LINE=49 COL=1 ALT=7
  CMD    FILENAME FILETYPE FM FORMAT LRECL      RECORDS      BLOCKS   DATE       TIME
         LVTOCD   VSEJCL   A1 F        80           10          1  8/29/86  9:22:14
         PAUSEBG  VSEJCL   A1 F        80            5          1  8/27/86 14:05:22
         PAUSEF1  VSEJCL   A1 F        80            5          1  8/27/86 14:05:49
         PRINTLOG VSEJCL   A1 F        80            5          1  8/27/86 14:07:19
         VSEUTIL  VSEJCL   A1 F        80          253         20  8/27/86 14:24:27
         CLG1     XEDIT    A1 V        30           11          1  9/19/86  9:19:39
         CLG2     XEDIT    A1 V        24            5          1  9/19/86  9:09:44
  *      PROF     XEDIT    A1 ** DISCARDED OR RENAMED **
         RN       XEDIT    A1 V        22           15          1  9/23/86  9:58:42




  1= HELP      2= REFRESH  3= QUIT    4= SORT(TYPE)  5= SORT(DATE)  6= SORT(SIZE)
  7= BACKWARD  8= FORWARD  9= FL /N  10=           11= XEDIT      12= CURSOR

  ====>
                                                            X E D I T  1 FILE
  ‾A                                                      ▭—▭04
```

**Figure 5-10**   Using the slash to indicate a file identifier in a command entered on the FILELIST display (part 3 of 4)

To make sure the file was renamed properly, press PF2 to refresh the screen, PF4 to resort the display by filetype, and PF8 to scroll to the end of the list where the new file identifier is

```
  STEVE      FILELIST A0  V 108   TRUNC=108 SIZE=57 LINE=49 COL=1 ALT=67
  CMD    FILENAME FILETYPE FM FORMAT LRECL      RECORDS      BLOCKS   DATE       TIME
         LVTOCD   VSEJCL   A1 F        80           10          1  8/29/86  9:22:14
         PAUSEBG  VSEJCL   A1 F        80            5          1  8/27/86 14:05:22
         PAUSEF1  VSEJCL   A1 F        80            5          1  8/27/86 14:05:49
         PRINTLOG VSEJCL   A1 F        80            5          1  8/27/86 14:07:19
         VSEUTIL  VSEJCL   A1 F        80          253         20  8/27/86 14:24:27
         CLG1     XEDIT    A1 V        30           11          1  9/19/86  9:19:39
         CLG2     XEDIT    A1 V        24            5          1  9/19/86  9:09:44
         PROFILE  XEDIT    A1 V        26            5          1  9/18/86 12:02:55
         RN       XEDIT    A1 V        22           15          1  9/23/86  9:58:42




  1= HELP      2= REFRESH  3= QUIT    4= SORT(TYPE)  5= SORT(DATE)  6= SORT(SIZE)
  7= BACKWARD  8= FORWARD  9= FL /N  10=           11= XEDIT      12= CURSOR

  ====>  _
                                                            X E D I T  1 FILE
  ‾A                                                      ▭—▭04
```

**Figure 5-10**   Using the slash to indicate a file identifier in a command entered on the FILELIST display (part 4 of 4)

instead of

```
RENAME / PROFILE XEDIT A
```

because the filetype and filemode of the file were to remain the same.

## How to use advanced FILELIST facilities

The chances are that most of the FILELIST work you do will involve the operations I just described. However, you might want to use a couple of advanced FILELIST features sometimes. This section describes (1) how to save FILELIST data in a file so you can use it later and (2) how to add data to an existing FILELIST display.

***How to save FILELIST data in a file and retrieve it later***    Because the file information you see when you use FILELIST is actually stored in a file, you can manipulate it like any other file. By default, the FILELIST procedure stores the data it accumulates for your files in a file with the filetype FILELIST and filename equal to your user-id. The file is created on your A-disk.

Normally, the file FILELIST uses is automatically deleted when you leave the FILELIST environment. However, you can issue either the XEDIT SAVE or FILE command from the FILELIST command line to store a copy of that file. (Remember, the FILELIST display is actually managed by XEDIT.) Both the SAVE and FILE commands cause the FILELIST data to be stored in a file you name; they differ only in that FILE ends your FILELIST session, while SAVE does not. For example, you could enter

```
SAVE MAY27 FILELIST A
```

on the command line to store the FILELIST data in a file called MAY27 FILELIST on your A-disk.

You might want to save a copy of the FILELIST file so you can print it later. In the example I just showed you, it's clear from the file identifier I used that the file contains FILELIST data (from the filetype) that was current on the 27th of May (from the filename).

If you save FILELIST data in a file, you can restore it for use in a later FILELIST session. To do that, you have to use an option when you invoke FILELIST. For example, suppose I want to access the data stored in MAY27 FILELIST A. To do that, I'd invoke FILELIST with this command:

```
FILELIST MAY27 FILELIST A (F
```

The F option tells the FILELIST procedure that the file identifier is not to be used to select the files that will be displayed, but rather that it's the name of a file that already contains FILELIST data. As a result, the procedure accesses that file and uses the stored data rather than building a new file for the current FILELIST session. (The F is an abbreviation for the FILELIST option of the FILELIST command.)

***How to add data to an existing FILELIST display***      Within the FILELIST environment, you can build a selective list by issuing additional FILELIST commands with the APPEND (or just A) option. The APPEND option causes the files selected to be added to the existing list; that's why you can only use it within FILELIST. If you use the APPEND option on the command that invokes FILELIST from the CMS command environment, you'll get an error message.

To understand how you can use APPEND, consider figure 5-11. To get the display in part 1 of the figure, I entered the command

```
FILELIST SC2*  *  B
```

The result is that the display contains one line for each file on the B-disk whose filename begins with the characters SC2. In this example, six files meet the search requirements. However, suppose I'm looking for a particular file, but it's not in the list. It might be on another disk, so I need to look for it elsewhere. Of course, it's possible to exit FILELIST, then invoke it again. It's more useful, though, to append additional information to the existing list.

To do that, you issue FILELIST from the command line on the FILELIST display and use the APPEND option. In part 1 of figure 5-11, I've requested information about all files whose filenames begin with the characters SC2, but that reside on the A-disk. Because I specified the APPEND option, that information will be added to the information already displayed for files on the B-disk. The result is the display in part 2 of the figure. Now, all of this information is stored in a single file and it can be manipulated with the FILELIST facilities you're already familiar with.

## Discussion

I think you'll agree that the FILELIST command offers a practical and workable environment in which to manage your CMS files. However, you should realize that there is some overhead involved in using FILELIST. In particular, if your system is a busy one, you might notice delays when you invoke FILELIST. As a result, if all you want is information about a small group of files, you should probably use the LISTFILE command directly rather than through FILELIST.

The FILELIST APPEND option says to add to the current display all the files on the A-disk whose names start with SC2

```
 PAT        FILELIST A0   V 108   TRUNC=108 SIZE=6 LINE=1 COL=1 ALT=0
 CMD     FILENAME FILETYPE FM FORMAT LRECL      RECORDS      BLOCKS   DATE      TIME
         SC2TAPE  EBCDIC   B1 F         80         8228         643  4/23/87 16:18:30
         SC22300  COBOL    B1 F         80          112           9 11/20/86  9:44:27
         SC22100  COBOL    B1 F         80           75           6 11/19/86 13:27:47
         SC21500  COBOL    B1 F         80          204          16 11/19/86 13:27:35
         SC2C5V1  ICCF     B1 F         80          227          18 11/17/86 14:31:14
         SC2C5V2  ICCF     B1 F         80          334          27 11/17/86 14:14:23




 1= HELP      2= REFRESH  3= QUIT    4= SORT(TYPE)  5= SORT(DATE)  6= SORT(SIZE)
 7= BACKWARD  8= FORWARD  9= FL /N  10=             11= XEDIT      12= CURSOR

====> FILELIST SC2* * A (APPEND_
                                                        X E D I T  1 FILE
 I∃                                                   ⊡–⊡04
```

**Figure 5-11**    Using the APPEND option of the FILELIST command (part 1 of 2)

The result of the FILELIST command with the APPEND option

```
 PAT        FILELIST A0   V 108   TRUNC=108 SIZE=26 LINE=1 COL=1 ALT=20
 CMD     FILENAME FILETYPE FM FORMAT LRECL      RECORDS      BLOCKS   DATE      TIME
         SC2TAPE  EBCDIC   B1 F         80         8228         643  4/23/87 16:18:30
         SC22300  COBOL    B1 F         80          112           9 11/20/86  9:44:27
         SC22100  COBOL    B1 F         80           75           6 11/19/86 13:27:47
         SC21500  COBOL    B1 F         80          204          16 11/19/86 13:27:35
         SC2C5V1  ICCF     B1 F         80          227          18 11/17/86 14:31:14
         SC2C5V2  ICCF     B1 F         80          334          27 11/17/86 14:14:23
         SC2C10   COBOL    A1 F         80          317          25 10/29/86  9:59:09
         SC2C2V1  COBOL    A1 F         80          115           9 11/14/86 15:17:59
         SC2C2V2  COBOL    A1 F         80          157          13 11/14/86 15:18:11
         SC2C2V3  COBOL    A1 F         80          149          12 11/14/86 15:18:21
         SC2C2V4  COBOL    A1 F         80          134          11 11/14/86 15:09:12
         SC2C2V5  COBOL    A1 F         80           96           8 11/14/86 15:17:46
         SC2C3V1  COBOL    A1 F         80           87           7 11/14/86 15:18:40
         SC2C3V2  COBOL    A1 F         80          138          11 11/14/86 15:18:50
         SC2C3V3  COBOL    A1 F         80          126          10 11/14/86 15:19:00
         SC2C3V4  COBOL    A1 F         80          235          19 11/20/86 10:33:07
         SC2C3V5  COBOL    A1 F         80          231          19 11/14/86 15:19:20
 1= HELP      2= REFRESH  3= QUIT    4= SORT(TYPE)  5= SORT(DATE)  6= SORT(SIZE)
 7= BACKWARD  8= FORWARD  9= FL /N  10=             11= XEDIT      12= CURSOR

====> _
                                                        X E D I T  1 FILE
 I∃                                                   ⊡–⊡04
```

**Figure 5-11**    Using the APPEND option of the FILELIST command (part 2 of 2)

## Terminology

mask

## Objectives

1. Use the FILELIST command to display information about any files on your accessed minidisks.

2. Issue CMS commands from the FILELIST display to view, rename, copy, edit, and delete files.

3. Save the data that appears in a FILELIST display, then retrieve it later.

4. Use the APPEND option of the FILELIST command to add file information to an existing FILELIST display.

**Topic two** | # How to use the TYPE command

In the last chapter, I introduced the basic operation of the CMS TYPE command, which you can use to "type," or display, the contents of a file on your terminal screen. In this topic, you'll learn how use some special features of the TYPE command.

Figure 5-12 presents the complete format of the TYPE command. Unless you specify otherwise, the TYPE command displays all the records in the file you name, presents them in character (EBCDIC) format, and shows you all columns. The advanced features you can request with the operands and options shown in figure 5-12 let you override these defaults.

### How to display a range of records with the TYPE command

If you want to view just a part of a file, you can specify a range of records to be displayed with the first-rec and last-rec operands of the TYPE command. For example, to view just records 100 through 110 of the file CASEC2P1 COBOL B, you'd enter

```
TYPE CASEC2P1 COBOL B 100 110
```

as in figure 5-13. As you can see, just the 11 lines I requested on the TYPE command are displayed.

Specifying a range of records for display can make it easier for you to use the TYPE command. However, it's obvious that you need to know the record numbers that bound the range you're interested in. A more flexible technique is to specify only the starting record number, then terminate the display with the HT immediate command when you've seen what you're interested in.

To understand this technique, consider figure 5-14. Here, I've keyed in a TYPE command that specifies a starting record number, but not an ending value:

```
TYPE CASEC2P1 COBOL B 100
```

When I press the enter key, the file is displayed in part 1 starting with the record I specified. However, more of the file is presented than I need to see. As a result, I key in the HT immediate command in part 1 and press the enter key. The HT command takes effect in the screen in part 2, and the TYPE command's operation is terminated. I press PA2 to respond to the MORE terminal status message, and the CMS ready message reappears, as you can see in part 3 of the figure. (CLOSE MNTTRAN was the last file line to be displayed before the HT command took effect.)

**The TYPE command**

```
TYPE fn ft [fm] [first-rec [last-rec]] [([HEX] [COL first-col - [last-col]]]
```

**Explanation**

| | |
|---|---|
| fn | Filename of the file to be displayed. |
| ft | Filetype of the file to be displayed. |
| fm | Filemode of the file to be displayed. If you specify *, all accessed drives are searched until a file matching the specified filename and filetype is found. If omitted, A is assumed. |
| first-rec | Specifies that the file display should begin with the indicated record number. If omitted, 1 is assumed. |
| last-rec | Specifies that the file display should end with the indicated record number. If omitted, the last record in the file is assumed. |
| HEX | Specifies that the file should be displayed in hex rather than character format. |
| COL first-col | Specifies that the display should contain only a range of columns in each record, beginning with the column identified by first-col. |
| last-col | Specifies that the column range to be displayed should end with the column indicated by last-col. If omitted, the last column in the record is assumed to be the end of the range. |

---

Figure 5-12        The TYPE command

### How to display selected columns with the TYPE command

To display just selected columns, you use the COL option. For example, if you want to view just columns 8-72 of a COBOL source file, you could enter a command like this:

```
TYPE CASEC2P1 COBOL B (COL 8-72
```

Figure 5-15 illustrates how to use this facility. I keyed in the TYPE command

```
TYPE CASEC2P1 COBOL B 100 110 (COL 8-72
```

to display columns 8 through 72 of records 100 through 110 of the indicated file. Notice here that the same records that were displayed in figure 5-13 appear, but they don't include columns 1-7 or 73-80. It's easy to see that the first seven columns aren't included because the data is shifted to the left and because the asterisks in column 7, which are obvious in figure 5-13, don't appear in figure 5-15.

The numbers after the file identifier in the TYPE command indicate the first and last records to be displayed

```
R; T=0.05/0.13 16:37:34
TYPE CASEC2P1 COBOL B 100 110

                    15   IM-UNIT-SALES-LAST-YEAR     PIC S9(5).
                    15   IM-UNIT-SALES-2-YEARS-AGO   PIC S9(5).
                    15   IM-UNIT-SALES-3-YEARS-AGO   PIC S9(5).
                    15   IM-UNIT-SALES-4-YEARS-AGO   PIC S9(5).
                    15   IM-UNIT-SALES-5-YEARS-AGO   PIC S9(5).
              05  FILLER
       *
       01  MASTER-HOLDING-AREA                       PIC X(128).
       *
       PROCEDURE DIVISION.
       *

R; T=0.09/0.39 16:37:58




 -
                                                           RUNNING
 IA                                                  □-□04
```

**Figure 5-13**   How to view a range of records in a file with the TYPE command

If you want the columns that will be displayed to start at a particular location, but to extend through the end of the record, you don't have to specify an ending location. For example,

```
TYPE CASEC2P1 COBOL B (COL 8
```

causes columns 8 through 80 of this file to be displayed. (Files with filetype COBOL contain 80-character records.)

### How to display data in hexadecimal format with the TYPE command

The last feature of TYPE this topic presents is the HEX option. You use it to display the contents of a file in hexadecimal rather than character (EBCDIC) format.

To understand how you might use the HEX option of the TYPE command, consider the example in figure 5-16. Here, I displayed a COBOL COPY member that contains 3270 field attribute definitions for use in COBOL CICS programs. To look at the first 10 records in the file in character format, I typed in the command

```
TYPE FACS COPY A 1 10
```

The TYPE command displays the file starting with record 100; to end the TYPE operation without displaying all the rest of the file, enter the HT command

```
R; T=0.05/0.13 16:39:18
TYPE CASEC2P1 COBOL B 100
                        15   IM-UNIT-SALES-LAST-YEAR     PIC S9(5).
                        15   IM-UNIT-SALES-2-YEARS-AGO   PIC S9(5).
                        15   IM-UNIT-SALES-3-YEARS-AGO   PIC S9(5).
                        15   IM-UNIT-SALES-4-YEARS-AGO   PIC S9(5).
                        15   IM-UNIT-SALES-5-YEARS-AGO   PIC S9(5).
                   05   FILLER
             *
             01  MASTER-HOLDING-AREA                    PIC X(128).
             *
             PROCEDURE DIVISION.
             *
             000-MAINTAIN-INVENTORY-FILE.
             *
                 OPEN INPUT   MNTTRAN
                              INVMAST
                        OUTPUT NEWMAST.
                 MOVE LOW-VALUE TO IM-BOOK-CODE.
                 PERFORM 300-PROCESS-MAINTENANCE-TRAN
                     UNTIL ALL-RECORDS-PROCESSED.
    HT_
                                                          MORE...
    Iª                                                  □—□04
```

**Figure 5-14**   How to use the HT immediate command to stop output of the TYPE command (part 1 of 3)

The HT command takes effect; press PA2 to respond to the MORE terminal status message

```
R; T=0.05/0.13 16:39:18
TYPE CASEC2P1 COBOL B 100
                        15   IM-UNIT-SALES-LAST-YEAR     PIC S9(5).
                        15   IM-UNIT-SALES-2-YEARS-AGO   PIC S9(5).
                        15   IM-UNIT-SALES-3-YEARS-AGO   PIC S9(5).
                        15   IM-UNIT-SALES-4-YEARS-AGO   PIC S9(5).
                        15   IM-UNIT-SALES-5-YEARS-AGO   PIC S9(5).
                   05   FILLER
             *
             01  MASTER-HOLDING-AREA                    PIC X(128).
             *
             PROCEDURE DIVISION.
             *
             000-MAINTAIN-INVENTORY-FILE.
             *
                 OPEN INPUT   MNTTRAN
                              INVMAST
                        OUTPUT NEWMAST.
                 MOVE LOW-VALUE TO IM-BOOK-CODE.
                 PERFORM 300-PROCESS-MAINTENANCE-TRAN
                     UNTIL ALL-RECORDS-PROCESSED.
    _
                                                          MORE...
    Iª                                                  □—□04
```

**Figure 5-14**   How to use the HT immediate command to stop output of the TYPE command (part 2 of 3)

The end of the TYPE output is displayed, and the CMS ready message appears

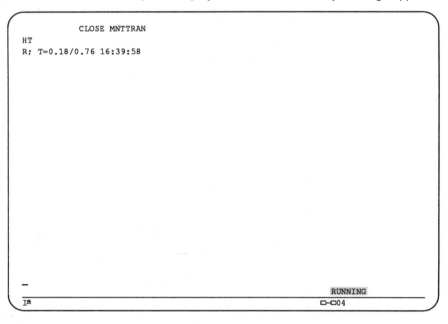

```
                    CLOSE MNTTRAN
HT
R; T=0.18/0.76 16:39:58
```

RUNNING

I ª                                              □—□04

---

**Figure 5-14**    How to use the HT immediate command to stop output of the TYPE command
(part 3 of 3)

Then, I wanted to find out if the value specified for the first field attribute definition was a space or some non-printable value. (The shaded character is what I
wanted to see in hexadecimal.)

To find out, I needed to use the TYPE command again, so I entered

**TYPE FACS COPY A 3 3 (HEX COL 44-72**

I limited the amount of data to be displayed to just the third record in the file
(both the starting and ending records are specified as 3) and to just columns 44
through 72 of that record. I was this specific to make it easier for me to find
that data I wanted in the output.

As you can see, the output identifies the record displayed and its length. (If
multiple records are displayed, each will have this sort of header line.) The hex
values of the character I'm interested in and its two limiting quote marks are also
shaded in the figure. The hex value of the attribute byte here is 40, which is a
space. (You can verify that by checking the hex values of the trailing spaces in
columns 67-72.)

```
R; T=0.05/0.13 16:40:14
TYPE CASEC2P1 COBOL B 100 110 (COL 8-72

            15   IM-UNIT-SALES-LAST-YEAR    PIC S9(5).
            15   IM-UNIT-SALES-2-YEARS-AGO  PIC S9(5).
            15   IM-UNIT-SALES-3-YEARS-AGO  PIC S9(5).
            15   IM-UNIT-SALES-4-YEARS-AGO  PIC S9(5).
            15   IM-UNIT-SALES-5-YEARS-AGO  PIC S9(5).
        05  FILLER

01  MASTER-HOLDING-AREA                     PIC X(128).

PROCEDURE DIVISION.


R; T=0.10/0.39 16:40:36




    -
                                                    RUNNING
Iª                                             □-□04
```

**Figure 5-15**    How to view only selected columns in a file with the TYPE command

```
R; T=0.05/0.09 16:43:54
TYPE FACS COPY A 1 10

        01   FIELD-ATTRIBUTE-DEFINITIONS.
        *
            05   FAC-UNPROT         PIC X        VALUE ' '.
            05   FAC-UNPROT-MDT     PIC X        VALUE 'A'.
            05   FAC-UNPROT-BRT     PIC X        VALUE 'H'.
            05   FAC-UNPROT-BRT-MDT PIC X        VALUE 'I'.
            05   FAC-UNPROT-DARK    PIC X        VALUE '<'.
            05   FAC-UNPROT-DARK-MDT PIC X       VALUE '('.
            05   FAC-UNPROT-NUM     PIC X        VALUE '&'.
            05   FAC-UNPROT-NUM-MDT PIC X        VALUE 'J'.

R; T=0.09/0.40 16:44:04
TYPE FACS COPY A 3 3 (HEX COL 44-72

RECORD          3 LENGTH=        80
 D7C9C340  E7404040  40404040  40E5C1D3  E4C5407D  407D4B40  40404040  40

R; T=0.05/0.17 16:44:29


    -
                                                    RUNNING
Iª                                             □-□04
```

**Figure 5-16**    How to view the contents of a file in hexadecimal with the TYPE command

### Discussion

The features of the TYPE command you've learned in this topic are for special operations. As a result, you'll probably use them infrequently. Frankly, you might find it easier to use XEDIT to look at the contents of a file. After all, with it, you can scroll back and forth, and you can easily exit whenever you need to.

### Objectives

1. Use the TYPE command to display a selected range of records from a file.
2. Use the TYPE command to display a selected range of columns within the records of a file.
3. Use the TYPE command to display the hexadecimal values of data stored in a file.

**Topic three**

## How to use the COPYFILE command

In the last chapter, I showed you how to use the COPYFILE command to perform its basic function: make a duplicate copy of a file. Although that's what you'll want to do most of the time, the COPYFILE command lets you do much more. The complexity of the command, illustrated in figure 5-17, suggests that. In this section, you'll learn how to (1) copy over an existing file, (2) copy multiple files with one command, (3) combine files, (4) copy only part of a file, (5) change the characteristics of a file, (6) perform character translations, and (7) enter specifications to alter specific fields. As you read about how to perform these tasks, keep in mind that you can combine options to do exactly what you need in particular cases.

### How to copy over an existing file with the COPYFILE command

Unless you specify otherwise, COPYFILE won't create an output file if another file already exists with the name you supplied. For example, suppose a file named MNT4130 COBOL B exists on your virtual machine. If you issue the command

```
COPYFILE MNT4130 COBOL A = = B
```

the command will fail, and CMS will display the message

```
FILE 'MNT4130 COBOL B1' ALREADY EXISTS -- SPECIFY 'REPLACE'.
```

Of course, one option is to use the ERASE command to delete the file before you issue the COPYFILE command again. However, it's easier to use the REPLACE option of the COPYFILE command, as the error message I just showed you suggests. If you enter

```
COPYFILE MNT4130 COBOL A = = B (REPLACE
```

the output file that results from the command replaces the existing file with the same name.

There are two exceptions to this basic technique that you need to know about; both are related to COPYFILE operations that copy a file to itself. (As you'll see later in this section, you might want to copy a file to itself to change one or more of its characteristics.) At any rate, if you specify

```
= = =
```

as the file identifier for the output file or you don't specify an output file identifier at all, the input file replaces itself, and you don't need to code the REPLACE option. As a result, the three commands

```
COPYFILE MNT4130 COBOL A
COPYFILE MNT4130 COBOL A = = =
COPYFILE MNT4130 COBOL A MNT4130 COBOL A (REPLACE
```

are equivalent.

### How to copy multiple files with the COPYFILE command

You already know how to copy multiple files to multiple files. All you have to do is specify an asterisk for one or more components of the input file identifier, and an equal sign for one or more components of the output file identifier. For instance,

```
COPYFILE * COBOL B = = C
```

copies every file with the filetype COBOL from your B-disk to your C-disk. The filenames and filetypes of the input files are used for the output files because I entered equal signs in the output file identifier.

When you copy multiple files, you might want to monitor the progress of the operation. If you include the TYPE option when you enter the command, the identifiers of the affected files are displayed as they're processed. For example, consider figure 5-18. This figure illustrates the displays I saw during an operation to copy all of my procedure files (filetype EXEC) from one minidisk to another. First, in part 1 of the figure, I issued the command

```
L * EXEC A
```

to display the identifiers of my procedure files; the resulting display (in part 2) shows that there were five EXEC files on my A-disk. Then, I entered

```
COPYFILE * EXEC A = OLDEXEC B (TYPE
```

to copy the files. Notice that I specified the TYPE option. As a result, one line for each copy operation performed was displayed, as you can see in part 3 of the figure.

### How to combine multiple files with the COPYFILE command

Now, consider this variation on the COPYFILE command:

```
COPYFILE * COBOL A ALLPROGS COBOL C
```

Here, I've specified multiple input files, but named only *one* output file. When you issue a command like this, all the input files are combined into the one output file. The second input file is added after the end of the first, the third is added after the end of the second, and so on. This process is called *concatenation*.

**The COPYFILE command**

```
COPYFILE infile-1 [infile-n...] [outfile] [ ([REPLACE]
                                            [TYPE]
                                            [APPEND]

                                            [(FROM start-rec   )]
                                            [(FRLABEL start-text)]

                                            [(FOR count        )]
                                            [(TOLABEL end-text  )]

                                            [OLDDATE]
                                            [LRECL record-length]
                                            [RECFM format]
                                            [TRUNC]
                                            [FILL fill-character]

                                            [(PACK  )]
                                            [(UNPACK)]

                                            [(UPCASE )]
                                            [(LOWCASE)]

                                            [TRANS]
                                            [SPECS]
                                            [OVLY]                ]
```

**Explanation**

| | |
|---|---|
| COPYFILE | The command may be abbreviated as COPY. |
| infile-1 | The file identifier (fn ft fm) of the first (or only) file to be copied. You may use the asterisk for any of the three components of this file identifier. |
| infile-n | The file identifier(s) for additional input file(s). You may use the asterisk or the equal sign for any of the three components of these file identifiers. However, all three components of the file identifiers may not be asterisks. |
| outfile | The file identifier of the output file(s) to be created. You may omit outfile to cause the input file to be copied to itself. |
| REPLACE | Specifies that if a file already exists with the name supplied for outfile, it should be replaced. |
| TYPE | Specifies that the identifiers of the files copied should be displayed on the terminal screen as they're processed. |
| APPEND | Specifies that the contents of infile-1 are to be added to the current contents of outfile. |

---

**Figure 5-17** The COPYFILE command (part 1 of 2)

| FROM start-rec | Specifies where in the input file a partial copy operation is to begin. For start-rec, supply the number of the first record from the input file to be copied. |
| --- | --- |
| FRLABEL start-text | Specifies where in the input file a partial copy operation is to begin. For start-text, supply from one to eight non-blank characters that appear at the start of the first record to be copied from the input file. |
| FOR count | Specifies how many records are to be copied from the input file in a partial copy operation. For count, supply the number of records to be copied. |
| TOLABEL end-text | Specifies where in the input file a partial copy operation is to end. For end-text, supply from one to eight non-blank characters that appear at the start of the last record to be copied from the input file. |
| OLDDATE | Specifies that the creation date and time of the input file should be used for the copy; the default is to use the current date and time. |
| LRECL record-length | Specifies that the record length for a fixed-length record file should be changed to the value supplied as record-length. Record-length cannot be larger than 65535. If omitted, the default is the record length of the input file. |
| RECFM format | Specifies that the record format of the output file should be fixed-length (if format is F) or variable-length (if format is V). If omitted, the record format of the input file is used. |
| TRUNC | Specifies that trailing pad characters (usually spaces) should be removed when converting a file with fixed-length records to one with variable-length records. (The default is for trailing pad characters not to be removed.) |
| FILL fill-character | For fill-character, specify either a single character value or a two-digit hexadecimal value to be used as the pad character. The space is the default. Do not enclose the value between quote marks. |
| PACK | Specifies that the file should be converted to compressed format. |
| UNPACK | Specifies that the compressed file should be converted back to normal format. |
| UPCASE | Specifies that all lowercase letters in the input file should be converted to uppercase in the output file. |
| LOWCASE | Specifies that all uppercase letters in the input file should be converted to lowercase in the output file. |
| TRANS | Specifies that you should be prompted to enter pairs of character translation values. See the text for more information. |
| SPECS | Specifies that you should be prompted to enter a specifications list. See the text for more information. |
| OVLY | Specifies that data from the input file should overlay data in an existing output file. Valid only when you use the SPECS option and a specifications list. |

**Figure 5-17**   The COPYFILE command (part 2 of 2)

The operands on the LISTFILE command specify that all the procedure files on the
A-disk should be displayed

```
R; T=1.95/3.59 14:52:35




















L * EXEC A_
                                                        RUNNING
 IA                                                  □—□04
```

**Figure 5-18**    How to copy multiple files with a single COPYFILE command (part 1 of 3)

The COPYFILE command says to copy the procedure files to the B-disk and assign
them the filetype OLDEXEC

```
R; T=1.95/3.59 14:52:35
L * EXEC A
BACKUP    EXEC    A1
BACKUP2   EXEC    A1
CLG       EXEC    A1
CLG2      EXEC    A1
PROFILE   EXEC    A1
R; T=0.08/0.17 14:56:15











COPYFILE * EXEC A = OLDEXEC B (TYPE_
                                                        RUNNING
 IA                                                  □—□04
```

**Figure 5-18**    How to copy multiple files with a single COPYFILE command (part 2 of 3)

The messages issued during the COPYFILE operation as a result of the TYPE option

```
R; T=1.95/3.59 14:52:35
L * EXEC A
BACKUP     EXEC      A1
BACKUP2    EXEC      A1
CLG        EXEC      A1
CLG2       EXEC      A1
PROFILE    EXEC      A1
R; T=0.08/0.17 14:56:15
COPYFILE * EXEC A = OLDEXEC B (TYPE
COPY 'BACKUP EXEC A1' TO 'BACKUP OLDEXEC B1' (NEW FILE).
COPY 'BACKUP2 EXEC A1' TO 'BACKUP2 OLDEXEC B1' (NEW FILE).
COPY 'CLG EXEC A1' TO 'CLG OLDEXEC B1' (NEW FILE).
COPY 'CLG2 EXEC A1' TO 'CLG2 OLDEXEC B1' (NEW FILE).
COPY 'PROFILE EXEC A1' TO 'PROFILE OLDEXEC B1' (NEW FILE).
R; T=1.70/3.55 14:56:38



                                                    RUNNING
 I                                                  □─□04
```

**Figure 5-18**     How to copy multiple files with a single COPYFILE command (part 3 of 3)

You can also concatenate files by naming them explicitly. That's why you can specify more than one input file on the COPYFILE command. (Notice the item infile-n in the syntax of the command in figure 5-17.) For example, suppose you edited the beginning of a COBOL program (through the Data Division) and stored it in a file called AR6310 DATA A, and you edited and stored the Procedure Division of the same program in another file called AR6310 PROCED A. You could use the command

```
COPYFILE AR6310 DATA A AR6310 PROCED A AR6310 COBOL A
```

to combine them in a single, complete source code file named AR6310 COBOL A. When you specify multiple input files for an operation like this, you can use the equal sign to make the command easier to enter. For instance,

```
COPYFILE AR6310 DATA A = PROCED = = COBOL =
```

is equivalent to the command I just showed you.

When you use these techniques to concatenate files, two or more input files are combined to produce a new output file. Sometimes, though, you might want to add the contents of a file to another existing file. To do so, you supply the target file's identifier for outfile on the COPYFILE command; infile is the identifier of the file to be added. In addition, you need to include the APPEND option on the command. If you don't, the command will fail because COPYFILE will try to open the output file as if it were new, but it already exists. Here's an example that illustrates how to use the APPEND option:

```
COPYFILE AR6310 PROCED A = DATA = (APPEND
```

In this case, the contents of the file AR6310 PROCED A will be added to the end of the file AR6310 DATA A.

## How to copy part of a file with the COPYFILE command

The next options in figure 5-17 (FROM, FRLABEL, FOR, and TOLABEL) are used when you want to copy only part of a file. To specify where in the input file to begin the copy operation, you can use either the FROM option (to indicate the number of the first record to be copied) or the FRLABEL option (to indicate a text string in the file that first appears at the beginning of the first record to be copied); if you don't specify a starting position, the beginning of the file is assumed.

To specify where to stop a copy operation, you can use either the FOR option (to indicate the number of records to be copied) or the TOLABEL option (to indicate a text string that first appears at the beginning of the last record to be copied); if you don't specify an ending position, the end of the file is assumed.

For example, the command

```
COPYFILE CUSTMAST DATA A = = B (FROM 50 FOR 25
```

copies records 50 through 74 from the file CUSTMAST DATA A to the file CUSTMAST DATA B. In contrast,

```
COPYFILE CUSTMAST DATA A = = B (FROM 50
```

copies records from the input file beginning with record 50 and continuing through the end of the file, regardless of how many records that involves. In other words, all of the records in the input file are copied except the first 49.

Often, instead of specifying absolute record numbers for the input file, you'll find it easier to specify the content of the records that mark the beginning and end of the range of records you want to copy. For example, suppose the file CUSTMAST DATA A contains unique, five-digit customer numbers in the first five bytes of each record and that the records in the file are sequenced according to the contents of that field. To copy just a selected range of records from the file, you could enter a command using the FRLABEL and TOLABEL options, like

```
COPYFILE CUSTMAST DATA A = = B (FRLABEL 01000 TOLABEL 01999
```

Here, the range of records from the customer file to be copied are those whose customer number values fall between 01000 and 01999. Notice that this does not necessarily mean 1000 records will be copied; that happens only if every customer number in the specified range is in use.

The text strings you specify on the FRLABEL and TOLABEL options can be from one to eight characters long and may not contain blanks. That's because blanks separate elements in the COPYFILE command line. These text strings must appear starting in column 1 of records in the file to be recognized. If the text you specify for FRLABEL isn't found, no copy is done; if the text you specify for TOLABEL isn't found, the copy operation continues to the end of the input file.

When you copy a range of records, you aren't restricted to using just the record number or string technique to specify starting and ending locations; it's OK to combine them. For instance,

```
COPY CUSTMAST DATA A = = B (FRLABEL 01000 FOR 100
```

starts the copy operation at the first record that begins with the characters 01000, but ends after exactly 100 records have been copied (or the end of the input file is reached), regardless of the contents of the last record.

## How to change the characteristics of a file with the COPYFILE command

The next two groups of COPYFILE options in figure 5-17 let you change the characteristics of a file. When you want to change a file's characteristics, you'll probably want the input file to be copied onto itself. (Remember, this is what happens when you don't specify an output file identifier.)

You use the first of these options, OLDDATE, to override the default time and date stamping performed when you use COPYFILE; normally, when you create a new file with COPYFILE, the current date and time are used.

Figure 5-19 illustrates the use of the OLDDATE option. On the screen in this figure, you can see a sequence of four commands I issued. Here, I first issued a LISTFILE command to display information for one file (LISTMAST COBOL A), whose date and time are 5/12/87 and 11:41:31. Then, I issued two COPYFILE commands (one with and the other without OLDDATE) to make copies of that file. Finally, I entered another LISTFILE command to display information for the new files. If you examine the output of the second LISTFILE command, you'll see that the file I created with the COPYFILE command without the OLDDATE option has a more recent time and date than the other copy.

If you want to change the logical record length of a file, you can use COPYFILE with the LRECL option. Simply specify the new length for the records in the file for record-length on the option; the value you specify cannot be larger than 65535. For example, to change the record length to 512 for the records in a file called CUSTMAST DATA A,

```
COPYFILE CUSTMAST DATA A (LRECL 512
```

```
R; T=2.18/3.92 15:16:17
L LISTMAST COBOL* A (LABEL
FILENAME FILETYPE FM FORMAT LRECL      RECS     BLOCKS   DATE     TIME     LABEL
LISTMAST COBOL    A1 F        80        236        19   5/12/87 11:41:31 STEVE1
R; T=0.06/0.11 15:16:31
COPYFILE LISTMAST COBOL A = COBOL1 =
R; T=1.30/2.70 15:16:49
COPYFILE LISTMAST COBOL A = COBOL2 = (OLDDATE
R; T=1.31/2.67 15:16:59
L LISTMAST COBOL* A (LABEL
FILENAME FILETYPE FM FORMAT LRECL      RECS     BLOCKS   DATE     TIME     LABEL
LISTMAST COBOL    A1 F        80        236        19   5/12/87 11:41:31 STEVE1
LISTMAST COBOL1   A1 F        80        236        19   6/02/87 15:16:49 STEVE1
LISTMAST COBOL2   A1 F        80        236        19   5/12/87 11:41:31 STEVE1
R; T=0.07/0.16 15:17:04



-
                                                             RUNNING
Iª                                                          □-□04
```

Figure 5-19     The effect of the OLDDATE option of the COPYFILE command

is all you have to enter. If you reduce the size of a file's records, they're truncated. If you increase the size of a file's records, they're padded with the current fill character. The default fill character is the space; you can specify a different one with the FILL option.

You use the RECFM option to change the records in a file from fixed-length to variable-length (if you specify RECFM V), or vice versa (if you specify RECFM F). You'll typically use the LRECL and RECFM F options together. If you want to change the record format of a file to variable-length, the longest record length is taken from the longest record in the input file; if you code the LRECL option when you specify RECFM V, it's ignored.

By default, if you convert a file with fixed-length records to one with variable-length records, trailing pad characters (which are almost always spaces) are not removed. In other words, records are not truncated in the conversion. However, if you want to override this default, you can specify the TRUNC option on the COPYFILE command.

When you convert a file with variable-length records to one with fixed-length records, the process is reversed. It's typically necessary to pad short records so they become the correct fixed-length. By default, spaces are used for that padding process.

If you wish, you can use the the FILL option of the COPYFILE command to specify a pad character other than the space. For example, if you want to use zeros as the fill character, you'd key in

```
FILL 0
```

```
R; T=2.18/3.90 16:20:14
L LISTMAST COBOL A (LABEL
FILENAME FILETYPE FM FORMAT LRECL        RECS     BLOCKS   DATE     TIME     LABEL
LISTMAST COBOL     A1 F        80          236        19   6/02/87 16:14:43 STEVE1
R; T=0.06/0.11 16:20:25
COPYFILE LISTMAST COBOL A (PACK
R; T=1.14/2.08 16:20:35
L LISTMAST COBOL A (LABEL
FILENAME FILETYPE FM FORMAT LRECL        RECS     BLOCKS   DATE     TIME     LABEL
LISTMAST COBOL     A1 F      1024            9         9   6/02/87 16:20:35 STEVE1
R; T=0.06/0.11 16:20:41
COPYFILE LISTMAST COBOL A (UNPACK
R; T=1.14/2.09 16:20:56
L LISTMAST COBOL A (LABEL
FILENAME FILETYPE FM FORMAT LRECL        RECS     BLOCKS   DATE     TIME     LABEL
LISTMAST COBOL     A1 F        80          236        19   6/02/87 16:20:55 STEVE1
R; T=0.06/0.11 16:20:57




-                                                          RUNNING
Iª                                                         ▯−▯04
```

**Figure 5-20**          The effect of the PACK and UNPACK options of the COPYFILE command

as one of COPYFILE's options. Then, either for truncating records being converted to variable-length or extending records being converted to fixed-length, the zero is used as the pad character instead of the space. Keep in mind that this is unusual; it's almost always the space that's used as the pad character.

Also, when you convert a file with variable-length records to one with fixed-length records, any records that are *longer* than the new fixed length are truncated. There's no option to override this default.

The PACK and UNPACK options let you manipulate files that will be or have been stored in compressed format. In a compressed file, repeating sequences of characters are represented in a coded form that reduces the amount of minidisk space required to store the file. In addition, records are combined so they can be stored more efficiently. To change a file from normal to compressed format, you copy it with the PACK option; to restore a compressed file to normal format, you copy it with the UNPACK option.

To understand how the PACK and UNPACK options work and what their effects are, consider figure 5-20. Here, I've issued a LISTFILE command for the file LISTMAST COBOL A. As you can see, the file contains 236 fixed-length, 80-byte records and uses 19 CMS blocks of minidisk space. Next, I compress the file with a COPYFILE command that specifies the PACK option, then I issue another LISTFILE command. Notice that the file has been significantly changed. Now, it consists of nine 1024-byte records, and it only uses nine CMS minidisk blocks. Finally, I convert the file back to its original format with a COPYFILE command that includes the UNPACK option, and I check the result with a third

LISTFILE command. The formats of the first and third versions of the file are the same.

If your minidisk space is limited, you might compress many of your files. Realize, though, that when a file is compressed, it must not be changed. For example, you shouldn't run an application program or utility that modifies a file stored in packed format.

## How to perform character translations with the COPYFILE command

The next options in figure 5-17 let you do character translations. The first two of these options, UPCASE and LOWCASE, are easy to understand. If you specify UPCASE, all lowercase letters in the input file are converted to uppercase in the output file. And if you specify LOWCASE, all uppercase letters in the input file are converted to lowercase in the output file.

If you want to perform more specific character translations, you can specify the TRANS option when you invoke the COPYFILE command. When you use TRANS, you're prompted to enter the translations you want performed. For each individual translation, you enter the character to be translated and what it should be translated to. You can enter as many pairs of values as you need.

To understand, consider the sequence of commands illustrated in figure 5-21. I created a small test file called TRANSTST INFILE A, which I listed with the TYPE command, the first command on the screen in the figure. As you can see, the file has three records with the repeating pattern ABCDEFG. Next, I keyed in

```
COPYFILE TRANSTST INFILE A = OUTFILE = (TRANS
```

Because I specified TRANS, CMS prompted me to enter the character translations I wanted performed.

In the next line, I requested four character translations:

```
A * B 40 C ! 40 -
```

These values request that all occurrences of the character A be replaced by asterisks, all occurrences of the character B be replaced by the character with the hexadecimal value 40 (the space), all occurrences of the character C be replaced by exclamation marks, and all spaces (hexadecimal 40) be replaced by hyphens. After the COPYFILE operation had finished, I entered the TYPE command to display the contents of the output file. If you compare the contents of the input and output files in the figure, you'll see that the four character translations I requested were performed properly.

As the example in figure 5-21 illustrates, you can specify the characters involved in a translation using either character or hexadecimal values. Although it's usually easiest to specify the character values, sometimes you'll need to use hex.

You can specify as many pairs of characters for translation as you need. If you need to enter more than one line of values, just type two plus signs at the

In the translation list, you enter pairs of values: first, the existing value, followed by the value you want to change it to (the values can be in hex)

```
R; T=2.22/4.01 11:19:40
TYPE TRANSTST INFILE A

ABCDEFG   ABCDEFG   ABCDEFG
    ABCDEFG   ABCDEFG   ABCDEFG
        ABCDEFG   ABCDEFG   ABCDEFG

R; T=0.06/0.20 11:19:55
COPYFILE TRANSTST INFILE A = OUTFILE = (TRANS
DMSCPY602R ENTER TRANSLATION LIST:
A * B 40 C ! 40 -
R; T=0.18/0.45 11:20:27
TYPE TRANSTST OUTFILE A

* !DEFG---* !DEFG---* !DEFG-------------------------------------------------
---* !DEFG   * !DEFG---* !DEFG-------------------------------------------------
------* !DEFG---* !DEFG---* !DEFG-------------------------------------------------

R; T=0.05/0.18 11:20:34



-                                                              RUNNING
Iª                                                            □─□04
```

Figure 5-21    How to perform character translations with the COPYFILE command

end of each line except the last. For example, the four lines

```
A  *  ++
B  40 ++
C  !  ++
40  -
```

are equivalent to the one-line reply I entered in figure 5-21.

### How to alter a file column-by-column with the COPYFILE command

You can resequence the data in a file's records when you use the SPECS option of the COPYFILE command. The SPECS option works similarly to TRANS; when you specify it, CMS prompts you to enter the specifications for the COPY-FILE operation.

The specifications you supply each contain two elements. The first element identifies the source of the data to be copied; it can be either a range of columns (a field) in the input file or a literal value that will be the same for all output records. The second element is the location where that data will be stored in the output file; it becomes the first column of that field in the output record.

For example, to copy the contents of the five-byte field that begins in column 32 of the input file to the first five bytes of the records in the output file, you supply this specification:

```
32-36 1
```

Or, to copy a literal to the output file, you supply it between slashes and specify the starting column for the target field in the output file. For instance,

```
/CALIFORNIA/ 40
```

copies the text string "CALIFORNIA" to columns 40-49 of each record written to the output file. You can also insert non-character literals by coding the literal using two-digit hexadecimal values for each byte in the literal, as long as a single *h* precedes the string. For example,

```
h000000FFFFFF 1
```

causes three bytes of binary zeros followed by three bytes of binary ones to be stored at the beginning of each record in the output file.

You can enter up to 20 field specifications for a single COPYFILE operation. Just separate them from each other with spaces. If you need to use more than one line, end each line except the last with two plus signs.

To understand how the SPECS option works, consider figure 5-22. For this illustration, I created a short test file named SPECSTST INFILE A and displayed it with the TYPE command. The file contains the letters A-J in columns 1-10, the digits 0-9 in columns 12-21, and the letters K-Z in columns 23-38. The next command I entered was a COPYFILE command to create a new file named SPECSTST OUTFILE A; because I included the SPECS option, CMS prompted me to enter the specifications for the operation.

This is the specifications line I entered:

```
1-10 40 12-21 10 23-38 50 /NUMBERS:/ 1 /LETTERS:/ 30
```

This might look imposing, but if you evaluate it one pair of specifications at a time, it's easy to interpret. The first three pairs of specs identify column ranges from the input file and locations in the output file where the fields should be stored. They cause the data in the input file to be resequenced in the output file and stored with different spacing. The last two pairs of specs cause the indicated literals (NUMBERS: and LETTERS:) to be inserted in the new file in columns 1 and 30.

The last command I issued on the screen in figure 5-22 was a TYPE command to display the contents of the new file. If you examine the output of that command, you'll see the effect of the specifications I supplied.

Also, notice that the output file's columns that aren't accounted for in the specifications are filled with the current pad character. Unless you specify an alternate pad character with the FILL option, the pad character will be the space.

In the specification list, you enter pairs of values: first, the data to be used (you can specify column numbers to move existing data or a literal value to add data), followed by the data's new starting position; the data in columns that aren't specified is shifted to accommodate the data that is moved or added

```
R; T=5.55/11.62 13:08:14
TYPE SPECSTST INFILE A

ABCDEFGHIJ 0123456789 KLMNOPQRSTUVWXYZ
ABCDEFGHIJ 0123456789 KLMNOPQRSTUVWXYZ
ABCDEFGHIJ 0123456789 KLMNOPQRSTUVWXYZ

R; T=0.06/0.21 13:08:21
COPYFILE SPECSTST INFILE A = OUTFILE = (SPECS
DMSCPY601R ENTER SPECIFICATION LIST:
1-10 40 12-21 10 23-38 50 /NUMBERS:/ 1 /LETTERS:/ 30
R; T=0.18/0.47 13:09:39
TYPE SPECSTST OUTFILE A

NUMBERS: 0123456789        LETTERS:   ABCDEFGHIJKLMNOPQRSTUVWXYZ
NUMBERS: 0123456789        LETTERS:   ABCDEFGHIJKLMNOPQRSTUVWXYZ
NUMBERS: 0123456789        LETTERS:   ABCDEFGHIJKLMNOPQRSTUVWXYZ

R; T=0.05/0.17 13:09:45


-                                                        RUNNING
Iª                                           □─□04
```

**Figure 5-22**    How to rearrange a file's fields with the COPYFILE command

The last option of the COPYFILE command shown in figure 5-17, OVLY, is used only in combination with the SPECS option and only when the output file you use is the same as the input file. OVLY lets you change specified columns, but leave other data unchanged.

Take a look at figure 5-23 to understand how OVLY works. The input for this COPYFILE example is the output of the example I just showed you. In this example, I want to replace the value of the literal in columns 1-9; instead of NUMBERS:, I want it to be NUMERALS:. Also, I want to shift the contents of the field that begins in column 10 two bytes to the right. However, I don't want to affect the rest of the data in the file.

To meet these goals, I invoked COPYFILE with the command

```
COPYFILE SPECSTST OUTFILE A (SPECS OVLY
```

and supplied two pairs of specifications:

```
/NUMERALS:  / 1 10-19 12
```

The first specification placed the new literal string I wanted starting in column 1, and the second shifted the column that contained the numerals themselves two positions to the right. However, as you can see in the screen in figure 5-23, the

The OVLY (overlay) option allows you to change specified columns only; the data in the other columns remains unchanged in its original position

```
R; T=0.20/0.51 13:39:02
TYPE SPECSTST OUTFILE A

NUMBERS: 0123456789          LETTERS:  ABCDEFGHIJKLMNOPQRSTUVWXYZ
NUMBERS: 0123456789          LETTERS:  ABCDEFGHIJKLMNOPQRSTUVWXYZ
NUMBERS: 0123456789          LETTERS:  ABCDEFGHIJKLMNOPQRSTUVWXYZ

R; T=0.05/0.18 13:39:08
COPYFILE SPECSTST OUTFILE A (SPECS OVLY
DMSCPY601R ENTER SPECIFICATION LIST:
/NUMERALS:  / 1 10-19 12
R; T=0.20/0.52 13:39:45
TYPE SPECSTST OUTFILE A

NUMERALS:  0123456789         LETTERS:  ABCDEFGHIJKLMNOPQRSTUVWXYZ
NUMERALS:  0123456789         LETTERS:  ABCDEFGHIJKLMNOPQRSTUVWXYZ
NUMERALS:  0123456789         LETTERS:  ABCDEFGHIJKLMNOPQRSTUVWXYZ

R; T=0.05/0.17 13:39:52

_

                                                          RUNNING
Iª                                                        ▭—▭04
```

**Figure 5-23**    How to use the OVLY option of the COPYFILE command

letters in the rest of the record were not affected because I included the OVLY option on the command. Note, too, that I had to include two trailing spaces in the literal NUMERALS:; otherwise, the characters *01* would still be in positions 10 and 11 of the output file.

## Terminology

concatenation

## Objectives

1. Copy multiple files with one COPYFILE command.
2. Concatenate files with the COPYFILE command.
3. Copy a part of a file with the COPYFILE command.
4. Change the characteristics of a file with the COPYFILE command.
5. Perform character translations with the COPYFILE command.
6. Rearrange the fields in a file's records with the COPYFILE command (SPECS option).
7. Alter specific fields in a file's records with the COPYFILE command (SPECS and OVLY options).

**Topic four**

## How to use the COMPARE and SORT commands

There are two other CMS commands for file manipulation that you should know about: COMPARE and SORT. The COMPARE command lets you find out if two files are the same; I'll describe it first in this topic. Then, I'll show you how to change the sequence of records in a CMS file with the SORT command.

### How to find out if two files are the same with the COMPARE command

The COMPARE command, whose syntax is presented in figure 5-24, is easy to use. In its simplest form, you supply two file identifiers. For example,

```
COMPARE LISTMAST COBOL A LISTMAST SAVE B
```

compares the two named files. CMS reads through both files at the same time. If they're identical, the CMS ready message is displayed and no additional indication is given. On the other hand, if any record in one of the files differs from the corresponding record in the other file, both records are displayed on your screen. And if one of the files has a different number of records than the other, a message telling you a "premature EOF (end of file)" was encountered for the shorter of the two is displayed.

Unless you specify otherwise, the comparison the command performs uses all the data in each record it reads. However, if you specify the COL option, you can restrict the columns the command evaluates as it compares the files. For instance, you'd enter

```
COMPARE LISTMAST COBOL A LISTMAST SAVE B (COL 8-72
```

if you wanted to compare the two files I used in the above example, but were only interested in the contents of columns 8-72. If you omit the ending column, the comparison continues through to the end of each record.

### How to resequence a file with the SORT command

To change the order of the records in a file, you use the SORT command. To invoke it, all you do is specify the command name and the input and output file identifiers, as the syntax in figure 5-25 indicates. The input and output files must be different; SORT cannot write a file back onto itself. If you specify an output file that already exists, it's automatically replaced by SORT.

After you've invoked SORT, CMS prompts you to enter the *control fields* whose values the SORT command will evaluate as it resequences the file. In response to the prompt, all you do is key in a pair of numbers to identify each control

## The COMPARE command

```
COMPARE file-1 file-2 [(COL start-col - end-col]
```

**Explanation**

| | |
|---|---|
| file-1 | The file identifier (fn ft fm) of one of the two files to be compared. |
| file-2 | The file identifier (fn ft fm) of the other of the two files to be compared. |
| COL | Specifies that the comparison is to be restricted to the indicated columns. |
| start-col | The first column in the range of columns to be used for the comparison. |
| end-col | The last column in the range of columns to be used for the comparison. |

---

**Figure 5-24**        The COMPARE command

field; the first of those numbers is the starting column position, and the second is the ending position.

The first pair of column positions you specify is the *major control field*. If any records have duplicate values for the major control field, they're sorted by the second control field, identified by the second pair of column numbers you enter. If there are still duplicates, they're resolved using the third control field, and so on.

The sort is performed in ascending sequence only and according to the EBCDIC collating sequence. There's no way to request that the sort be in descending sequence for one or more of the control fields or to use a different collating sequence.

To understand how to use the SORT command, take a look at figure 5-26. In part 1 of the figure, I've entered a TYPE command to display a file called NAMES INFILE A, and in part 2, you can see its contents. The file contains five names, which are in sequence by first name. For this example, I want to sort the file by last name. As a result, I've keyed in the command

```
SORT NAMES INFILE A NAMES OUTFILE A
```

at the bottom of the screen in part 2. This will invoke the SORT command and cause it to use NAMES INFILE A as its input file and NAMES OUTFILE A as its output file.

Next, the SORT command prompts me to enter the specifications for the sort operation (part 3). I've keyed in

```
10 19
```

to specify that the major control field (indeed, the only control field) for this

**The SORT command**

```
SORT file-1 file-2
```

**Explanation**

file-1                    The file identifier (fn ft fm) of the input file; that is, the file to be sorted.

file-2                    The file identifier (fn ft fm) of the output file.

---

Figure 5-25    The SORT command

sort operation is in columns 10 through 19. As you can see, that's where the last names are located. When I press the enter key, the SORT command sequences the records according to my specifications and ends.

To verify the operation, I've keyed in a TYPE command to display the output file in part 4 of the figure. In part 5, you can see that the output file was sorted correctly.

## Terminology

control field
major control field

## Objectives

1. Use the COMPARE command to determine if two files are the same.

2. Use the SORT command to resequence the records in a file.

The TYPE command says to display a file called NAMES INFILE A

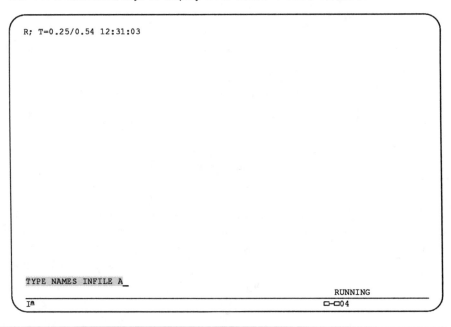

**Figure 5-26**    How to use the SORT command (part 1 of 5)

The SORT command says to sort NAMES INFILE A into a file called NAMES OUTFILE A

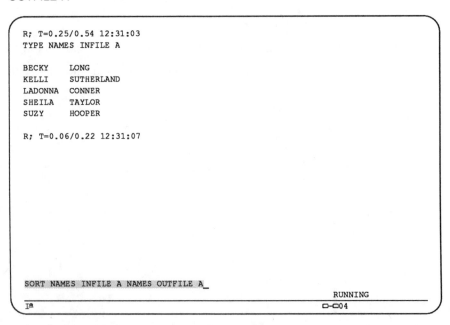

**Figure 5-26**    How to use the SORT command (part 2 of 5)

CMS asks for the sort fields; in this case, the file will be sorted according to the data in positions 10-19 of each record (the last-name field)

```
R; T=0.25/0.54 12:31:03
TYPE NAMES INFILE A

BECKY     LONG
KELLI     SUTHERLAND
LADONNA   CONNER
SHEILA    TAYLOR
SUZY      HOOPER

R; T=0.06/0.22 12:31:07
SORT NAMES INFILE A NAMES OUTFILE A
DMSSRT604R ENTER SORT FIELDS:




10 19_
                                        VM READ
Iª                                   □─□04
```

**Figure 5-26**    How to use the SORT command (part 3 of 5)

Once the sort is complete, the TYPE command is used to view the output file

```
R; T=0.25/0.54 12:31:03
TYPE NAMES INFILE A

BECKY     LONG
KELLI     SUTHERLAND
LADONNA   CONNER
SHEILA    TAYLOR
SUZY      HOOPER

R; T=0.06/0.22 12:31:07
SORT NAMES INFILE A NAMES OUTFILE A
DMSSRT604R ENTER SORT FIELDS:
10 19
R; T=0.14/0.48 12:31:43




TYPE NAMES OUTFILE A_
                                        RUNNING
Iª                                   □─□04
```

**Figure 5-26**    How to use the SORT command (part 4 of 5)

The sorted file is in last-name sequence

```
R; T=0.25/0.54 12:31:03
TYPE NAMES INFILE A

BECKY     LONG
KELLI     SUTHERLAND
LADONNA   CONNER
SHEILA    TAYLOR
SUZY      HOOPER

R; T=0.06/0.22 12:31:07
SORT NAMES INFILE A NAMES OUTFILE A
DMSSRT604R ENTER SORT FIELDS:
10 19
R; T=0.14/0.48 12:31:43
TYPE NAMES OUTFILE A

LADONNA   CONNER
SUZY      HOOPER
BECKY     LONG
KELLI     SUTHERLAND
SHEILA    TAYLOR

-
                                    MORE...
Iᵃ                                  ▭-▭04
```

**Figure 5-26**  How to use the SORT command (part 5 of 5)

# Chapter 6

## How to manage your minidisks

Although you can use CMS productively with the background you already have, you'll be able to get more out of your system if you understand the advanced minidisk management functions this chapter presents. First, this chapter reviews the essential concepts and commands you must know to use DASD storage effectively under CMS and introduces some additional concepts that you should be aware of. Then, it describes the concepts and commands you need to know to use shared minidisks. Next, the chapter shows you how to use temporary minidisks, which are allocated only for the duration of a terminal session. And in some shops, users are responsible for backing up their own files, so this chapter ends with a brief discussion of backup strategies.

### A deeper look at minidisk concepts

As you already know, DASD storage is provided for virtual machines through the minidisk facility. A minidisk is simply a range of real disk storage that has been allocated to a virtual machine and has been properly formatted for use by it. VM manages access to the real tracks and cylinders that contain users' minidisks. As a result, users can think of their minidisks just as if they were real disk units with a certain fixed amount of storage.

The real disk extent that is used to store a single minidisk is specified in the VM system directory. In the directory entry that defines each virtual machine, the systems programmer codes one MDISK statement for each minidisk that virtual machine will own. Figure 6-1 presents a sample directory entry that contains

**145**

```
USER STEVE ECKOLS 1M 3M ABCDEG
 IPL CMS
 CONSOLE 009 3215
 SPOOL 00C 2540 READER *
 SPOOL 00D 2540 PUNCH A
 SPOOL 00E 1403 A
 LINK MAINT 190 190 RR
 LINK MAINT 19D 19D RR
 LINK MAINT 19E 19E RR
 LINK DOSVSE 240 240 RR
 LINK DOSVSE 241 241 RR
 MDISK 191 FB-512 041218 003262 VMSRES MW ALL
 MDISK 192 FB-512 000016 001984 VMSEXT MW ALL
```

**Figure 6-1**    Sample VM directory entry

definitions for two owned minidisks. (This is the same sample directory entry I presented in chapter 3.) In this example, two minidisks are defined (with addresses 191 and 192).

The minidisks that are defined in a directory entry are permanent minidisks. In other words, the DASD space they use is permanently allocated, and they're part of your virtual machine configuration each time you start a terminal session. (As I mentioned a moment ago, you can also use temporary minidisks, which are allocated to your virtual machine just for the duration of a single terminal session; I'll show you how later in this chapter.)

You should also remember from chapter 4 that before a CMS user can read or write data to or from a minidisk, a filemode letter must be associated with it. Your 191 minidisk is automatically associated with filemode letter A, and your 192 minidisk, if you have one, is automatically associated with filemode letter D. For additional minidisks, ACCESS commands must be supplied that provide filemodes. Usually, ACCESS commands for minidisks that are part of your virtual machine's permanent configuration are stored in your user profile so they're executed automatically when you start a terminal session. However, you can also issue the ACCESS command directly. For example,

```
ACCESS 194 B
```

associates the minidisk at virtual address 194 with filemode letter B.

*Minidisk access modes: Read/write or read/only*    In the directory control statements that define the minidisks for a user's virtual machine, the systems programmer specifies the *access modes* for the user's minidisks. A minidisk can be accessed in *read/write mode* or in *read/only mode*. The names imply exactly what the modes mean. Files on a minidisk accessed in either mode can be read; however, files can be updated (written) only if the minidisk on which they reside is defined for read/write mode.

This distinction is significant because, as you know, minidisks can be shared by multiple users under VM, and some mechanism must be provided to insure that those users don't try to update the same data at the same time. When I describe disk sharing in a moment, I'll discuss access modes in more detail. I'm introducing them now because you need to understand the difference between read/write and read/only access to understand another CMS minidisk management facility: filemode extensions.

*Filemode extensions*       An advanced CMS minidisk facility, *filemode extensions*, lets you specify that one or more minidisks should be considered an extension of another minidisk, called the *parent*. When you use extensions, they're searched for files you request right after the parent, regardless of where the extension falls in the normal CMS search order. However, files cannot be written on the extension; extensions are always treated as though they were defined with read/only access.

To understand how extensions might be used, consider a virtual machine with minidisks accessed as A (at virtual address 191), B (at 192), C (at 193), D (at 194), and E (at 195). The A-disk, as you'd expect, is the user's primary working disk; the others are used for a variety of other purposes. In this example, though, suppose the E-disk is used to store archive copies of completed source programs that the user needs to access frequently. If that's the case, it can be defined as an extension of the A-disk with the command

```
ACCESS 195 E/A
```

As the complete syntax of the ACCESS command in figure 6-2 shows, you separate the filemode extension from the parent filemode with a slash.

With this arrangement, the user can issue commands that will search for files on the A-disk. If they're not found there, the command will automatically search the E-disk also. The result is that to access files on the E-disk, the user does not always have to specify E as the filemode, nor does he have to know that a file is on the E-disk instead of the A-disk. In addition, the virtual machine doesn't have to look first for the file on the B, C, and D disks, as the default CMS search order would require. Remember, though, that the user can only read files retrieved from the extension. (By the way, extension searches work for most CMS commands, but LISTFILE and FILELIST are exceptions; they do not search extensions.)

If you explicitly specify the filemode letter of a file you want to access, extensions are not necessarily used. For example, if you enter the command

```
TYPE MNT5120 COBOL E
```

the requested file is retrieved directly from the E-disk. Although the E-disk is an extension of the A-disk, the A-disk is not searched. Also, if you specify an asterisk

**The ACCESS command**

```
ACCESS [virtual-address filemode-letter[/parent [file-id]]] [(NOPROF]
```

**Explanation**

virtual-address    The virtual address of the minidisk to be accessed. If you omit the virtual address, 191 is used as the default.

filemode-letter    The letter to be associated with the accessed minidisk. If you omit the filemode letter, A is used as the default.

parent    The filemode letter associated by a previous ACCESS command with the minidisk to which this minidisk should be a read/only extension.

file-id    The file identifier mask to be used to select files for inclusion in the directory image for a read/only extension.

NOPROF    Specifies that your user profile should be bypassed; this option is valid only when you issue the ACCESS command immediately after you IPL CMS.

---

**Figure 6-2**    The ACCESS command

for the filemode, extensions are not used; instead, the default alphabetical CMS search order is used.

A parent disk can have as many extensions as you'd like. For example, the A-disk in the example I just described could have the C-disk as an extension as well as the E-disk. However, only one level of extensions is allowed. In other words, you couldn't request that the C-disk be the extension of the E-disk, which itself is an extension of the A-disk.

Because extensions are always treated as read/only disks, you can protect a minidisk by accessing it as an extension of itself. For example, if you issue the command

```
ACCESS 196 E/E
```

your E-disk is accessed as an extension of itself and, as a result, is treated as though it were defined with the read/only access mode, regardless of how it actually was defined. You'll seldom have an occasion to use this technique, but it might be useful if you're involved in reorganizing the files on your minidisks and you're doing extensive copying, renaming, and deleting.

The relationship between a parent minidisk and an extension remains in effect until one of the disks is released or reaccessed. You need to be aware of a couple of details of this, though. If you release an extension, then access another minidisk with the same filemode letter, the new disk is not an extension of the original parent unless you explicitly indicate so on its ACCESS command. However, if you release a parent, then access another minidisk with its filemode letter, any extensions that belonged to the first parent are automatically attached to the new one.

When you use extensions, you can also specify that just a subset of the files on the extension be included in your view of the disk. For example, if you're only interested in files with a particular filetype on an extension, you can access the extension with a command like

```
ACCESS 196 E/A * COBOL E
```

Here, the E-disk is accessed as an extension of the A-disk, and only files with filetype COBOL will be available. The way this works has to do with the way CMS handles directory information from a minidisk when you access it.

*Minidisk file directories*     When you first access a minidisk, its file directory is read by your virtual machine. A minidisk's file directory contains information about each file on the minidisk that you can access.

Normally, information about *all* of the files on the disk is read when the disk is accessed. However, if you specify that only certain files should be accessed for an extension, as in the example I just showed you, only information for them is read. You can limit the files accessed only when you specify an extension, as the syntax of the ACCESS command indicates.

When you have read/write access to a minidisk, any changes you make to that minidisk are reflected in both the directory stored on the minidisk and in the directory image in storage in your virtual machine. However, if you have read/only access to a minidisk, the situation is different. It's possible that another user who has read/write access to that minidisk might make changes to a file that would affect the directory. Unfortunately, the image of the directory in your virtual machine is not updated when this occurs. As a result, it's possible that the directory image you use for a read/only minidisk and the actual status of the disk can disagree. You can get around this problem by issuing the ACCESS command for that minidisk using its current filemode from time to time as you work. That refreshes the directory image in your virtual machine with data from the minidisk itself and brings it up to date.

The image of a minidisk's directory that's in your virtual machine is removed when you issue a RELEASE command for that minidisk. However, if you just issue the CP DETACH command (which I'll describe in a moment) to remove the minidisk from your virtual machine's configuration, the minidisk's directory image is not removed. That means some confusion can result if you then try to use that minidisk. CMS thinks the disk is still present, and a processing error occurs. As a result, you should always issue a RELEASE command before you detach a minidisk from your virtual machine. These considerations are most important when you change your machine's configuration, and particularly when you share minidisks with other users.

**The CP LINK command**

```
LINK [TO] user-id vaddr-1 [AS] vaddr-2 [access-mode] [[PASS= ]pwd]
```

**Explanation**

TO user-id
The operand *user-id* specifies the user-id of the owner of the minidisk to which link access is being requested. The TO keyword can be omitted unless the value of user-id is TO or T. You can specify * to refer to your own user-id.

vaddr-1
The virtual address assigned in the owner's directory entry for the minidisk to which link access is being requested.

AS vaddr-2
The operand *vaddr-2* specifies the virtual address to be used on your virtual machine for the minidisk to which link access is being requested. As long as the virtual address to be used for vaddr-2 is not A (an abbreviation of 00A), you can omit AS.

access-mode
One or two letters to indicate the primary or the primary and secondary access modes to be used for the minidisk to which link access is being requested. Acceptable values are R, W, M, RR, WR, MR, and MW. See figure 6-4 for details on what these values mean. If you omit the access mode when accessing another user's minidisk, R is assumed.

PASS = pwd
The operand *pwd* is the access mode password assigned in the owner's directory entry to the minidisk to which link access is being requested. If you use the keyword PASS =, one space must separate the equal sign from the *pwd* value.

Figure 6-3　The CP LINK command

## How to access another user's minidisks

In addition to the MDISK statements that define the minidisks you own, your VM system directory entry also contains LINK statements that give you access to minidisks owned by other users. (In figure 6-1, there are five LINK statements.) Typically, those statements give you access to the minidisks that contain CMS program files all users need to share.

Minidisks specified in LINK statements in your directory entry are available as part of your virtual machine configuration each time your virtual machine is started. Because you have automatic access to these minidisks each time you start a terminal session (unless, of course, the specifications in your VM system directory entry have been changed), they're called *permanent links*.

***The LINK command***　　You can also request *temporary links*, which last only as long as your current terminal session, by issuing the CP LINK command. Figure 6-3 gives its format. Basically, the LINK command specifies the disk you want to access (by owner and virtual address on the owner's virtual machine) and the virtual address you want to use for it on your virtual machine. For example,

```
LINK MAINT 192 202
```

| Access mode | Description |
|---|---|
| R | Requests primary read/only access. If no other user has the disk in read/write status, read/only access is granted. This is the default value for access mode. |
| W | Requests primary read/write access. If no other user has a link to the disk, read/write access is granted. |
| M | Requests primary multiple access. If no other user has the disk in read/write status, read/write access is granted. |
| RR | Requests primary read/only access and alternate read/only access. Read/only access is granted regardless of how other users are accessing the disk. |
| WR | Requests primary read/write access and alternate read/only access. If no other user has a link to the disk, read/write access is granted; otherwise, read/only access is granted. |
| MR | Requests primary multiple access and alternate read/only access. If no other user has the disk in read/write status, read/write access is granted; otherwise, read/only access is granted. |
| MW | Requests primary multiple access and alternate read/write access. Read/write access is granted in all cases. |

**Figure 6-4**    Access mode operand values for the CP LINK command

specifies that the minidisk defined in the MAINT user's directory entry with virtual address 192 should be linked to my virtual machine with the address 202. I could also enter

```
LINK TO MAINT 192 AS 202
```

which makes the command a little easier to understand, but the keywords TO and AS aren't required.

The other operands you can code on the LINK command, access mode and password, are for specialized purposes. The next sections describe both.

*Sharing files and access modes*    The access mode operand of the LINK command lets you specify whether you'll have read/write or read/only access to the minidisk for which you're requesting a link. However, it's not as simple as just asking for what you want and getting it. What's allowed depends on what you're authorized to do and on what other users on the system are doing.

To understand, take a look at figure 6-4; it lists the seven possible values you can code for the access mode operand on the LINK command. If you specify one of the one-letter access mode values, you are indicating that you'll accept the link only if that access mode is available.

For example, access mode W specifies that you require exclusive read/write access to the disk. If any other users have access to the disk, your link won't be granted. Similarly, a primary multiple link (M), which lets you have read/write access to a disk, won't be granted if any other users already have read/write access to it. However, if the other users have just read/only access to the disk, a primary multiple link will be granted to you.

If you don't specify an access mode value when you issue a LINK command for another user's minidisk, the default value is R, which requests primary read/only access. With primary read/only access, you can use a minidisk for read/only operations as long as no other users already have access to it with read/write access.

The other four access mode values in figure 6-4 supply not only a primary access mode, but an alternate access mode as well. If the link you request cannot be provided with the primary access mode you specify, then the system will provide the link with the alternate mode. Usually, if the alternate access mode has to be used, it results in a link with read/only access.

However, if you specify MW for the access mode operand on the LINK command, you're given read/write access regardless of what other users are doing with the minidisk. As a general rule, shops avoid the MW option of the LINK command. If two or more users have update access to the same minidisk at the same time, data can be lost, and system actions are unpredictable.

In some cases, you might have to issue the LINK command to add your own disks to your virtual machine's configuration. If it's possible for other users to access your disks, you might discover when you logon that another user has one of your minidisks in read/write access. When that's the case, you'll be given read/only access to the minidisk, even though it's yours and is usually available for update. If you need read/write access to the minidisk, send a message to the other user (with the MSG command) and ask that he detach your disk. Then, you can link to it and request the M access mode to enable you (and only you) to update files on it, although other users may be granted read/only access.

Don't let all of these combinations and circumstances confuse you. When you issue a LINK command, the access mode granted to you is displayed by the command. And typically, read/only access is what's appropriate when you access other users' minidisks. You can nearly always get it with the RR access mode value, provided you know the password necessary to access the disk.

*Passwords*    The last operand you can specify when you issue the LINK command is the access mode password. When the system administrator codes the statements that define minidisks, she can specify up to three passwords that users must specify if they want to establish a temporary link to that minidisk. The three passwords correspond to the three kinds of primary access I just described; there can be a *read password*, a *write password*, and a *multiple password*.

To be able to access a disk in any of these modes, the appropriate password must be supplied. Depending on how your VM system is configured, you can enter the password in one of two ways. If password displays are not suppressed on your system, you enter the password on the command line. For example,

```
LINK TO MAINT 193 AS 195 RR PASS= READPW
```

**The CP DETACH command**

```
DETACH virtual-address . . .
```

**Explanation**

virtual-address     The virtual address of the device to be removed from your virtual machine's configuration. You can specify multiple virtual addresses (up to 48) on one DETACH command.

---

Figure 6-5     The CP DETACH command

---

requests that the MAINT user's 193 disk be attached to your virtual machine with address 195 for read/only access. The read password associated with the minidisk in the MAINT user's directory entry is READPW.

On the other hand, if your shop uses a facility that does suppress password display, you don't key in the password on the command line. Instead, you enter the LINK command without the password operand. Then, you're prompted to enter the password, and your screen is formatted so the characters you key in aren't displayed as you type. For instance, you might be prompted

```
ENTER MULT PASSWORD:
```

if you requested a link for multiple access. You'd key in the password, but it wouldn't be displayed.

*How to release a linked minidisk*     When you end a terminal session by logging off, any linked minidisks you've been using are automatically released. If you want to remove a linked minidisk from your virtual machine's configuration without logging off, you can issue RELEASE and DETACH commands to do so.

First, issue the RELEASE command to break the relationship between the virtual disk and its associated CMS filemode letter and to remove its directory image from storage. Then, issue the CP DETACH command to remove the device from your virtual machine; figure 6-5 presents its syntax. As you can see, all you have to specify on the DETACH command is the virtual address of the device to be removed from your virtual machine's configuration. For example, you might enter

```
RELEASE 196
```

and

```
DETACH 196
```

to remove the minidisk with virtual address 196 from your virtual machine.

### How to use temporary minidisks

The minidisks I've described so far, whether they're (1) owned by you, (2) owned by others but permanently linked to you via statements in your directory entry, or (3) owned by others and accessed by you for the duration of the terminal session via the LINK command—all have something in common. They're all permanently defined to VM in the directory. But VM also provides support for minidisks that are created dynamically (rather than just accessed dynamically, as with the LINK command). They're called *temporary minidisks*.

*Temporary minidisk concepts*     Most of the real DASD space on VM systems is allocated permanently to user minidisks. However, a portion of the real DASD storage available is reserved for temporary minidisks. When a user requests a temporary minidisk, the DASD storage required for it is drawn from this pool, which is shared among all virtual machines. At the end of a terminal user's session, the temporary DASD space allocated for that user is released and is again available for other users.

To use a temporary minidisk, two preliminary steps are required. First, you have to tell VM that you want to use a temporary minidisk. You do this by issuing a CP DEFINE command to request that another virtual device be defined for your virtual machine. After the temporary minidisk has been allocated to your virtual machine, you have to format it. For most applications, you'll use the CMS FORMAT command to prepare the temporary minidisk for CMS files. This section shows you how to use these two commands.

*How to request a temporary minidisk with the DEFINE command*     The CP DEFINE command provides many options that you can use to configure your virtual machine. For example, you can use it to change the amount of storage provided for your virtual machine or to alter its channel operating mode. Although the DEFINE command provides a wide range of features, you'll seldom use most of them. Of its many features, the one you're most likely to use lets you define temporary minidisks.

Figure 6-6 presents the syntax of the CP DEFINE command that's related to defining temporary minidisks. To request a space allocation for a temporary minidisk, you have to specify three items of information: (1) the kind of real DASD on which the allocation should be made, (2) the virtual address to be used for your temporary minidisk, and (3) the amount to storage to be allocated (in cylinders for CKD devices or in blocks for FBA units).

For example, to allocate a 750-block temporary minidisk with virtual address 205 on a fixed-block architecture DASD, you'd enter

```
DEFINE TFB-512 205 750
```

**The CP DEFINE command (to define a temporary minidisk)**

```
DEFINE real-device-type virtual-address storage
```

**Explanation**

real-device-type      Specifies what type of real device should be used to define the temporary minidisk. Enter one of the following values (other than TFB-512, the numbers all correspond to the actual device type):

TFB-512   (any available FBA device—that is, either a 3310 or a 3370)
T3310
T3370
T2305
T2314
T2319
T3330
T3340
T3350
T3375
T3380

virtual-address      Specifies the virtual address to be used for the temporary minidisk.

storage      Specifies the amount of DASD storage to be allocated to the temporary minidisk. If you specify an FBA device (TFB-512, T3310, or T3370), storage is the number of FBA blocks to be allocated. Otherwise, storage is the number of CKD cylinders to be allocated.

---

**Figure 6-6**      The CP DEFINE command (to define a temporary minidisk)

The command to allocate a temporary minidisk on a CKD device is similar. For example,

```
DEFINE T3380 198 2
```

requests a two-cylinder temporary minidisk on a 3380 DASD; the temporary minidisk will have the virtual address 198. In either case, the virtual address you use must not already be in use by your virtual machine, or CMS will issue an error message and the minidisk won't be defined.

When you define a temporary minidisk on an FBA DASD, it's possible to specify an unrealistically small number of blocks for the disk. CMS uses some disk space for its purposes, and you must allow enough space for it. If you always allocate 48 FBA blocks more than you think you'll need for the files you expect to create, you shouldn't have any problems.

*How to prepare a CMS minidisk for use with the FORMAT command*      After you've added a temporary minidisk to your virtual machine's configuration with the CP DEFINE command, you have to format it before you can store files on it. To use a minidisk for CMS files, you format it with the CMS FORMAT command.

Figure 6-7 presents the basic syntax of the FORMAT command. Most of the time, all you need to specify on the command are the virtual address of the minidisk you want to format and the CMS filemode letter that will be associated with it. For example, to format a temporary minidisk with virtual address 198 and associate the filemode letter T with it, I'd enter

```
FORMAT 198 T
```

If any other minidisk is currently accessed with the filemode you specify, that minidisk is automatically released. As a result, you'll usually use a filemode letter that isn't already associated with one of your minidisks.

After you press the enter key, the FORMAT command verifies that you want to proceed with the format operation by advising you that any files already on the minidisk will be erased. Pay close attention to what you're doing here. It's all too easy to format an existing minidisk by specifying the wrong virtual address on the command. If you do, you'll wipe out the files on that minidisk.

If you indicate the operation should continue by replying YES, CMS prompts you for a six-character disk label, which, for a temporary disk, can be any value you like. (In contrast, minidisks formatted for permanent use probably have to be labelled according to an installation standard.)

The complete syntax of the FORMAT command lets you specify the CMS block size to be used on the minidisk. Almost always, the default (1024 bytes) is the best choice. Although you might see slight performance improvements in some special cases with alternate block sizes, estimating optimum block sizes is beyond the scope of this book. As a result, I'm not going to show you the command syntax for specifying other values.

After the FORMAT command has completed, the temporary minidisk is available to you to use like a permanent minidisk. The filemode letter you specified on the FORMAT command is associated with the minidisk and determines its position in the CMS search order. You'll have read/write access to it, so you can create files as you wish. Just remember not to leave files there that you want to keep; the space used for a temporary minidisk is released for use by others at the end of a terminal session, regardless of the data stored there.

*How to return a temporary minidisk to the system with the DETACH command*
Because temporary minidisks are automatically removed from your virtual machine's configuration and the real DASD space they used is freed when you end a terminal session, you don't have to take any explicit action to return a temporary mini-

**The FORMAT command**

```
FORMAT virtual-address filemode
```

**Explanation**

virtual-address     The virtual address of the minidisk to be formatted.

filemode            The CMS filemode letter to be associated with the new minidisk.

---

Figure 6-7     The FORMAT command

disk to VM. However, if you wish, you can issue the CMS RELEASE and the CP DETACH commands to give up your temporary minidisk. For example,

```
RELEASE 198
```

and

```
DETACH 198
```

remove the virtual device at address 198.

## How to backup your minidisks

You can protect yourself from accidental loss of data in the event of a hardware, software, or operator error in a variety of ways. Because almost all shops are scrupulous about performing a system-wide backup on a regular basis, it's unlikely that a hardware or software error will result in much lost work, if any. As a result, it's more likely that if you do lose data, it will be due to your own operational mistakes. For example, if you make a keying error when you enter an ERASE command or you specify the wrong virtual address on the FORMAT command, you can destroy a lot of files.

As a result, then, you might consider performing your own, personalized backups. Again, a variety of ways are available to do this. You might maintain multiple copies of your files on different minidisks or with different names or types on the same minidisks. You can do that using the commands you've already learned.

Another way to make backups is to copy disk files to tape with either the CMS TAPE command or the CMS DASD Dump and Restore program, called DDR. You can use either to dump disk files to tape, then restore them later if necessary. You'll learn how to perform these and other tape processing functions in the chapters in section 3.

## Terminology

access mode
read/write mode
read/only mode
filemode extension
parent
permanent link
temporary link
read password
write password
multiple password
temporary minidisk

## Objectives

1. Describe how you can use filemode extensions.

2. Explain why it's a good practice to issue an ACCESS command periodically when you have read/only access to another user's minidisk.

3. Explain why you should always issue a RELEASE command before you DETACH a minidisk from your virtual machine's configuration.

4. Use the LINK command to establish a temporary link to another user's minidisk.

5. Define and format a temporary minidisk, then remove it from your virtual machine's configuration.

# Chapter 7

```
┌─────────────────────────────────┐
│                                 │
│                                 │
│                                 │
│        How to use the           │
│           VM File               │
│       Storage Facility          │
│                                 │
│                                 │
└─────────────────────────────────┘
```

In some shops an optional program product, the *VM File Storage Facility* (also called *VMFSF* or just *FSF*), is used to make file management and disk use operations easier. Although not all shops use FSF, it is widely installed. If your shop doesn't use FSF, you can skip this chapter. However, if it does, you're almost certain to have to know how to use this facility.

## File Storage Facility concepts

FSF has two main components: the *Data Space and Sharing Facility* (*DSSF*) and the *Loaned Minidisk Facility* (*LMF*). DSSF provides a large pool of disk space in which all users can store data. DSSF keeps track of who owns particular files that have been placed under its control. As a result, DSSF relieves users of the disk space limitations imposed by necessarily small owned minidisks. In addition, DSSF lets you add high-level qualifiers to the identifiers of CMS files you place under its control.

The Loaned Minidisk Facility provides users with a way to acquire additional minidisk space they can retain from one terminal session to another. LMF manages a number of preformatted minidisks that it can allocate to users who request them. Such minidisks are called *borrowed minidisks*. To gain access to a borrowed minidisk, a user requests one of a particular size for a specified time period (which can be up to 9999 hours). Because borrowed minidisks remain allocated to the users who requested them after those users have logged off, they're different from temporary minidisks created with the CP DEFINE command. As you'll recall from chapter 6, temporary minidisks are automatically released at the end of the user's terminal session.

DSSF and LMF are independent functions. As a result, I'll describe them in separate sections of this chapter. But before I do, I want to give you some background on how FSF works.

## How FSF works

To request an FSF service, such as to store or retrieve a file, you issue the FSF command and specify one of its functions. (You'll learn the syntax of the command in a moment.) As you can see in figure 7-1, several virtual machines are active when FSF is in use. When you enter an FSF command, it's transferred by VM from your virtual machine to another called the FSF *control virtual machine*. The control virtual machine owns the pool of minidisk space used for DSSF and the preformatted minidisks used for LMF.

Depending on the function you request, the control virtual machine will either perform it itself or will direct one of its subordinate *task virtual machines* to manage the operation. As a general rule, if the function you request involves a file transfer, a task virtual machine will manage it, not the control virtual machine. For example, if you issue a command to retrieve a file from FSF, the control virtual machine passes that command to a task virtual machine which actually retrieves the file and passes it to your virtual machine.

The number of task virtual machines in a particular FSF configuration can vary from one to many. The number is determined by the systems programmer and is based on how many users will request FSF services. (IBM recommends one task virtual machine be defined for every 30 FSF users. As a result, a system with 120 active users should be configured with four task virtual machines.)

Because the control virtual machine doesn't manage all of the FSF file I/O, it can service a large number of users. And because multiple task virtual machines can be part of an FSF configuration, multiple file transfers to and from users' virtual machines can occur at the same time.

It's possible for two or more FSF control virtual machines, each with its own minidisk allocations and subordinate task virtual machines, to be active on the same system at the same time. When that's the case, each control virtual machine is considered to be a separate FSF *node*. (Figure 7-1 illustrates a single FSF node.) Each FSF node is independent of all others; they do not share minidisks.

Regardless of the number of FSF nodes that are active, one of them will be your *standard node*. Unless you specify otherwise when you issue FSF commands, all of your FSF operations will be automatically performed at your standard node.

If you want to use FSF services through some other node, you have to identify that node on the commands you issue. Each node is assigned a unique name by the system programmer. It's that name you supply to identify the particular node you want to process a given command. Keep this in perspective, though. Most of your FSF work will be through your standard node, where you don't need to supply a node name.

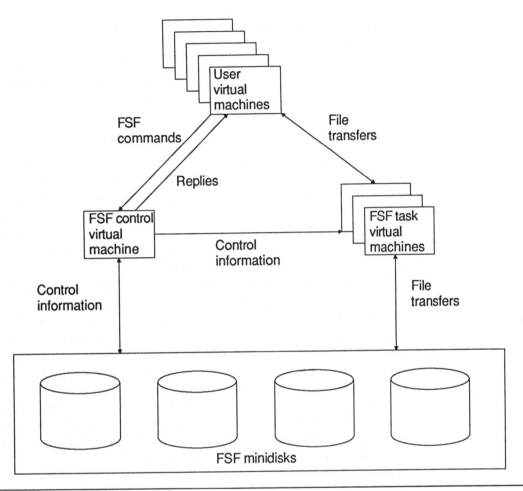

**Figure 7-1**    How the File Storage Facility works

## How to use DSSF functions for file management

From the outset, you need to know that the DSSF component of FSF is used as an archive facility. If you want to use the full range of CMS functions to work on a file, that file needs to reside on one of your CMS minidisks. You store files with DSSF to free space on your owned minidisks or to organize your data more rigorously than you can with basic CMS facilities.

In this section, you'll learn how to save and retrieve files using the DSSF functions of FSF. After I describe how to copy files to and from the FSF environment, I'll show you how to issue commands to rename, delete, or get information about your FSF files. As you'll see, for simple operations, the FSF command functions are easy to use. After I've discussed FSF's basic operation, I'll show you how to use two advanced FSF features: password protection and directory paths.

## Simple file management techniques

FSF keeps track of the files you put under its control by associating your virtual machine's user-id with them. As a result, as long as you don't introduce any additional naming complexities by using directory paths (which I'll describe in a moment), FSF will be able to find your files if you supply only their filenames and filetypes.

You don't use the filemode component of a standard CMS file identifier for files you've placed under the control of FSF. You're completely insulated from where and how FSF stores your data. In addition, FSF automatically compresses data it stores and expands data it returns to you. However, you hardly even need to know that occurs, and you certainly don't need to know how it's done.

***How to save an FSF file: The STORE function of the FSF command***      To place a file under the control of FSF, you use the STORE function of the FSF command, illustrated in figure 7-2. The FSF STORE command does not affect your original CMS file; it remains on its minidisk. It's a copy of the original CMS file that's stored under the control of FSF.

For simple transfers to FSF, you're likely to enter the command in one of just two ways. First, to create a new FSF file, all you'll need to do is supply the file identifier of the file you're copying. For example,

```
FSF STORE LISTMAST COBOL B
```

would copy the CMS file LISTMAST COBOL from my current B-disk to FSF. If I had already transferred a file to FSF with that name and I wanted to replace the first version, I'd have to include the COND REP option:

```
FSF STORE LISTMAST COBOL B ( COND REP
```

(COND is a keyword parameter and REP is an option of the parameter. There's only one other option of the COND parameter for FSF STORE: NEW. Because NEW is the default, you never need to code it.) Notice one point here: there's a single space between the first option and the left parenthesis that delimits the options from the first part of the command. That's unlike other CMS commands where a space isn't required.

Unless you specify otherwise, files you transfer to FSF are stored in your standard node. However, if you want to store a file in another node, you can specify its name on the NODE option. For instance

```
FSF STORE LISTMAST COBOL B ( NODE FSFSYS2
```

stores the file LISTMAST COBOL at the node named FSFSYS2. The other three option keywords (RPW, WPW, and APW) and the path operand are for advanced FSF features I'll describe in a moment.

## The STORE function of the FSF command

```
                             ┌  [RPW read-pw]   ┐
                             │  [WPW write-pw]  │
FSF STORE fn ft [fm [path]]  (  [APW add-pw]    │
                             │  [COND REP]      │
                             └  [NODE node-id]  ┘
```

### Explanation

| | |
|---|---|
| fn | The filename of the CMS file to be copied into FSF space. The filename is used to identify the FSF file. |
| ft | The filetype of the CMS file to be copied into FSF space. The filetype is used to identify the FSF file. |
| fm | The CMS filemode letter of the minidisk from which the CMS file should be copied. If omitted, the default is the asterisk. |
| path | The FSF path to be used for the file. If omitted, the default is your user-id at your standard node. |
| RPW read-pw | For read-pw, specify the read password to be used for the file. Valid only for a new file. If omitted, the default is your user-id. |
| WPW write-pw | For write-pw, specify the write password to be used for the file. If omitted, the default is your user-id. |
| APW add-pw | For add-pw, specify the password to be used to add the file to a directory path you don't own. If omitted, the default is your user-id. |
| COND REP | Specify this option if a file with the same name is already under the control of FSF and you want to replace it. |
| NODE node-id | To save the file at a local node other than your standard node, supply its name for node-id. |

Figure 7-2    The STORE function of the FSF command

*How to get information about FSF files: The LIST and LOCATE functions of the FSF command*    To find out what files you've stored with FSF, you can use the LIST and LOCATE functions; figure 7-3 presents their syntax. They work similarly. For either, you supply the filename and filetype you're interested in. (You may use the asterisk wild-card for both.) The two functions differ in scope: LIST looks just within a single node for the files you want, while LOCATE searches all the nodes on your system.

If you use the LIST or LOCATE function to retrieve information about a specific file, the information displayed shows you how many times the file has been read and updated, its record format and size, the number of records in the

**The LIST and LOCATE functions of the FSF command**

```
FSF   {LIST  }   [fn [ft]]   [path]   [( [RPW read-pw]  ]
      {LOCATE}                          [  [NODE node-id] ]
```

**Explanation**

LIST            Searches a single node for the specified files and gives information on them.

LOCATE          Searches all nodes for the specified files and gives information on them.

fn              The filename of the file(s) for which information is to be displayed. The default is the asterisk.

ft              The filetype of the file(s) for which information is to be displayed. The default is the asterisk.

path            The FSF path to be used for the search. If omitted, the default is your user-id at your standard node. If you identified a specific file with fn and ft, you may code ALL for path to indicate that all directory paths should be searched.

RPW read-pw     For read-pw, specify the read password to be used for the file. Not required if you own the file.

NODE node-id    For the LIST function, specify node-id to have FSF search a node other than your standard node. For the LOCATE function, you never need to code this option.

---

**Figure 7-3**      The LIST and LOCATE functions of the FSF command

file, its current status, and who owns it. On the other hand, if you retrieve information for a group of files, all you see is a list of filenames and when and by whom they were last updated.

*How to retrieve an FSF file: The GET function of the FSF command*      To retrieve a file you've placed under the control of FSF, you use the GET function of the FSF command, illustrated in figure 7-4. You supply the filename and filetype of the file you want, and the filemode of the CMS minidisk where you want the file you're retrieving to be placed. (If you want the file to be returned on your A-disk, you can omit filemode.) If you already have a CMS file with the identifier you specify, it will be replaced by the file from FSF.

You use the COND option with the GET function to specify whether you intend to update and replace the FSF file or whether you want to retrieve the file if another user has declared an intention to update it. If you specify

```
COND ANY
```

the file is retrieved regardless of its update status. (ANY is the default.) If you specify

```
COND NOU
```

**The GET function of the FSF command**

```
                                  ┌                    ┐
                                  │ [RPW read-pw]      │
FSF GET fn ft [fm [path]]  (      │ [WPW write-pw]     │
                                  │ [COND cond]        │
                                  │ [NODE node-id]     │
                                  └                    ┘
```

**Explanation**

| | |
|---|---|
| fn | The filename of the FSF file to be retrieved. The filename is used as the name for the target CMS file. |
| ft | The filetype of the FSF file to be retrieved. The filetype is used for the target CMS file. |
| fm | The CMS filemode letter of the minidisk to which the FSF file should be copied. If omitted, the default is A. |
| path | The FSF path to be used for the file. If omitted, the default is your user-id at your standard node. |
| RPW read-pw | For read-pw, specify the file's read password. If omitted, the default is your user-id. |
| WPW write-pw | For write-pw, specify the file's write password. Required only if you declare your intention to update the file with COND UPD. If omitted, the default is your user-id. |
| COND cond | You may specify one of three values for cond; they all relate to the update status of the file: |

|  |  |  |
|---|---|---|
| | UPD | Indicates that you intend to alter the file, then replace it; when you specify UPD, you receive the file only if no other user has declared an intent to update it. |
| | NOU | Indicates that you do not intend to update the file, but that you want it only if no other users have declared an intention to update it. |
| | ANY | Indicates that you want to retrieve the file whether or not another user has declared an intention to update it; ANY is the default. |

| | |
|---|---|
| NODE node-id | To retrieve the file from a local node other than your standard node, supply its name for node-id. |

---

**Figure 7-4**   The GET function of the FSF command

(NOU stands for NOUPDATE), the file is returned to you only if no other user intends to update it. And if you specify

```
COND UPD
```

(UPD stands for UPDATE), you're declaring that you plan to update and replace the file. When you use UPD, you will not be given the file if some other user has it in update status.

**The RENAME function of the FSF command**

```
FSF RENAME fn ft new-fn new-ft [path] [( [WPW write-pw]
                                         [NODE node-id]]
```

**Explanation**

| | |
|---|---|
| fn | The old filename of the FSF file to be renamed. |
| ft | The old filetype of the FSF file to be renamed. |
| new-fn | The new filename for the FSF file. |
| new-ft | The new filetype for the FSF file. |
| path | The FSF path of the file. If omitted, the default is your user-id at your standard node. |
| WPW write-pw | For write-pw, specify the file's write password. If the write password isn't your user-id, this option is required. |
| NODE node-id | If the file is stored at a local node other than your standard node, supply its name for node-id. |

---

Figure 7-5    The RENAME function of the FSF command

*How to rename and delete FSF files: The RENAME and ERASE functions of the FSF command*    Figures 7-5 and 7-6 present two other FSF command functions you'll find useful. To change the name of an FSF file, use the RENAME function, illustrated in figure 7-5. You supply the current filename and filetype, then the new filename and filetype. For example,

```
FSF RENAME LISTMAST COBOL LISTMAST COBSAVE
```

changes the name of the FSF file LISTMAST COBOL to LISTMAST COB-SAVE. You can only change the names of files you own.

To delete an FSF file, you use the ERASE function, presented in figure 7-6. For instance, I'd enter

```
FSF ERASE LISTMAST COBSAVE
```

to delete the file I just renamed.

## Password protection for files

Under FSF, many users can share the same disk space. So to make your data more secure, FSF provides a password facility you can use to impose various levels of

**The ERASE function of the FSF command**

```
FSF ERASE fn ft [path]  ⎡ ( [WPW write-pw]  ⎤
                        ⎣   [NODE node-id] ⎦
```

**Explanation**

| | |
|---|---|
| fn | The filename of the FSF file to be deleted. |
| ft | The filetype of the FSF file to be deleted. |
| path | The FSF path of the file. If omitted, the default is your user-id at your standard node. |
| WPW write-pw | For write-pw, specify the file's write password. If the write password isn't your user-id, this option is required. |
| NODE node-id | If the file is stored at a local node other than your standard node, supply its name for node-id. |

---

Figure 7-6    The ERASE function of the FSF command

access restrictions on your files. The default is for your user-id to be used as a password. Therefore, unless you specify other passwords, someone who knows your user-id can access your files. You use the options RPW, WPW, and APW (which you probably noticed in figures 7-2 through 7-6) to supply other passwords for your files.

When you store a file with FSF, you can code the RPW option on the FSF STORE command to cause a one- to eight-character *read password* value to be associated with your file. Then, when any user tries (1) to access the file to list its characteristics with the FSF LIST or FSF LOCATE command or (2) to retrieve it with the FSF GET command, he must also code the RPW option and supply the password value you assigned.

For example, if you save a file with the command

```
FSF STORE LISTMAST COBOL A ( RPW PW123
```

you have to supply the password to retrieve the file later:

```
FSF GET LISTMAST COBOL A ( RPW PW123
```

Even though you're the owner of the file, you have to supply the password to access it.

Although it doesn't seem like it, this sort of password checking is always taking place. Remember, if you don't supply particular passwords, the defaults are your user-id. So for me, the pairs of commands

```
FSF STORE LISTMAST COBOL A ( RPW STEVE
FSF GET LISTMAST COBOL A ( RPW STEVE
```

and

```
FSF STORE LISTMAST COBOL A
FSF GET LISTMAST COBOL A
```

are equivalent.

The read password keeps other users from accessing your files. The second kind of password, the *write password*, keeps other users from altering your FSF files. Like the read password, you specify the write password when you store a file with FSF. For it, you use the WPW option. Then, to retrieve a file with intent to update it (that is, with the COND UPD option of the FSF GET command), to rename it, or to delete it, you must supply the write password.

If you want to alter the read or write password associated with one of your FSF files, you can use the FSF PASSWORD command, illustrated in figure 7-7. Only the owner of a file can change its passwords, so don't try to use this command for another user's FSF files. Notice that you have to supply the current write password of the file (with the option OPW) to be able to change either the read or write password.

There are two special values you can use for your read and write passwords. If you use ANY as a password, any user can access your file without supplying a password. At the other extreme, if you use OWNER as a password, no other user may access your file under any circumstances (in other words, the user-id that was logged on when the password was assigned is the user-id that has to be logged on to access the file).

There is a third kind of password you might have to supply when you store a file: the *add password*. It's required when you want to store a file on a particular path and that path is password protected. To understand how this password is used, you need to be familiar with FSF directory paths.

## FSF directory paths

To manage data, FSF has to know more than just files' names and types. After all, many users share the same FSF node, and they can store files with the same names and types. In addition to filenames and filetypes, FSF uses paths to identify files.

As I mentioned a moment ago, each user's data is actually identified not only by filename and filetype, but also by that user's id. For simple file handling operations, FSF automatically uses your user-id as a *path* to store and retrieve your files at your standard node; you don't have to be aware that it's happening. However, you can create and use other path names. And when you do, you have to understand what's going on.

**The PASSWORD function of the FSF command**

```
                                    ⎡ [OPW current-write-pw] ⎤
                                    ⎢ [RPW read-pw]          ⎥
FSF PASSWORD fn ft [path]    (      ⎢ [WPW new-write-pw]     ⎥
                                    ⎣ [NODE node-id]         ⎦
```

**Explanation**

| | |
|---|---|
| fn | The filename of the FSF file whose passwords are to be changed. |
| ft | The filetype of the FSF file whose passwords are to be changed. |
| path | The FSF path of the file. If omitted, the default is your user-id at your standard node. |
| OPW current-write-pw | For current-write-pw, code the file's current write password. Required unless your user-id is the current write password. |
| RPW read-pw | For read-pw, specify the new read password for the file. The current read password is the default. |
| WPW new-write-pw | For new-write-pw, code the new write password for the file. The default is the file's current write password. |
| NODE node-id | For node-id, code the name of the node where the file is located. Required if the file is at a node other than your standard node. |

Figure 7-7    The PASSWORD function of the FSF command

Why bother with paths other than your default path? Well, there are a couple of reasons. First, if you need to access files owned by others, you have to supply their path names to do so. So using path names makes data sharing possible. Second, you can create paths other than the default which let you group files and create hierarchical relationships among the groups. (From a user's viewpoint, this is similar to the tree-structured directories supported by MS-DOS on personal computers and to the use of qualified data set names under OS-family operating systems.)

*How to use FSF command PATH functions*    To create and manage paths, you use the FSF command's PATH function and its subfunctions DEFINE, PASSWORD, LIST, and DELETE. Figures 7-8 through 7-11 illustrate them.

To create a new path, you use FSF PATH DEFINE, shown in figure 7-8. On it, you specify the name of the new path as an operand. As options, you can specify (1) password values to apply to the new path and (2) the node at which the path is to be created, if it's not your standard node.

Path names can be up to 64 characters long. Spaces are not allowed, but you can use the period to separate parts of a path name, if you wish. Each part

**The PATH DEFINE function of the FSF command**

```
                          ┌ [APW add-pw]          ┐
                          │ [EPW extension-pw]     │
FSF PATH DEFINE path    ( │ [DPW delete-pw]        │
                          └ [NODE node-id]         ┘
```

**Explanation**

path                  The complete path name to be added.

APW add-pw            For add-pw, code the add password users must supply to store a file on this path. The default is your user-id.

EPW extension-pw      For extension-pw, code the extension password users must supply to be able to extend this path. The default is your user-id.

DPW delete-pw         For delete-pw, code the delete password a user must supply to be able to delete this path. The default is your user-id.

NODE node-id          For node-id, code the name of the node where this path should be created. Required if you want the path to be defined at a node other than your standard node.

---

**Figure 7-8**    The PATH DEFINE function of the FSF command

of a path name should be eight or fewer characters long. So to create a path named STEVE.DOS.JOBS,

```
FSF PATH DEFINE STEVE.DOS.JOBS
```

is the command I'd enter.

You can use three kinds of passwords on the paths you create. The APW option lets you specify an add password, which users must supply to store files on this path. You can code the EPW option to provide an *extension password*. A user who wants to extend your path must supply the extension password. (Extensions are easy to understand by example: STEVE.DOS.JOBS.APRIL is an extension of the path STEVE.DOS.JOBS.) The third kind of password you can provide for a new path is a *delete password* (you code it on the DPW option.) The password you code on the DPW option must be provided to delete this path, unless the password is the same as your user-id. (The default value for each of the three path passwords is your user-id.)

To change the passwords associated with a path, you use the FSF PATH PASSWORD command; figure 7-9 presents its syntax. Code the name of the path to be affected as the operand and supply one or more options identifying the password to be changed and its new value. If the delete password in effect for the path is not the same as your used-id, you must supply the delete password with the OPW option to change any of the passwords.

**The PATH PASSWORD function of the FSF command**

```
                                  ┌                          ┐
                                  │ [OPW current-delete-pw]  │
                                  │ [APW add-pw]             │
FSF PATH PASSWORD path   ( │ [EPW extension-pw]       │
                                  │ [DPW new-delete-pw]      │
                                  │ [NODE node-id]           │
                                  └                          ┘
```

**Explanation**

path                      The complete path name for which a password change is to be made.

OPW current-delete-pw     For current-delete-pw, code the path's current delete password. Required unless your user-id is the current delete password.

APW add-pw                For add-pw, code the new add password users must supply to store a file on this path. The default is the path's current add password.

EPW extension-pw          For extension-pw, code the new extension password for this path. The default is the path's current extension password.

DPW new-delete-pw         For new-delete-pw, code the new delete password for this path. The default is the path's current delete password.

NODE node-id              For node-id, code the name of the node where this path is located. Required if the path is at a node other than your standard node.

---

**Figure 7-9**     The PATH PASSWORD function of the FSF command

To process files using paths other than your default path, you supply the alternate path name as the path operand on the STORE, GET, LIST, LOCATE, RENAME, and ERASE functions of the FSF command. So to store a file in the path I just defined, I'd enter a command like

```
FSF STORE CLG PROCED B STEVE.DOS.JOBS
```

This command would cause FSF to store the CMS file CLG PROCED on my B-disk on the FSF path STEVE.DOS.JOBS. If I hadn't specified the alternate path name, my default path would have been used instead.

To find out what paths have been defined, you use FSF PATH LIST, shown in figure 7-10. The only operand it requires is a comparison string to use as it evaluates path names. For example,

```
FSF PATH LIST S
```

lists every path at the standard node that begins with the letter S. In contrast,

```
FSF PATH LIST STEVE
```

lists paths that begin with the letters STEVE.

**The PATH LIST function of the FSF command**

```
FSF PATH LIST {ALL
              {path-mask}  [( NODE node-id]
```

**Explanation**

ALL                 Specifies that all paths you own should be displayed.

path-mask           Specifies that all paths that start with the characters that match path-mask should
                    be displayed, regardless of who owns them.

NODE node-id        For node-id, code the name of the node that should be searched for paths. Required
                    if you want to search for paths at a node other than your standard node.

---

Figure 7-10     The PATH LIST function of the FSF command

Another way to use FSF PATH LIST is to code ALL as the path name operand. When you do, all of the paths that you own are displayed. (When you supply a comparison value, all paths that match it, regardless of who owns them, are displayed.) If you want information on paths that are not stored at your standard node, you must name the alternate node with the NODE option.

To get rid of a path, use FSF PATH DELETE. As you can see in figure 7-11, its only operand is the name of the path to be erased. If the path has a delete password that is different from your user-id, you must supply it on the DPW option. And if the path is not at your standard node, you must identify the alternate node with the NODE option. Also, you should know that you can't delete a path if files are stored on it.

***How to identify paths by number instead of by name***     Coding complete path names each time you issue an FSF file management command can be an error-prone and time-consuming process. As a result, FSF includes a shortcut you can use. You can associate the path names you use often with numbers from 1 to 99. Then, you can supply just those numbers in file management commands in place of full path names.

For example, if I associated the number 12 with the path STEVE.DOS.JOBS, I could enter just

```
FSF STORE CLG PROCED B 12
```

instead of

```
FSF STORE CLG PROCED B STEVE.DOS.JOBS
```

However, for this to work, you must record the numbers you want to use and the path names that are associated with them.

**The PATH DELETE function of the FSF command**

```
FSF PATH DELETE path ⎡( ⎡DPW delete-pw⎤ ⎤
                     ⎣   ⎣NODE node-id⎦ ⎦
```

**Explanation**

path                The complete path name to be deleted.

DPW delete-pw       For delete-pw, code the delete password for this path. The default is your user-id.

NODE node-id        For node-id, code the name of the node where this path is stored. Required if the path is stored at a node other than your standard node.

---

Figure 7-11    The PATH DELETE function of the FSF command

---

To do that, create a file on one of your CMS minidisks that contains one line for each number/path combination you want to use. The number must be first in the record, followed by one or more spaces and the path name. The file's filename must be your user-id, and its filetype must be FSFPATHS. You can store the file on any of your accessed CMS disks. You can also assign a path name to number 0 in your FSFPATHS file. If you do, that path name becomes your default path instead of your user-id.

## How to use LMF functions for loaned minidisks

When the File Storage Facility is installed, some of the minidisks it owns are reserved for use by the Loaned Minidisk Facility. You can ask FSF to let you "borrow" one or more of these minidisks when you need additional storage. When you borrow a minidisk, you tell FSF how long you intend to keep it. FSF retains the borrowed minidisk for you until you give it up or the time you requested has run out.

As I mentioned above, this is an advantage of borrowed minidisks over the temporary minidisks provided by basic VM facilities. A temporary minidisk is available for use only during the terminal session in which you define and format it. In contrast, borrowed minidisks are maintained for you from one terminal session to another.

Another advantage of borrowed minidisks is that they're already formatted when you receive them. As a result, you don't have to go through that step, as you do with temporary minidisks.

You request borrowed minidisk services from the Loaned Minidisk Facility by using the FSF command's TDISK function. It has four subfunctions you need to know: BORROW, USE, QUERY, and RETURN.

**The TDISK BORROW function of the FSF command**

```
FSF TDISK BORROW disk-name [size] [( [WITH co-owner] [TIME hours]]
```

**Explanation**

| | |
|---|---|
| disk-name | An identifying name you assign to the minidisk you're borrowing. If you use more than one borrowed minidisk, each must have a unique name. You can select any value you like, as long as it doesn't exceed 32 characters. |
| size | The minimum acceptable size for the minidisk you want to borrow. Express size in kilobytes. For example, for a minidisk with at least 1 megabyte of storage, code 1024 for size. The default is 400, which gives you a minidisk with at least .4 megabyte of storage. |
| WITH co-owner | If you want to share ownership of the borrowed minidisk with another user, code that user's user-id for co-owner. |
| TIME hours | For hours, code the number of hours you want to retain the borrowed minidisk. You can specify a value up to 9999; the default is 1. |

---

**Figure 7-12**    The TDISK BORROW function of the FSF command

## How to borrow a minidisk:
## The TDISK BORROW function of the FSF command

Figure 7-12 shows the FSF TDISK BORROW command, which you use to get a minidisk from the LMF. The only operand you must supply on the command is a name you make up that you'll use to refer to the disk when you issue subsequent commands to FSF. The name can be anything you like, as long as it's not longer than 32 characters.

Although the disk name is the only value you *must* supply when you use TDISK BORROW, you'll probably also specify the size of the minidisk you want and how long you intend to keep it. For the size operand, code the number of kilobytes you want. For example, if you need two megabytes of minidisk space, code 2048 for the size operand (one megabyte consists of 1024 kilobytes). If you don't code a size value, FSF uses 400 as the default value. FSF will allocate the smallest minidisk it has available that contains at least as much space as you request. So you might find yourself with a borrowed minidisk that's considerably larger than what you requested.

You code the TIME option to specify how long you want to use the borrowed minidisk. The value you code is in hours. The default for this option is just one hour, so you're almost sure to want to ask for a longer time period. The maximum value you can code is 9999; that's over a year.

The last option you can use is WITH; it lets you specify the user-id of another user who, along with you, will be co-owner of the minidisk you're borrowing. If you're working on a project with a partner, this can be a useful feature.

**The TDISK USE function of the FSF command**

```
FSF TDISK USE disk-name [virtual-address] [fm] [( ACCESS {READ }]
                                                        {WRITE}
```

**Explanation**

| | |
|---|---|
| disk-name | The identifying name you assigned to the minidisk when you borrowed it. |
| virtual-address | The virtual address that should be used for this minidisk. The default is 333. |
| fm | The CMS filemode letter to be associated with this minidisk. The default is T. |
| ACCESS READ | Specifies that you should be given read/only access to the minidisk whether or not your co-owner has access to it. |
| ACCESS WRITE | Specifies that you should be given read/write access to the minidisk. If the minidisk's co-owner already has read/write access to it, you will not be given access to the mini-disk. ACCESS WRITE is the default. |

**Figure 7-13**     The TDISK USE function of the FSF command

Here's an example of how to request a minidisk from the LMF:

```
FSF TDISK BORROW STEVETDISK1 5000 ( TIME 96
```

In this case, I've asked for a minidisk with nearly five megabytes of storage, and I've declared that I want to be able to use it for four days (96 hours). I've called the disk STEVETDISK1, and I have not specified a co-owner.

### How to access a borrowed minidisk:
### The TDISK USE function of the FSF command

After you've borrowed a minidisk from the LMF, you have to assign it a virtual address and access it with a CMS filemode letter to be able to use it. To perform both tasks, issue the FSF TDISK USE command, illustrated in figure 7-13. As with FSF TDISK BORROW, the only value you must code is the disk-name operand. For it, use the same name you specified when you borrowed the disk.

If I entered

```
FSF TDISK USE STEVETDISK1
```

I'd be able to use the minidisk I borrowed in the example I just showed you. Here, because I didn't provide either a virtual address or a filemode for the mini-disk, it's accessed at address 333 with filemode T. You can override those defaults by coding either or both of the optional operands in figure 7-13. So

```
TDISK USE STEVETDISK 196 G
```

**The TDISK QUERY function of the FSF command**

```
FSF TDISK QUERY  {disk-name}
                 {ALL      }
```

**Explanation**

disk-name          The identifying name you assigned to the minidisk when you borrowed it.

ALL                Specifies that information for all of your borrowed minidisks should be displayed.
                   ALL is the default.

---

**Figure 7-14**    The TDISK QUERY function of the FSF command

would assign the virtual address 196 to my borrowed minidisk and would associate it with filemode letter G.

If you're sharing a borrowed minidisk with a co-owner, you might need to use the ACCESS option. If you code ACCESS READ when you issue the FSF TDISK USE command, you'll be given read/only access to your borrowed minidisk. The LMF allows only one user at a time to have read/write access to a borrowed minidisk. So if you request read/write access with the ACCESS WRITE option, it will be granted only if your co-owner is not already using the disk with read/write access. (ACCESS WRITE is the default.)

You need to use the FSF TDISK USE command each time you want to access a borrowed minidisk. Typically, that means you'll need to use the command once during each terminal session when you use the borrowed disk. (In contrast, you use FSF TDISK BORROW only once to borrow the minidisk.)

## How to get information about borrowed minidisks: The TDISK QUERY function of the FSF command

If you want to find out what the status of a borrowed minidisk is, you can use the FSF TDISK QUERY command, illustrated in figure 7-14. If you enter simply

```
FSF TDISK QUERY
```

the ALL operand is assumed, and information for all of your borrowed minidisks is displayed. This information shows the names you assigned to your disks when you borrowed them, how large they are, who their co-owners are, when you borrowed them, and when the LMF will take them back. If you want information for just one borrowed minidisk, specify the name you assigned to it right after QUERY.

**The TDISK RETURN function of the FSF command**

```
FSF TDISK RETURN disk-name
```

**Explanation**

disk-name                    The identifying name you assigned to the minidisk when you borrowed it.

Figure 7-15          The TDISK RETURN function of the FSF command

You'll use this command for two reasons. First, if you forget the name you assigned to a borrowed minidisk (which you must know to issue the FSF TDISK USE command to access it), you can find out what the name is with this command. And second, you can find out how much longer you'll be able to use a borrowed minidisk. You need to keep track of that because if the time you requested for a borrowed minidisk expires, the LMF reclaims the disk and any data you've stored there is lost. If you're about to run out of time for a borrowed minidisk, probably the easiest approach is to borrow another. Then, you can transfer your files from the older borrowed minidisk to the newer one.

## How to release a borrowed minidisk:
## The TDISK RETURN function of the FSF command

If you want to return a borrowed minidisk to FSF before its time period has expired, you can issue the FSF TDISK RETURN command, shown in figure 7-15. On it, specify the name you assigned to the disk when you borrowed it. I'd enter

```
FSF TDISK RETURN STEVETDISK1
```

to return the minidisk I borrowed in the example above.

## Terminology

| | |
|---|---|
| VM File Storage Facility | task virtual machine |
| VMFSF | node |
| FSF | standard node |
| Data Space and Sharing Facility | read password |
| DSSF | write password |
| Loaned Minidisk Facility | add password |
| LMF | path |
| borrowed minidisk | extension password |
| control virtual machine | delete password |

## Objectives

1. Describe how the VM File Storage Facility can service multiple users' virtual machines.

2. Use FSF to store and retrieve files.

3. Use FSF to gain access to a borrowed minidisk.

# Section 3

Tape file handling

Although most of the work you do under VM will involve disk files, you may need to use tape files from time to time. In this section, you'll learn basic tape-processing concepts (chapter 8), how to store data off-line on tapes and retrieve that data (chapter 9), and how to use tapes to transport data from one system to another (chapter 10).

Chapter 8

+----------------------------------+
|                                  |
|                                  |
|                                  |
|          Basic tape              |
|         concepts and             |
|          commands                |
|                                  |
|                                  |
|                                  |
+----------------------------------+

To use CMS commands to process tape files of any kind, you need to understand how data is organized on tape. So in this chapter, you'll learn general concepts about how tape data is stored (like density, blocking, and labelling). Then, you'll learn the basic CMS commands and concepts you need to know to perform the tape file processing functions chapters 9 and 10 present.

## How data is stored on a tape

As you'll recall from chapter 1, a *tape drive*, or *magnetic tape drive*, reads and writes data on a *magnetic tape*. The tape is a continuous strip of plastic that's coated on one side with a metal oxide material. Most tape drives process a tape that's wrapped around a *reel*, as figure 8-1 shows. However, some newer tape drives process a tape that's sealed within a special *cartridge*.

How much data a reel or cartridge of tape can contain depends on the length of the tape and the *density* used to record the data. Density is a measure of how many bytes of data are recorded in one inch of tape. Tape densities for standard reel tapes are usually 1600 or 6250 bytes per inch (bpi); cartridge tape drives record data at 38,000 bpi.

Of course, meaningful data on a tape isn't a random collection of bytes. A number of bytes are strung together along the tape to form a record. Between the records are *inter-record gaps*, or *IRGs*; they're illustrated in figure 8-1. When *blocking* is used, more than one record is stored between IRGs. Then a group of records stored together is called a block, and the IRG is an *inter-block gap*, or

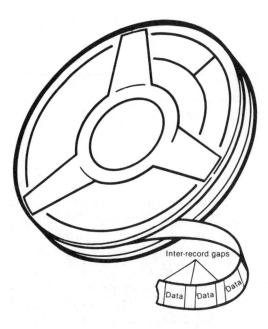

**Figure 8-1**    Inter-record gaps on a magnetic tape

| Gap | Record 1 | Record 2 | Record 3 | Record 4 | Record 5 | Gap |

**Figure 8-2**    Blocked records on tape

*IBG.* Figure 8-2 shows a segment of tape that uses a *blocking factor* of five; the blocking factor is the number of records that are stored in each block.

The term "record" can be confusing when you're working with blocked tape files. When records are unblocked, both the *logical records* (as they're viewed by applications that use the file) and *physical records* (as they're stored on the tape) are the same. In contrast, when blocking is used, multiple logical records are stored in one physical record (that is, in the area between two gaps). As a result, the term "record" can be ambiguous, and you'll often have to figure out from context what its meaning is. In any event, a block is the same thing as a physical record, regardless of the number of logical records it contains.

| File 1 | TM | File 2 | TM | File 3 | TM | TM |

**Figure 8-3**     Tapemarks used to separate files on an unlabelled tape

## Tape files and volumes

A series of related logical records (or groups of logical records packed in blocks) makes up a file. Depending on the size of the file, it may require one block, a few, hundreds, or thousands. Regardless, the end of a file is indicated on the tape by a special sequence of data called a *tapemark*. Because tapemarks are used to indicate where files end, it's possible to store multiple files on a single tape, as long as they're separated by tapemarks. For example, figure 8-3 shows a tape with three files, which are separated from each other by tapemarks. (To simplify this figure, I haven't shown the blocks or IBGs within each file, but you should understand that they're present.) The two tapemarks in a row after the last file mean there's no more data on the tape.

The number of ways files can be combined on tapes is limitless. Nevertheless, there are three basic tape types I want you to know about. Figure 8-4 illustrates them. As you can see in the figure, a single tape reel or cartridge is called a *volume*. A *volume* is simply a unit of external storage medium that can be mounted on an input/output device.

The first file and volume relationship in figure 8-4 is the simplest. In it, only one file is stored on one volume, and the file is completely contained within the volume. Such a tape is called a *single-file volume*. The second relationship figure 8-4 illustrates is a *multi-file volume*. Obviously, it's a single tape that contains more than one file. (The example in figure 8-3 is a multi-file volume.) The third relationship figure 8-4 presents is the *multi-volume file*. If a file is too large to fit on a single tape, it can often be stored on multiple volumes. In the example in figure 8-4, the multi-volume file requires five tapes.

In the examples in figures 8-3 and 8-4, you have to know where on a tape a file is located to access it; there is no mechanism on those tapes to identify the file or files they contain. For example, to access File-E in figure 8-4, you have to know that it's the fourth file on the volume and make sure the tape is positioned there before processing starts.

## Tape labels

Tape volumes that contain only file data are called *unlabelled tapes* because they don't have any internal identification of the data stored on them. Much of the work you'll do in CMS will involve unlabelled tapes. However, for data that's

**Single-file volume**

Tape volume

| File-A | Unused |
|---|---|

**Multi-file volume**

Tape volume

| File-B | File-C | File-D | File-E | File-F | File-G |
|---|---|---|---|---|---|

**Multi-volume file**

Tape volume

| File-H (part 1 of 5) |
|---|

Tape volume

| File-H (part 2 of 5) |
|---|

Tape volume

| File-H (part 3 of 5) |
|---|

Tape volume

| File-H (part 4 of 5) |
|---|

Tape volume

| File-H (part 5 of 5) | Unused |
|---|---|

**Figure 8-4**     File and volume relationships

transported between VM and other operating systems, you'll often need to work with labelled tapes.

As I'm sure you've figured out, a *labelled tape* is one that contains, in addition to files, extra information—*labels*—that identify the files on the tape and the tape volume itself. The different labelling schemes you can use vary widely. However, I'm going to focus on *IBM standard labels* because it's likely that they're what you'll use most often.

On a tape with IBM standard labels, the first data recorded on the tape identifies the tape itself. It's called the *volume label*. The volume label contains a *volume serial number* (or *volser*), which was written on the tape when it was created

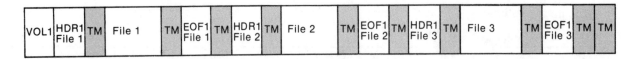

**Figure 8-5** ⫶ Tapemarks used to separate labels and files on a labelled tape

and identifies the tape volume. You'll often see a tape's volume label called the *VOL1 label*; that's because the characters VOL1 are stored at the beginning of the label.

Each file on a tape with IBM standard labels is identified at its beginning with a *file-header label* (*HDR1 label*) and at its end with an *end-of-file label* (*EOF1 label*). The HDR1 label contains information about the file that follows; the most important item is the file's name. For a multi-volume file, another kind of label, called the *end-of-volume*, or *EOV1*, *label* is the last data on each volume except the last. The last volume of the set ends with an EOF1 label. (By the way, other labels, with names like HDR2, might be stored on labelled tapes you process; don't worry about them.)

Figure 8-5 shows how labels are organized on a tape. I particularly want you to notice that labels are separated from each other and from file data with tapemarks. (An exception is between the VOL1 and the first HDR1 label, where there isn't a tapemark.) I stress this point because it's possible to process a labelled tape as an unlabelled tape. When you do that, labels are treated as files. So in that case, the tape in figure 8-5 would seem to have nine files. Data file 1 would be treated as the second file on the tape, data file 2 would be treated as the fifth file on the tape, and data file 3 would be treated as the eighth file on the tape.

## Basic CMS tape processing commands and concepts

To do tape processing from your virtual machine, you must access and refer to tape drives. Because tape drives are under the control of the system operator, you must be able to ask the operator to let you use them and to mount and dismount the volumes you want. In addition, you need to know how to refer to the tape drives that are made available for your use. And once you've gained access to a tape unit and you know how to refer to it, you need to be able to use the tape control functions of the CMS TAPE command. In this section, you'll learn how to perform all of these tasks.

### How to gain access to and release tape drives

Figure 8-6 shows a typical sequence of interactions with a system operator to gain access to a tape drive. In parts 1 and 2 of the figure, I keyed in two CP MSG commands to ask the system operator to mount a particular tape on a tape drive, then attach that tape drive to my virtual machine.

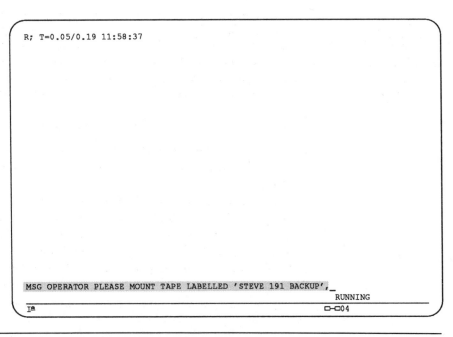

```
R; T=0.05/0.19 11:58:37




















MSG OPERATOR PLEASE MOUNT TAPE LABELLED 'STEVE 191 BACKUP',_
                                                        RUNNING
  I≜                                                  ▢—▢04
```

**Figure 8-6** Interacting with the system operator to gain access to a tape drive (part 1 of 5)

```
R; T=0.05/0.19 11:58:37
MSG OPERATOR PLEASE MOUNT TAPE LABELLED 'STEVE 191 BACKUP',
R; T=0.04/0.06 11:58:55

















MSG OPERATOR THEN ATTACH THE TAPE DRIVE TO MY VIRTUAL MACHINE._
                                                        RUNNING
  I≜                                                  ▢—▢04
```

**Figure 8-6** Interacting with the system operator to gain access to a tape drive (part 2 of 5)

```
R; T=0.05/0.19 11:58:37
MSG OPERATOR PLEASE MOUNT TAPE LABELLED 'STEVE 191 BACKUP',
R; T=0.04/0.06 11:58:55
MSG OPERATOR THEN ATTACH THE TAPE DRIVE TO MY VIRTUAL MACHINE.
R; T=0.04/0.06 11:59:21
 12:02:33


 MSG FROM OPERATOR:   5 MIN. WAIT; STAND BY FOR ADD'L MSG.
```

```
 _                                                RUNNING
 Ị꜡                                               ▭⊶▭04
```

**Figure 8-6**    Interacting with the system operator to gain access to a tape drive (part 3 of 5)

```
R; T=0.05/0.19 11:58:37
MSG OPERATOR PLEASE MOUNT TAPE LABELLED 'STEVE 191 BACKUP',
R; T=0.04/0.06 11:58:55
MSG OPERATOR THEN ATTACH THE TAPE DRIVE TO MY VIRTUAL MACHINE.
R; T=0.04/0.06 11:59:21
 12:02:33


 MSG FROM OPERATOR:   5 MIN. WAIT; STAND BY FOR ADD'L MSG.


 TAPE 181 ATTACHED
```

```
 _                                                RUNNING
 Ị꜡                                               ▭⊶▭04
```

**Figure 8-6**    Interacting with the system operator to gain access to a tape drive (part 4 of 5)

```
R; T=0.05/0.19 11:58:37
MSG OPERATOR PLEASE MOUNT TAPE LABELLED 'STEVE 191 BACKUP',
R; T=0.04/0.06 11:58:55
MSG OPERATOR THEN ATTACH THE TAPE DRIVE TO MY VIRTUAL MACHINE.
R; T=0.04/0.06 11:59:21
 12:02:33


 MSG FROM OPERATOR:  5 MIN. WAIT; STAND BY FOR ADD'L MSG.



 TAPE 181 ATTACHED
 12:05:06


 MSG FROM OPERATOR:  ALL SET; GO AHEAD.




 _
                                                         RUNNING
 Iᴬ                                                      ☐–☐04
```

**Figure 8-6**       Interacting with the system operator to gain access to a tape drive (part 5 of 5)

---

The screen in part 3 of the figure shows the operator's reply. As you can see, the operator told me I had to wait for a tape unit to be available. Soon, another message was displayed indicating that a tape unit with virtual address 181 was attached to my virtual machine; that message is in part 4 of the figure.

In part 5 of the figure, the system operator told me that I could go ahead with my tape processing. With this message, I could assume that the tape volume I requested had been mounted on the tape drive the operator attached to my virtual machine. At this point, I was able to issue tape processing commands.

After you've finished your work with a tape drive, you should remove it from your virtual machine's configuration so it's available for other users. Use the CP DETACH command and specify the virtual address of the tape unit to be released. For example,

```
DETACH 181
```

releases the tape drive attached to my virtual machine at virtual address 181. CP replies with a message like

```
TAPE 181 DETACHED
```

after it has removed a tape unit from your virtual machine's configuration.

### How to find out what tape drives are attached to your virtual machine: The QUERY VIRTUAL TAPES command

To find out what tape drives are part of your virtual machine's configuration, you can issue the command

```
QUERY VIRTUAL TAPES
```

or just the abbreviation

```
Q V TA
```

The output of this command looks like this:

```
TAPE 181 ON TAPE 300
```

Here, the message indicates that the tape unit that's attached to my virtual machine with virtual address 181 is the one at real address 300. If more than one tape drive is attached to your virtual machine, one line appears for each. You can check with a co-worker or ask the system operator via a MSG command what kind of device is located at a particular real address, if you need to know.

### How to refer to the tape drives attached to your virtual machine

Depending on the commands you want to use, you can refer to a tape unit either with its virtual address or with a *symbolic name*. Symbolic names are used by CMS to refer to specific virtual addresses which are typically used for tape drives. Figure 8-7 shows the symbolic names that are supported and their corresponding virtual addresses. As you can see, the symbolic names range from TAP0 to TAPF (where the fourth character is a hexadecimal value) and correspond to tape drives that can be attached to your virtual machine with virtual addresses 180 through 187 and 288 through 28F. (These virtual addresses are seldom used for devices other than tape units.)

For example, if a tape unit is attached to your virtual machine with virtual address 181, some commands will let you refer to it with the symbolic name TAP1. Symbolic names are easy to use, but you must remember that each corresponds to one and only one virtual address. To be able to use a symbolic name, two conditions must be met. First, the command you want to issue must support symbolic names in its syntax. And second, a tape drive must be attached to your virtual machine with the corresponding virtual address.

### How to perform tape control functions: The TAPE command

Although the TAPE command has a variety of functions, they fall into two groups: tape control functions and file processing functions. I'll present the tape control functions in this chapter; the next chapter describes the file processing functions.

| Tape unit virtual address | Symbolic name |
|---|---|
| 180 | TAP0 |
| 181 | TAP1 |
| 182 | TAP2 |
| 183 | TAP3 |
| 184 | TAP4 |
| 185 | TAP5 |
| 186 | TAP6 |
| 187 | TAP7 |
| | |
| 288 | TAP8 |
| 289 | TAP9 |
| 28A | TAPA |
| 28B | TAPB |
| 28C | TAPC |
| 28D | TAPD |
| 28E | TAPE |
| 28F | TAPF |

**Figure 8-7**     Symbolic tape unit names

As you can see in figure 8-8, the TAPE command provides ten functions to control tape operations. The first, MODESET, lets you change the recording density for a tape drive. The next four (BSF, FSF, BSR, and FSR) let you move a tape forward or backward a specified number of files or records. The WTM function lets you write a tapemark on a tape. The next two functions, REW and RUN, let you rewind a tape either to its beginning or entirely off the take-up reel so it can be removed from the tape drive. Finally, the DVOL1 and WVOL1 functions let you display and write VOL1 labels on tapes.

*How to set recording density: The TAPE command's MODESET function*    As I said before, density is a measure of how many bytes of data are recorded in one inch of tape. Recording densities for standard reel tapes are usually 1600 or 6250 bytes per inch (bpi); cartridge tape drives record data at 38,000 bpi.

Although a primary advantage of tapes is that they can be transported from one system to another, for a tape drive to be able to read a tape, it must operate at the density that was used to create the tape. Similarly, when you create a tape, you need to be sure that it's created with a density that's compatible with the tape drives on which it will eventually be read.

You can use the MODESET function of the TAPE command to set recording density. Just how often you need to use MODESET depends on what you use tapes for and on how your shop manages its tape drives. If your shop's tape drives are always used with the same settings, you don't need to use MODESET

**The tape control functions of the TAPE command**

**To change the recording density for a tape drive**

```
TAPE MODESET [([tape-unit] DEN density]
```

**To position a tape**

```
TAPE BSF [count] [(tape-unit]

TAPE FSF [count] [(tape-unit]

TAPE BSR [count] [(tape-unit]

TAPE FSR [count] [(tape-unit]
```

**To write a tapemark**

```
TAPE WTM [count] [(tape-unit]
```

**To rewind a tape**

```
TAPE REW [(tape-unit]

TAPE RUN [(tape-unit]
```

**To handle VOL1 labels**

```
TAPE DVOL1 [([tape-unit] [REWIND]]

TAPE WVOL1 volume-id [owner] [([tape-unit] [REWIND]]
```

---

Figure 8-8    The tape control functions of the TAPE command (part 1 of 2)

at all. That's because unless you specify otherwise, the setting that was last used at a particular tape drive remains in effect.

However, if your shop regularly uses different tape densities, you'll probably want to use MODESET. Even though a tape drive might be set at the recording density you want from a previous operation, you can't be sure of that. As a result, it's a safe practice to issue a TAPE MODESET command whenever you gain access to a tape drive if varying recording densities are used on it.

Figure 8-8 presents MODESET's syntax. For the MODESET function, the information you supply is specified as command options. The first option specifies the tape unit to be affected by the command, and the second specifies the recording density.

**Explanation**

tape-unit    Specifies the tape unit to be affected. May be specified as a symbolic name (TAP0 through TAPF) or as a virtual address. The default is TAP1 (virtual address 181). See figure 8-7 for more information on symbolic names.

density    The recording density at which the tape unit should operate. Acceptable values are 800, 1600, and 6250 for 9-track standard reel tapes and 38K for 18-track cartridge tapes.

BSF
FSF
BSR
FSR    BSF means backward-space file; FSF means forward-space file; BSR means backward-space record; and FSR means forward-space record.

count    The number of times the operation should be performed; the default is 1.

REW
RUN    REW means rewind the tape to its load point; RUN (rewind and unload) means rewind the tape all the way off the take-up reel.

DVOL1
WVOL1    DVOL1 means display the VOL1 label; WVOL1 means write a VOL1 label.

REWIND    Specifies that the tape should be rewound to the load point after the function is complete. If omitted, the tape remains positioned at the record that follows the VOL1 label when the function is complete.

volume-id    The one- to six-character value stored in the VOL1 label and used to identify the tape.

owner    A value (up to eight characters long) that's stored in the owner-name field of the VOL1 label.

**Figure 8-8**    The tape control functions of the TAPE command (part 2 of 2)

You can specify the tape unit with either a virtual address or a symbolic name. (You can look back to figure 8-7 for valid symbolic names.) The default for this option value is TAP1/181. As a result, if the tape drive you're using is attached to your virtual machine with virtual address 181, you can omit this option value. This is the case not only with MODESET, but with all the functions of the TAPE command. (Most system operators know this and routinely use address 181 when they attach a tape drive to a user's virtual machine.)

The other option value you specify for the MODESET function is the recording density. As figure 8-8 shows, acceptable values are 800, 1600, and 6250 for 9-track tapes, and 38K for cartridge tape units; however, because cartridge tape units can operate at no other density than 38K, there's no reason to ever specify that value. There are also values for use with 7-track tapes, but because such tapes are uncommon today, I haven't presented them here. (If you're interested, you can look in the *CMS Command and Macro Reference* manual.)

In practical terms, then, the density values you might need to change are for standard 9-track reel tapes. For some older tape drives, you might need to specify 800 as the density, but that would be unusual. Most likely, you'll have to select between 1600 and 6250. For example,

```
TAPE MODESET (TAP2 DEN 1600
```

sets the recording density to 1600 bpi on the tape drive at virtual address 182 (symbolic name TAP2).

You issue the MODESET command right after the system operator has attached a tape drive to your virtual machine, mounted a tape, and positioned it at its beginning, or *load point*. The load point is a reflective marker that separates the tape's leader from the usable portion of the tape.

*How to position a tape: The TAPE command's BSF, FSF, BSR, and FSR functions*
Most of the time, the load point is where you'll want to start your tape processing. However, sometimes you'll need to position the tape elsewhere. To control tape positioning, you can use the TAPE command's BSF, FSF, BSR, and FSR functions. The first letter in the function name tells you which direction the tape will move: B stands for backward, and F stands for forward. The middle letter stands for space, and the third letter stands for the unit of measure to be used in the operation: F means file, and R means physical record (block). For example, the FSF function means "forward-space file." For most purposes, you'll use FSF and BSF. The record-oriented positioning functions (FSR and BSR) commands aren't commonly used.

The syntax for these four functions is the same. As figure 8-8 shows, you can specify the tape unit to be affected by coding either a symbolic name or a virtual address as an option. If you're using a tape unit with virtual address 181, you can omit this option. For example, you can enter

```
TAPE FSF
```

or

```
TAPE FSF (TAP1
```

or

```
TAPE FSF (181
```

to cause the tape mounted on the tape drive with virtual address 181 to be forward-spaced one file.

The count operand of these functions specifies the number of times the function should be performed. The default is 1, so the commands I just showed you all achieve the same result. If you wanted to forward-space a tape more than one file, you could issue a command like

```
TAPE FSF 4 (TAP1
```

This command causes the tape mounted on the unit at virtual address 181 to be positioned after the next four files. Keep in mind as you use the FSF and BSF functions that they operate based on tapemarks. As you should recall, tapemarks separate physical files on a tape.

*How to write a tapemark: The TAPE command's WTM function*      If you want to write a tapemark at a specific location on a tape, you use the WTM (Write TapeMark) function of the TAPE command. Like the tape positioning functions, you specify the number of times the operation is to be performed as an operand (1 is the default) and the tape unit to be affected as an option (TAP1/181 is the default).

The function is performed wherever the tape is currently positioned. As a result, you should be careful with the WTM function; it's easy to destroy a file if the tape is positioned in the middle of it and you write a tapemark there.

If you want to write one tapemark on the tape mounted on the tape unit with the default tape unit address, you can enter

```
TAPE WTM 1 (TAP1
```

or simply

```
TAPE WTM
```

If you want to write multiple tapemarks or use a tape unit other than TAP1 (virtual address 181), you have to supply information that varies from the defaults. For instance,

```
TAPE WTM 2 (300
```

causes CMS to write two tapemarks at the current position on the tape mounted on the tape unit attached with virtual address 300.

*How to rewind a tape: The TAPE command's REW and RUN functions*
The TAPE command provides two options you can use to rewind a tape: REW and RUN. REW causes the tape to be rewound and positioned back at its load point. RUN causes it to be rewound all the way off the take-up reel. This is called *unloading*; RUN stands for Rewind and UNload.

The only other information you need to supply for either of these functions is the tape drive to be affected, if it's not TAP1. For example,

```
TAPE RUN (300
```

causes the tape mounted on the tape unit with virtual address 300 to be rewound and unloaded.

*How to handle VOL1 labels: The TAPE command's DVOL1 and WVOL1 functions*
The DVOL1 and WVOL1 functions help you when you have to work with labelled tapes. The DVOL1 function displays the VOL1 label of the tape mounted on the tape drive you specify (or the TAP1 unit if you don't specify another one). If a VOL1 label isn't present, an error message is displayed at your terminal telling you so. The WVOL1 function lets you initialize a labelled tape by writing a VOL1 label on it. I'll describe both of these functions in more detail in chapter 10 when I cover labelled-tape processing.

## Discussion

You'll apply the information you've learned in this chapter as you read the two that follow. For example, to use the TAPE command's file processing functions, you need to understand the physical layout of a tape. To read and write tapes for or from other systems, you need to be aware of the labels they might have so you can supply the appropriate information to identify the files they contain. And of course, to do any tape processing, a tape unit must be part of your virtual machine's configuration.

## Terminology

tape drive
magnetic tape drive
magnetic tape
reel
cartridge
density
inter-record gap
IRG
blocking
inter-block gap
IBG
blocking factor
logical record
physical record
tapemark
volume
single-file volume
multi-file volume
multi-volume file
unlabelled tape
labelled tape
label

IBM standard labels
volume label
volume serial number
volser
VOL1 label
file-header label
HDR1 label
end-of-file label
EOF1 label
end-of-volume label
EOV1 label
symbolic name
load point
unload

## Objectives

1. Describe how logical records are organized on tape, either with or without blocking.

2. Describe how files are separated and identified on unlabelled tapes and on IBM standard labelled tapes.

3. Communicate with the system operator to request that a tape be mounted on a tape unit and that the device be attached to your virtual machine.

4. Use the CP QUERY command to find out if any tape units are attached to your virtual machine.

5. Remove a tape unit from your virtual machine's configuration.

6. Describe how symbolic names can be used to refer to tape drives that are attached to your virtual machine.

7. Use the MODESET function of the TAPE command to set the recording density for a tape unit.

8. Use the FSF, FSR, BSF, BSR, REW, and RUN functions of the TAPE command to position a tape at any specified location.

9. Use the WTM function of the TAPE command to write tapemarks.

Chapter 9

# How to store and retrieve tape files: The TAPE and DDR commands

This chapter teaches you two ways to store CMS files on tape and retrieve them. First, you'll learn how to use the TAPE command's file management functions. With them, you can process individual or grouped CMS files. Then, you'll see how to backup and restore complete minidisks with another CMS facility, the DASD Dump and Restore program (DDR).

## How to use the TAPE command's file processing functions

The TAPE command's functions you learned in the last chapter are for utility operations that can make tape processing easier to accomplish. Although they're useful functions, the primary purpose of the TAPE command is to transfer CMS files between disk and tape. In this section, I'll show you how to use the four file processing functions of the TAPE command: DUMP (to copy CMS files from minidisk to tape), LOAD (to copy CMS files from tape to minidisk), and SKIP and SCAN (to position a tape at a particular file and/or to list the CMS files stored on it).

As you'll see in the syntax figures for these commands, they have some options in common. Just as with the tape control functions, you can specify the tape unit to be involved in any of the file processing functions with the tape-unit option. For it, you code either the virtual address of the tape unit you want to use or its symbolic name. (If the tape unit has virtual address 181, you can omit this option.)

Also, the DUMP, LOAD, SKIP, and SCAN commands include options that let you control whether or not information about the CMS files they process

**The DUMP function of the TAPE command**

```
                              ┌                                       ┐
                              │           (NOPRINT)                   │
TAPE DUMP fn ft [fm]          │([WTM] [{PRINT  }] [tape-unit]         │
                              │           (DISK   )                   │
                              └                                       ┘
```

**Explanation**

fn            The filename of the file(s) to be dumped. You may specify ★ to indicate all files that
              meet your ft and fm specification should be dumped.

ft            The filetype of the file(s) to be dumped. You may specify ★ to indicate all files that
              meet your fn and fm specification should be dumped.

fm            The filemode letter of the minidisk from which files to be dumped will be read. If you
              omit fm, A is assumed. If you code ★, all currently accessed disks are searched for
              files that meet your fn and ft specifications. If you wish to restrict the dump operation
              to files with a particular filemode number, append that number to the filemode letter
              you specify.

WTM           Specifies that a tapemark should remain after each file dumped to tape. If you do
              not code WTM, the default value (NOWTM) is in effect. Then, a tapemark remains
              only after the last file is dumped; the files dumped are stored in a single physical
              tape file when NOWTM is in effect.

NOPRINT       Normally, the names of files dumped are echoed back on your terminal as they are
PRINT         processed. NOPRINT suppresses that display; PRINT routes that display to your vir-
DISK          tual printer; DISK causes the list of files dumped to be stored in a CMS file named
              TAPE MAP A5.

tape-unit     Specifies the tape unit to which files should be dumped. May be specified as a sym-
              bolic name (TAP0 through TAPF) or as a virtual address. The default is TAP1 (virtual
              address 181). See figure 8-7 for more information on symbolic names.

---

Figure 9-1          The DUMP function of the TAPE command

will be displayed. Normally, the identifier of each CMS file processed by any
of these functions is displayed at your terminal. You can disable this display if
you specify the NOPRINT option. If you want to route the list of files to your
virtual printer, you code the PRINT option. And if you want to store the list
in a disk file, you code the DISK option. (When you specify the DISK option,
the list is stored in a file named TAPE MAP A5.)

## How to store selected files on tape: The DUMP function

To copy a file from a minidisk to a tape, you use the DUMP function of the
TAPE command; figure 9-1 presents its syntax. In this section, I'll show you how
to specify the files that will be dumped to tape. Then, I'll describe how you can
control the way the CMS files you dump are stored in physical tape files. By
specifying where tapemarks are written, you can store several CMS files in a single physical tape file.

*How to specify the files to be dumped*     When you use the DUMP function of the TAPE command, you must specify the identifier(s) of the file(s) you want to move to tape. For example, to move the file named INV2350 COBOL on your A-disk to tape, you'd enter

```
TAPE DUMP INV2350 COBOL A
```

As with the other commands you've seen that require file identifiers, if you omit the filemode, only the A-disk is searched. As a result,

```
TAPE DUMP INV2350 COBOL
```

has the same effect as the first version of the command.

You can also use the asterisk as a wild-card character in file identifiers for the DUMP function. If you specify the asterisk for either the filename or filetype component of the identifier, all files that match the other parts of the identifier are copied to tape. For example,

```
TAPE DUMP * * A
```

copies all of the files on my A-disk to tape, while

```
TAPE DUMP * COBOL A
```

copies only files on my A-disk with filetype COBOL. If you specify the asterisk for filemode, CMS looks on all of your currently accessed disks for the file(s) you named. So

```
TAPE DUMP * COBOL *
```

copies all files with filetype COBOL on all of my currently accessed minidisks to tape. By the way, when you use the asterisk, it indicates any value in that component of the file identifier is acceptable; you cannot combine it with other characters to create a mask for a part of a file identifier, as you can with some other CMS commands.

*How to control how CMS files are stored in physical tape files*     As I mentioned earlier, a variable number of CMS files can be stored by the TAPE command in a single physical tape file. Therefore, there isn't necessarily a one-to-one relationship between CMS files stored on a tape and physical files (delimited by tape-marks) on that tape.

By default, the TAPE command writes a tapemark after it dumps each CMS file. However, if it dumps another CMS file right afterward, it backspaces the tape and writes over that tapemark. As a result, multiple CMS files can follow one another back-to-back, and only the last one is followed by a tapemark. This is how the TAPE command stores multiple CMS files in one physical tape file.

(In addition to the actual data in the files stored, the TAPE command also writes information to the tape that lets it later identify and recreate those files.)

You can explicitly issue the TAPE command with the WTM function (presented in the last chapter) after an execution of the TAPE command with the DUMP function if you want to combine multiple CMS files into groups of physical tape files. For example, the commands

```
TAPE DUMP * COBOL A
TAPE WTM
TAPE DUMP * EXEC A
```

copies all of the COBOL files on my A-disk into one physical tape file and all of the procedure files on my A-disk into a second. If I had issued these two TAPE DUMP commands without the intervening TAPE WTM command, both the COBOL and EXEC files would have been stored in a single physical tape file.

If you want to store each CMS file you dump in a separate physical tape file, you can code the WTM option with the DUMP function. Then, after it dumps a CMS file, the TAPE command writes *two* tapemarks instead of one. When it dumps the next file, it still backs up one tapemark and writes over the top of it. However, the first of the two tapemarks it wrote remains on the tape and separates the two CMS files into two physical tape files.

## How to retrieve files from tape: The LOAD function

You use the LOAD function of the TAPE command to retrieve CMS files stored with the DUMP function. Figure 9-2 presents the syntax of the LOAD function. Unless you're working with a tape that has multiple physical files, all you have to do is supply the identifier of the file(s) you want to load.

***How to specify the files to be loaded***     The filename and filetype components of the file identifier you specify for the LOAD function identify the file(s) to be retrieved from the tape. However, the filemode specifies the CMS minidisk to which the file(s) should be restored. For example, the commands

```
TAPE LOAD INV2350 COBOL A
```

and

```
TAPE LOAD INV2350 COBOL B
```

retrieve the same file from tape. They differ in that the first restores it to the currently accessed A-disk, while the second restores it to the B-disk. If you omit the filemode, A is assumed.

You can specify the wild-card asterisk for either the filename or the filetype. If you do, all of the files that match your specification are copied from the tape

**The LOAD function of the TAPE command**

```
TAPE LOAD [fn ft [fm]]    [([ {NOPRINT}    ] [ {EOT   } ]   [tape-unit] ]
                          [  {PRINT  }  ]  [ {EOF n } ]              ]
                          [  {DISK   }  ]                            ]
```

**Explanation**

fn                  The filename of the file(s) to be loaded. You may specify * to indicate all files that
                    meet your ft and fm specification should be loaded. If you omit fn and ft, all files within
                    the range specified by EOT or EOF are loaded.

ft                  The filetype of the file(s) to be loaded. You may specify * to indicate all files that
                    meet your fn and fm specification should be loaded. If you omit fn and ft, all files
                    within the range specified by EOT or EOF are loaded.

fm                  The filemode letter of the minidisk to which files are to be loaded from the tape. If
                    you omit fm, A is assumed. If you only wish to load files with a particular filemode
                    number, append that number to the filemode letter you specify.

NOPRINT             Normally, the names of files loaded are echoed back on your terminal screen as they
PRINT               are processed. NOPRINT suppresses that display; PRINT routes that display to your
DISK                virtual printer; DISK causes the list of files loaded to be stored in a CMS file named
                    TAPE MAP A5.

EOT                 Specifies that unless the indicated file is located, the operation should continue until
                    an end-of-tape indication is received.

EOF n               Specifies that unless the indicated file is located, the operation should continue until
                    n tapemarks have been encountered. (Note: The EOF option refers to physical tape
                    files delimited by tapemarks; any number of CMS files can be stored by the TAPE
                    command between tapemarks.) The default is EOF 1, which restricts the LOAD oper-
                    ation to one physical file.

tape-unit           Specifies the tape unit from which files should be loaded. May be specified as a sym-
                    bolic name (TAP0 through TAPF) or as a virtual address. The default is TAP1 (virtual
                    address 181). See figure 8-7 for more information on symbolic names.

---

**Figure 9-2**        The LOAD function of the TAPE command

---

to the minidisk. If two or more CMS files with the same name are stored on
the same tape, the first one encountered from the tape's current position is the
one that's restored.

*How to load files when the input tape contains multiple physical files*     As you
learned when you read about the DUMP function, it's possible for CMS files
stored on tape to be contained in a variety of combinations of physical files. In
the simplest case, all the CMS files stored on the tape are contained within one
physical file. When that's the case, you don't need to worry about physical files.
However, it's also possible for all the CMS files on a tape to be stored in separate

physical files (if the WTM option was in effect when the files were dumped), or for some CMS files to be grouped in one physical file, while other CMS files are grouped in other physical files.

When you have to retrieve files from a tape that contains CMS files in more than one physical file, you probably need to deal with another option of the LOAD function; EOT and EOF are its keywords. They control how many physical files are processed by the LOAD function.

The default value for this option is

```
EOF 1
```

which tells the TAPE command to look only in the current physical file for the specified CMS file(s). If you know that the CMS files you want to load are in the current physical file, that's fine; you don't need to code EOT or EOF.

However, if the CMS files you want to load are located in a physical file that's beyond the current one, you need to extend the scope of the load operation. You can do that by forward-spacing the tape a certain number of tapemarks (with the FSF function of the TAPE command). Or, you can direct the TAPE command to look beyond the current physical tape file when it executes the LOAD function.

To understand, consider this example:

```
TAPE LOAD INV2350 COBOL (EOF 5
```

Here, the EOF option tells CMS to look for the file INV2350 COBOL in the current physical tape file and beyond it until five tapemarks have been encountered. The search for the file stops when INV2350 COBOL is found, or the end of the fifth file from the current position has been reached.

The EOF option gives you a high degree of control over the scope of a load operation. However, it requires that you know approximately where the CMS file you want to retrieve is stored on the tape. A simpler approach is to use EOT instead. When you code EOT, the TAPE command searches for the file you requested until it finds it or reaches an end-of-tape indicator. When you use EOT, you don't have to know where the file you want is located.

### How to review a tape's contents and position the tape: The SKIP and SCAN functions

To find out what files have been stored on a tape created with the TAPE command, you can use the command's SKIP and SCAN functions. Figure 9-3 presents their syntax.

The commands work similarly; they only differ in where they leave the tape positioned when they end. SKIP leaves the tape positioned after the CMS file you name, while SCAN leaves the tape positioned before it. In either case, as the tape is processed, the names of the files stored on it are displayed at your terminal.

**The SKIP and SCAN functions of the TAPE command**

$$\text{TAPE} \quad \left\{ \begin{matrix} \text{SKIP} \\ \text{SCAN} \end{matrix} \right\} \quad \text{[fn ft]} \quad \left[ \text{( [} \left\{ \begin{matrix} \text{NOPRINT} \\ \text{PRINT} \\ \text{DISK} \end{matrix} \right\} \text{] [} \left\{ \begin{matrix} \text{EOT} \\ \text{EOF n} \end{matrix} \right\} \text{] [tape-unit]} \right]$$

**Explanation**

SKIP
: Causes the tape to be positioned after the specified file at the end of the SKIP operation.

SCAN
: Causes the tape to be positioned before the specified file at the end of the SCAN operation.

fn
: The filename of the file before or after which the operation should stop. If you omit fn and ft, all files within the range specified by EOF or EOT are listed.

ft
: The filetype of the file before or after which the operation should stop. If you omit fn and ft, all files within the range specified by EOF or EOT are listed.

NOPRINT
PRINT
DISK
: Normally, the names of files skipped or scanned are echoed back on your terminal screen as they are processed. NOPRINT suppresses that display; PRINT routes that display to your virtual printer; DISK causes the list of files skipped or scanned to be stored in a CMS file named TAPE MAP A5.

EOT
: Specifies that unless the specified file is located, the operation should continue until an end-of-tape indication is received.

EOF n
: Specifies that unless the specified file is located, the operation should continue until *n* tapemarks have been encountered. (Note: The EOF option refers to physical tape files delimited by tapemarks; any number of CMS files can be stored by the TAPE command between tapemarks.) The default is EOF 1, which restricts the SKIP or SCAN operation to one physical file.

tape-unit
: Specifies the tape unit to be used for the SKIP or SCAN operation. May be specified as a symbolic name (TAP0 through TAPF) or as a virtual address. The default is TAP1 (virtual address 181). See figure 8-7 for more information on symbolic names.

**Figure 9-3**    The SKIP and SCAN functions of the TAPE command

As with the LOAD function, the SKIP and SCAN functions operate only on the current file (that is, up to the next tapemark), unless you specify a wider range with either EOT or EOF.

## How to backup and restore complete minidisks with the DASD Dump and Restore (DDR) program

In this section, you'll learn how to use the *DASD Dump and Restore program*, called *DDR*, to make tape backups of your minidisks and, if necessary, restore your minidisks from those tapes. You can also use DDR to copy from disk to

**The DDR command**

```
DDR [file-identifier]
```

**Explanation**

file-identifier     The CMS file identifier of the file that contains the control statements to be used for this execution of DDR. If you omit the filemode letter, * is assumed, and your mini-disks are searched in the standard CMS sequence for a file with the filename and filetype you specified. If you omit the file identifier altogether, you're prompted to enter control statements from your terminal.

---

**Figure 9-4**     The DDR command

disk or tape to tape, but those functions are just as easily accomplished using the commands you already know.

As you can tell from the syntax of the DDR command in figure 9-4, it works somewhat differently from the commands you've already learned. DDR expects an input file of control statements to direct its operations. In contrast, the other commands you've learned get their direction from operands and options you specify on the command line, or they issue explicit messages at your terminal to prompt you to enter specific information.

When you invoke DDR, you can supply the name of the CMS file that contains its control statements on the DDR command line. For example,

```
DDR BACKUP SPECS A
```

invokes DDR and tells it to read its control statements from the CMS file BACKUP SPECS on the current A-disk.

If you don't specify a file that contains control statements when you invoke DDR, the program expects them from the virtual console and prompts you with the message

```
ENTER:
```

This isn't a particularly descriptive prompt. It's just an indicator that DDR wants you to key in a control statement. It's up to you to know what control statement values to enter. As a result, regardless of whether you use DDR interactively or through a control statement file, you have to know how to code control statements. The control statements you supply to DDR fall into two groups: *I/O definition control statements* and *functional control statements*.

## The DDR I/O definition control statements: INPUT and OUTPUT

The I/O definition control statements, INPUT and OUTPUT, specify the devices DDR will use; figure 9-5 presents their syntax. They're required for each DDR

**The DDR INPUT and OUTPUT control statements**

```
INPUT   vaddr device   [{{disk-label}}]
                        [{{SCRATCH  }}]
                        [{ alt-tape }}]
```

```
OUTPUT vaddr device   [{{disk-label}}]
                       [{{SCRATCH  }}][([MODE tapemode] [COMPACT]]
                       [{ alt-tape }}]
```

**Explanation**

vaddr
The virtual address of the input or output device. Be sure that the disk and tape units you specify are attached to your virtual machine before you run DDR.

device
The real input or output device type. Acceptable values for disk devices are:

FB-512 (for 3310 and 3370 FBA devices)
2305-1
2305-2
2314
2319
3330
3330-11
3340-35
3340-70
3350
3375
3380

Acceptable values for tape devices are:

3410
3420
3430
3480
8809

disk-label
SCRATCH
Disk-label is the volume label of a minidisk to be used in a DDR operation. The value you code is compared with the actual label on the minidisk with the virtual address you specified to verify the operation; DDR asks you if you want to continue if they disagree. If you code SCRATCH for this operand, verification is not done. If you omit this operand, DDR prompts you with the disk label it reads from the minidisk and asks if it's really the minidisk you want to process.

alt-tape
Specifies the virtual address of an alternate tape unit to be used if the primary unit reaches the end of its tape during processing. Processing picks up automatically on the alternate unit while the tape on the primary unit is unloaded and, if necessary, replaced.

---

**Figure 9-5** ⫶ The INPUT and OUTPUT control statements of the DDR command (part 1 of 2)

MODE tapemode

Specifies the recording density to be used for a tape unit. Values allowed are:

6250
1600
800
38K

The default is 1600 for all units except the 3480; 38K is the default for the 3480. Although these values are allowed syntactically, they're not all supported by all tape units. For example, 8809 tape units don't support the 6250 and 38K options, and 3480 tape units support only the 38K option. (Since 38K is the default for the 3480, you don't need to specify the MODE option if you're using that kind of tape unit.)

COMPACT

Specifies that the output tape should be written using data compression. Tapes written in this format can only be read by DDR.

---

**Figure 9-5**    The INPUT and OUTPUT control statements of the DDR command (part 2 of 2)

operation. For both the INPUT and OUTPUT statements, you always have to specify two items: the virtual address of the device and the type of the real device associated with that address. For example, suppose you want to backup a minidisk with virtual address 192 which is stored on a real FBA device to an 8809 tape drive attached to your virtual machine with virtual address 181. The control statements

```
INPUT 192 FB-512
OUTPUT 181 8809
```

define those units. Although the minidisks you're likely to want to copy using DDR will already be part of your virtual machine's configuration, you'll have to be sure that the tape drives you'll use are attached before you run DDR.

When an INPUT or OUTPUT statement identifies a minidisk, DDR by default checks the label on the minidisk to verify that you've specified the right virtual address. If you enter an I/O definition control statement for a minidisk and specify just its virtual address and real device type, DDR displays the volume label it read from that minidisk and asks you to verify that it's correct.

If you want to avoid this prompt, you can code the disk-label operand on I/O definition control statements that refer to minidisks. For example,

```
INPUT 192 FB-512 STEVE2
```

specifies that the volume label of the minidisk at virtual address 192 is STEVE2. If the label you specify isn't correct, DDR advises you with an error message and lets you abort the operation. If you want to bypass label checking altogether, code SCRATCH in place of a disk label.

If your I/O definition control statement refers to a tape drive, you might want to specify the alt-tape operand. It's the address of an alternate tape unit to which processing should be automatically switched if the primary unit reaches the end of its tape. Using an alternate tape unit can improve processing efficiency because your DDR operation can continue without having to wait for the tape on the primary unit to be rewound, unloaded, and replaced. If you specify alt-tape, the tape unit it identifies should be attached to your virtual machine just like the primary tape unit, but—of course—with a different virtual address.

For output files created on tapes, you can specify two additional options: MODE and COMPACT. The MODE option lets you specify the recording density that should be used for the output tape. The specific value you use depends on the kind of tape unit you're using. For example, the 6250 and 38K options aren't supported for 8809 tape units, while 38K is the only option supported for 3480 tape units. The default MODE value for all device types except the 3480 is 1600; for the 3480, it's 38K.

For other tape units, the general rule I suggest you follow is to use the highest density value your tape drive supports. That results in more efficient processing and requires less tape. If you aren't sure which density value to use, ask your system operator when you request that the tape unit be attached to your virtual machine.

The second option you can specify on the OUTPUT statement for tape devices is COMPACT. It specifies that the data written to the tape should be in a compressed format that uses less space. DDR is able to read tapes written in this format to restore data from them, but other programs are not. But because DDR tapes are intended for backup purposes, that really doesn't present a problem. Therefore, because the COMPACT option can result in faster processing and uses less tape, I encourage you to use it.

### The DDR functional control statements: DUMP and RESTORE

After you've provided the INPUT and OUTPUT control statements that define the devices involved in the operation, you tell DDR what to do with a functional control statement. Although there are several DDR control statements, I'm only going to present two here: DUMP and RESTORE. DUMP copies data from a minidisk to a tape, and RESTORE performs the reverse operation.

It's possible to use DUMP and RESTORE to direct DDR to perform selective operations based on ranges of DASD storage locations. However, those capabilities are beyond the scope of what you'll need to do to backup and restore minidisks. As a result, I'm going to focus on the simplest forms of these statements, illustrated in figure 9-6. As you can see, the only operand I'm going to use is ALL, which for both the DUMP and RESTORE functions directs DDR to perform the requested operation on the entire minidisk involved.

**The DDR DUMP and RESTORE control statements**

```
DUMP ALL

RESTORE ALL
```

**Explanation**

ALL                Specifies that the DUMP or RESTORE operation should be performed on the entire
                   minidisk.

---

**Figure 9-6**          The DUMP and RESTORE control statements of the DDR command

*A typical DDR DUMP operation*        To understand how to perform a backup
of a minidisk using DDR, consider figure 9-7. It illustrates a complete sequence
of terminal interactions for running DDR and supplying the proper control statements to it. Before you use DDR, be sure that a tape unit is attached to your
virtual machine, that you know what kind of real device it is, and that the tape
you want to use is mounted on it and is positioned at its load point. (You can
look back to chapter 8 to review how to perform these tasks.)

In part 1 of the figure I started the program by keying in the command

```
DDR
```

and pressing enter. Next, in part 2, DDR prompted me for the first control statement by displaying

```
ENTER:
```

Notice here that the terminal status message was VM READ, which indicates
that DDR was waiting for me to make an entry.

In response, I keyed in the first control statement:

```
INPUT 191 FB-512
```

It specified that the input device was the FBA minidisk at virtual address 191.
When I pressed the enter key, DDR prompted me for another control statement,
and, as you can see in part 3, I keyed in

```
OUTPUT 181 8809 (COMPACT
```

to specify that the output device was an 8809 tape unit with virtual address 181.
The COMPACT option told DDR to compress the minidisk data it was about
to write to tape.

The DDR command starts the DDR program

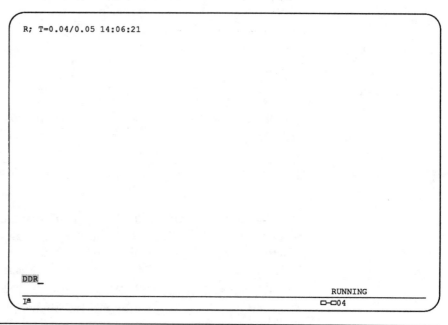

**Figure 9-7**    Backing up a minidisk with the DDR command (part 1 of 8)

The program asks for a control statement; in this case, the control statement speci-fies the input device

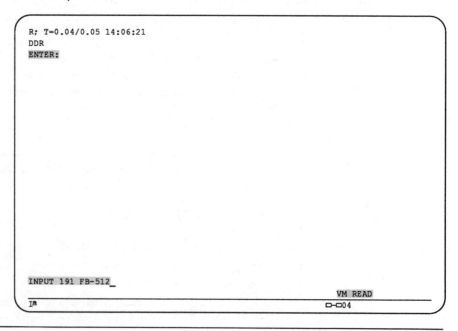

**Figure 9-7**    Backing up a minidisk with the DDR command (part 2 of 8)

After the next prompt, a second control statement is entered to specify the output device

```
R; T=0.04/0.05 14:06:21
DDR
ENTER:
INPUT 191 FB-512
ENTER:




















OUTPUT 181 8809 (COMPACT_
                                                    VM READ
  I4                                              □-□04
```

**Figure 9-7**   Backing up a minidisk with the DDR command (part 3 of 8)

After the next prompt, a DUMP ALL control statement tells DDR to copy the contents of the input device to the output device

```
R; T=0.04/0.05 14:06:21
DDR
ENTER:
INPUT 191 FB-512
ENTER:
OUTPUT 181 8809 (COMPACT
ENTER:

















DUMP ALL_
                                                    VM READ
  I4                                              □-□04
```

**Figure 9-7**   Backing up a minidisk with the DDR command (part 4 of 8)

DDR displays the volume label for the input minidisk and asks for verification of the operation; key in YES and press the enter key to continue

```
R; T=0.04/0.05 14:06:21
DDR
ENTER:
INPUT 191 FB-512
ENTER:
OUTPUT 181 8809 (COMPACT
ENTER:
DUMP ALL
DMKDDR711R VOLID READ IS STEVE1
DO YOU WISH TO CONTINUE?  RESPOND YES, NO, OR REREAD:




YES_
                                                        VM READ
IᵃΞ                                                     □─□04
```

**Figure 9-7**    Backing up a minidisk with the DDR command (part 5 of 8)

The dump operation has begun

```
R; T=0.04/0.05 14:06:21
DDR
ENTER:
INPUT 191 FB-512
ENTER:
OUTPUT 181 8809 (COMPACT
ENTER:
DUMP ALL
DMKDDR711R VOLID READ IS STEVE1
DO YOU WISH TO CONTINUE?  RESPOND YES, NO, OR REREAD:
YES
DUMPING   STEVE1




-
                                                        RUNNING
IᵃΞ                                                     □─□04
```

**Figure 9-7**    Backing up a minidisk with the DDR command (part 6 of 8)

At the end of the dump operation, DDR asks for a new control statement; to end
the program, press the enter key

```
R; T=0.04/0.05 14:06:21
DDR
ENTER:
INPUT 191 FB-512
ENTER:
OUTPUT 181 8809 (COMPACT
ENTER:
DUMP ALL
DMKDDR711R VOLID READ IS STEVE1
DO YOU WISH TO CONTINUE?  RESPOND YES, NO, OR REREAD:
YES
DUMPING    STEVE1
END OF DUMP
ENTER:




                                                          VM READ
 I▲                                                    □–□04
```

**Figure 9-7**    Backing up a minidisk with the DDR command (part 7 of 8)

The DDR run ends, and the CMS ready message appears

```
R; T=0.04/0.05 14:06:21
DDR
ENTER:
INPUT 191 FB-512
ENTER:
OUTPUT 181 8809 (COMPACT
ENTER:
DUMP ALL
DMKDDR711R VOLID READ IS STEVE1
DO YOU WISH TO CONTINUE?  RESPOND YES, NO, OR REREAD:
YES
DUMPING    STEVE1
END OF DUMP
ENTER:

END OF JOB
R; T=0.04/0.05 14:11:06




                                                          RUNNING
 I▲                                                    □–□04
```

**Figure 9-7**    Backing up a minidisk with the DDR command (part 8 of 8)

In part 4 of the figure, DDR prompted me for a third control statement, and I keyed in

```
DUMP ALL
```

to direct it to copy the contents of the entire input device to the output device.

Next, in part 5, DDR asked me to verify the operation I requested. I replied that the program should continue, and the dump operation began, as you can see in part 6. When the dump operation was complete, DDR prompted me for another control statement (part 7). Because I didn't want to perform any more DDR operations, I entered a null (blank) line by pressing the enter key, and the program ended (part 8).

*A typical DDR RESTORE operation*        Now, I'll show you how to perform a restoration of data you've backed up using the DUMP control statement. In this example, I'll demonstrate how to supply control statements to DDR not from your terminal but rather from a file.

For this example, assume that the data to be restored is that written to the output tape in figure 9-7. All you have to do is use XEDIT to store the necessary DDR control statements in a CMS file, then specify its file identifier when you invoke DDR.

To restore the data backed up in figure 9-7, I'd store these statements in a file:

```
INPUT 300 8809
OUTPUT 191 FB-512 STEVE1
RESTORE ALL
```

You don't need to specify the COMPACT option when you use a tape file for input. If the tape data is stored in compressed format, DDR automatically expands it before it writes it to the minidisk. I did code the volume identifier on the description of the output minidisk to avoid being prompted by DDR for verification, as I was in figure 9-7. Note, too, that the tape unit is at a different virtual address than it was in figure 9-7. To execute DDR with these control statements, the command

```
DDR RESTBACK SPECS A
```

is all I have to enter, assuming I stored the three control statements above in a file named RESTBACK SPECS on my A-disk.

## Discussion

Because the DDR backup and restore examples I've just shown you work on an entire minidisk, you need to take some special precautions if that isn't what you want to do. For example, suppose you want to retrieve a backup copy of a single file. If you use DDR to restore the entire volume, you'll get an old copy not just of the file you want to retrieve, but of every other file on the volume as well. In other words, you'll lose the current copies of all the files on the volume. To avoid this problem, you should perform the restoration to an empty minidisk, then use file management commands to copy the files from it that you're interested in. To get an empty minidisk for this purpose, you can create a temporary minidisk using the CP DEFINE and CMS FORMAT commands.

### Terminology

DASD Dump and Restore program
DDR
I/O definition control statement
functional control statement

### Objectives

1. Use the DUMP function of the TAPE command to copy minidisk files to tape in any specified arrangement of physical tape files.

2. Use the LOAD function of the TAPE command to retrieve CMS files stored on tape by the command's DUMP function. The input may be stored in any arrangement of physical tape files.

3. Use the SKIP and SCAN functions of the TAPE command to review the contents of a tape created with the command's DUMP function.

4. Use the DDR program to make backup copies of your minidisks on tape; supply control statements either from your terminal or from a CMS file.

5. Use the DDR program to restore a minidisk from a backup tape; supply control statements either from your terminal or from a CMS file.

Chapter 10

```
+-----------------------------------+
|                                   |
|                                   |
|     How to process               |
|     non-CMS tapes:               |
|     The MOVEFILE,                |
|     FILEDEF, and                 |
|     LABELDEF commands            |
|                                   |
+-----------------------------------+
```

As you know, one of the advantages of tapes is that they're transportable. In other words, files stored on tape on one system can be moved to another system relatively easily. So far in this book, the tape processing features you've learned have been for tapes that are restricted to the CMS environment.

In this chapter, I'll present the concepts and commands you need to know to (1) create tapes under CMS that will be read on other systems, and (2) read data into CMS disk files from tapes that were written on other systems. You'll learn how to process two kinds of non-CMS tapes: unlabelled tapes and tapes with IBM standard labels. To process either kind of tape, you use two new CMS commands: MOVEFILE and FILEDEF.

### The MOVEFILE and FILEDEF commands

To transfer files to and from labelled and unlabelled tapes, you use the MOVE-FILE command. But to be able to use MOVEFILE, you also have to use FILEDEF, which provides detailed specifications about the files that are processed by MOVE-FILE. In practical terms, you always use the two commands together.

*The MOVEFILE command*     MOVEFILE is a general-purpose command that lets you move files between any devices supported by VM. For example, you can use MOVEFILE to copy a file from your virtual card reader to a disk file, or to move an OS-format data set into a CMS file. For many of the functions of MOVEFILE, more specialized CMS commands are provided. For example, it's

**The MOVEFILE command**

```
MOVEFILE [input-ddname [output-ddname]]
```

**Explanation**

| | |
|---|---|
| MOVEFILE | The command may be abbreviated as MOVE. |
| input-ddname | The ddname specified on the FILEDEF statement that defines the file to be used for input. If omitted, the default ddname INMOVE is used. |
| output-ddname | The ddname specified on the FILEDEF statement that defines the file to be used for output. If omitted, the default ddname OUTMOVE is used. |

---

Figure 10-1    The MOVEFILE command

easier to use the PRINT command to print the contents of a file than it is to define the input and output files for MOVEFILE, then invoke the MOVEFILE command. However, for handling non-CMS tape files, MOVEFILE is the command you'll use.

By itself, MOVEFILE is simple, as you can see in figure 10-1. All you do is enter the command name (or its abbreviation MOVE) followed by two file specifications, which are called ddnames. A *ddname* is simply a name that an application program uses to refer to a file it processes. To relate the ddnames you code on the MOVEFILE command to real file names, you use the CMS FILEDEF command.

*The FILEDEF command*    Figure 10-2 presents the syntax elements of the FILEDEF command that you're most likely to need to know. In addition to the features figure 10-2 illustrates, you can use the FILEDEF command to create definitions for other device types and for OS and VSE disk files. Here, I want to concentrate on transferring tape files to and from CMS, so the syntax in this figure is limited to elements you need to know to process them.

First, notice that you can issue the FILEDEF command with no operands. If you do, all the file definitions created during your terminal session are displayed. This can be convenient, because once you create a file definition, it remains in effect until you end your terminal session or explicitly remove the definition.

If you want to remove all of the FILEDEFs currently in effect, you can issue this command:

```
FILEDEF * CLEAR
```

Although this might be useful in some circumstances, you'll seldom need to use it. If a program or command needs a file definition for a ddname that's already

**The FILEDEF command**

**To display all current file definitions**

```
FILEDEF
```

**To clear all file definitions**

```
FILEDEF * CLEAR
```

**To define CMS disk files**

```
FILEDEF ddname DISK [fn [ft [fm]]]    ⎡ [RECFM rec-format] ⎤
                                      ⎢ ([LRECL rec-length] ⎥
                                      ⎣ [BLOCK block-size] ⎦
```

**To define unlabelled tape files**

```
FILEDEF ddname TAPn LABOFF    ⎡ [RECFM rec-format] ⎤
                              ⎢ ([LRECL rec-length] ⎥
                              ⎣ [BLOCK block-size] ⎦
```

**To define IBM standard-label tape files**

```
FILEDEF ddname TAPn SL [file-position] [VOLID volser]    ⎡ [RECFM rec-format] ⎤
                                                         ⎢ ([LRECL rec-length] ⎥
                                                         ⎣ [BLOCK block-size] ⎦
```

**To route output to your terminal**

```
FILEDEF OUTMOVE TERMINAL
```

---

Figure 10-2    Various functions of the FILEDEF command (part 1 of 2)

in use, you just enter a new FILEDEF command for it, and the new specifications you code replace the old ones. There's no need to delete all the other active FILEDEFs.

To define a CMS disk file, all you have to do is supply a FILEDEF command like this:

```
FILEDEF INMOVE DISK AR6540 COBOL
```

This command creates a file definition for the ddname INMOVE (the default input file name MOVEFILE uses) and associates it with the disk file AR6540 COBOL on my A-disk. If you omit the filemode, as I did in this example, A

**Explanation**

| | |
|---|---|
| ddname | The one- to eight-character name to be associated with the specified file; used by the application program or command for which the definition is being made. The ddname must begin with a letter or a national character (@, #, or $). |
| fn | The filename of the CMS disk file to be processed. If omitted, the default is FILE. |
| ft | The filetype of the CMS disk file to be processed. If omitted, the default is the value you supplied for ddname. |
| fm | The filemode of the CMS disk file to be processed. If omitted, the default is A1. |
| RECFM rec-format | For rec-format, code one of the following: |

|    |                                   |
|----|-----------------------------------|
| F  | Fixed-length records              |
| FB | Fixed-length records, blocked     |
| V  | Variable-length records           |
| VB | Variable-length records, blocked  |

| | |
|---|---|
| LRECL rec-length | For rec-length, code the length of logical records in the file. The value may not exceed 32760. |
| BLOCK block-size | For block-size, code the number of bytes each block uses. The value may not exceed 32760. |
| TAPn | Symbolic name of the tape unit on which the specified tape file will be processed; *n* is a single hex value between 0 and F. (See figure 8-7 for valid symbolic names.) |
| file-position | The position of the file to be processed on a multifile volume. If you omit this value, the default is 1. |
| VOLID volser | For volser, code the one- to six-character volume serial number of the tape to be processed. If you don't code volser, the volume serial number on the tape is not checked. (This value may also be specified on the LABELDEF command; if both specifications are in effect, the one made most recently is used.) |

---

**Figure 10-2**     Various functions of the FILEDEF command (part 2 of 2)

is assumed. You can omit the entire file identifier if you like. When you do, the default filename is FILE and the default filemode is A; the filetype is the same as the ddname you specified.

You can use any ddnames you like, as long as they're no longer than eight characters and begin with a letter or a national character (@, #, or $). But because the MOVEFILE command uses the ddnames INMOVE and OUTMOVE as defaults for its input and output files, it makes sense to use those names so you don't have to key in ddnames when you use MOVEFILE.

As you can see in figure 10-2, you code the FILEDEF command differently for labelled and unlabelled tape files. I'll describe the details when I show you how to process those two kinds of files. The complete syntax of the FILEDEF command includes even more options for tape processing. But because I think you're unlikely to use them, I'm not covering them here. If you encounter a tough tape processing problem you can't solve with what you've learned in this chapter, you should refer to the *CMS Command and Macro Reference* manual.

The last FILEDEF option in figure 10-2 can be used if you want to look at the contents of a tape file. You code a FILEDEF command for the ddname INMOVE that identifies the file you want to view. Then, you enter

```
FILEDEF OUTMOVE TERMINAL
```

This specifies that the MOVEFILE command should copy the input file to your terminal screen. (You can also use this technique to view a disk file, but that would be silly because it's easier to use the TYPE command.)

### How to process unlabelled tapes

To process an unlabelled tape, you can define the tape with a FILEDEF command like this:

```
FILEDEF INMOVE TAP1 LABOFF
```

This specifies that a tape file on the tape unit attached with virtual address 181 (TAP1) should be associated with the ddname INMOVE. LABOFF tells CMS to disable all label processing. That puts the tape drive completely under your control. You can retrieve data from it with the MOVEFILE command, and you can position it with the TAPE command.

For example, to retrieve the data stored in the third file on a tape and store it in a CMS disk file called TAPEFILE DATA A, you'd have to acquire a tape unit and make sure the tape you want is mounted. Then, you'd enter these commands:

```
FILEDEF INMOVE TAP1 LABOFF
FILEDEF OUTMOVE DISK TAPEFILE DATA A
TAPE REW
TAPE FSF 2
MOVEFILE
```

The first FILEDEF command specifies that input (using the MOVEFILE command's default ddname INMOVE) will come from the tape unit at virtual address 181 (symbolic name TAP1), and that the tape to be processed there is unlabelled (LABOFF). The second FILEDEF command specifies that the output (default ddname OUTMOVE) will be stored in a CMS disk file (DISK) named TAPE-FILE DATA on my current A-disk. Next, a TAPE command with the REW function insures the tape is positioned at its load point, and another TAPE command with the FSF function skips two tapemarks to position the tape at the start of the third file. (This assumes that there is not a tapemark at the beginning of the tape.) Finally, a MOVEFILE command starts the data transfer.

Because I specified the default ddnames INMOVE and OUTMOVE on the FILEDEF commands above, I didn't need to specify ddnames on the MOVE-FILE command. If I had used ddnames other than INMOVE and OUTMOVE, though, they would have been required on the MOVEFILE command. For example, the commands

```
FILEDEF TAPEIN TAP1 LABOFF
FILEDEF DISKOUT DISK TAPEFILE DATA A
TAPE REW
TAPE FSF 2
MOVEFILE TAPEIN DISKOUT
```

achieve the same results as the commands in the first group I showed you.

If you wanted to copy the contents of the disk file to the tape, you would simply reverse the ddname assignments made by the FILEDEF commands:

```
FILEDEF OUTMOVE TAP1 LABOFF
FILEDEF INMOVE DISK TAPEFILE DATA A
MOVEFILE
```

Of course, before the MOVEFILE command is issued, you need to be sure the tape is positioned where you want the output file stored.

The situation is a little more complicated when you're processing blocked tape files. When that's the case, be sure to supply information to VM about the file's record format (FILEDEF's RECFM option), logical record length (FILEDEF's LRECL option), and block size (FILEDEF's BLKSIZE option). If you don't, each block is treated as a single record; the chances are that's not what you want.

To understand what can happen when you use a blocked input file, consider the two screens in figure 10-3. In the first screen, I've issued a series of commands to copy a tape file that contains COBOL source code to one of my mini-disks. When the copy operation was complete, I issued a LISTFILE command to verify that it was successful. Notice that the logical record length of the new disk file is 800 bytes, not 80 as you'd expect for a source program; that's because the tape records were blocked, ten to a block.

To correct the problem, I issued the commands in part 2 of the figure. Here, I specified the RECFM, LRECL, and BLOCK options for both the input and output files. This time, the operation was successful, as the LISTFILE output at the end of the display in part 2 shows.

When you work with blocked files, you need to be aware of what you're doing. I suggest you verify your work, as I did in figure 10-3, to make sure the results you get are what you expect.

The techniques you've learned in this section also apply to processing labelled tapes. Just remember, if you treat a labelled tape as though it's unlabelled, labels are considered to be files. That's because they're separated from the files they identify by tapemarks. If you don't know whether a tape is labelled or not, you can treat it as an unlabelled tape and view the contents of its files by routing

The LISTFILE output for AR6420A COBOL A, a file of COBOL source statements just copied from tape to disk using FILEDEF and MOVEFILE, shows the file has 800-character records instead of 80-character records as expected (that's because the tape records were blocked, ten to a block)

```
R;
TAPE REW
R;
TAPE FSF
R;
FILEDEF INMOVE TAP1 LABOFF
R;
FILEDEF OUTMOVE DISK AR6420A COBOL A
R;
MOVEFILE
R;
LISTFILE AR6420* COBOL A (LABEL
FILENAME FILETYPE FM FORMAT LRECL       RECS    BLOCKS   DATE      TIME     LABEL
AR6420A  COBOL    A1 V       800          42        33  8/14/87   9:16:57  STEVE1
R;




-                                                               RUNNING
I▪                                                              □-□04
```

**Figure 10-3**   Using the RECFM, LRECL, and BLOCK options of the FILEDEF command (part 1 of 2)

The copy operation is repeated using the RECFM, LRECL, and BLOCK options in the FILEDEF commands; the records in the new output file are the correct length

```
R;
TAPE REW
R;
TAPE FSF
R;
FILEDEF INMOVE TAP1 LABOFF (RECFM FB LRECL 80 BLOCK 800
R;
FILEDEF OUTMOVE DISK AR6420B COBOL A (RECFM F LRECL 80 BLOCK 80
R;
MOVEFILE
R;
LISTFILE AR6420* COBOL A (LABEL
FILENAME FILETYPE FM FORMAT LRECL       RECS    BLOCKS   DATE      TIME     LABEL
AR6420A  COBOL    A1 V       800          42        33  8/14/87   9:16:57  STEVE1
AR6420B  COBOL    A1 F        80         420        33  8/14/87   9:19:04  STEVE1
R;




-                                                               RUNNING
I▪                                                              □-□04
```

**Figure 10-3**   Using the RECFM, LRECL, and BLOCK options of the FILEDEF command (part 2 of 2)

them to your terminal. If you see files that contain label data, you'll know the tape is labelled. (I'll show you an example of this technique later in this chapter.)

## How to process labelled tapes

When you work with labelled tapes, you again use the MOVEFILE and FILEDEF commands to move data between tape and disk. But the FILEDEF syntax for labelled tapes allows for two new functions: checking the VOL1 label on the tape and positioning the tape at a particular file. I'll show you how to perform these operations first in this section. To find out if a tape has a VOL1 label and to write one, you can use the DVOL1 and WVOL1 functions of the TAPE command. The second part of this section shows you how to use them. And to perform label processing that involves file labels (HDR1 and EOF1), you need to use another command: LABELDEF. The third part of this section shows you how to use it.

Regardless of the facility you use when you process labelled tapes, you need to be prepared to deal with errors that are found during processing. Realize that you might need to communicate with the system operator to change tapes (if the volume serial number you specify does not agree with that on the mounted tape), issue TAPE commands to position the tape at another file, or reissue FILEDEF or LABELDEF commands to specify values that agree with the data stored in the tape's labels.

*Labelled tape processing through the FILEDEF command*      To perform volume label (VOL1) checking on a labelled tape, you code the VOLID operand on the FILEDEF command that identifies the tape. For example, to specify that the mounted tape should be checked to insure that its volume serial number is 042301, you'd use a FILEDEF command like this:

```
FILEDEF INMOVE TAP1 SL VOLID 042301
```

Notice that I coded SL instead of LABOFF in this command; SL tells FILEDEF that the tape file has standard labels.

If you're using a multi-file volume that contains standard labelled files, you can use the file-position operand of the FILEDEF command to position the tape at the specified file. For example, the command

```
FILEDEF INMOVE TAP1 SL 3 VOLID 042301
```

directs CMS to perform VOL1 label checking and position the tape at the third file. I think you'll agree that it's easier to use this feature than it would be to issue a separate TAPE command with the FSF function. Remember that if you use TAPE with FSF, you have to count tape labels as files too; that isn't the case with the file-position operand of the FILEDEF command.

**The DVOL1 and WVOL1 functions of the TAPE command**

```
TAPE DVOL1 [([tape-unit] [REWIND])]

TAPE WVOL1 volser [owner] [([tape-unit] [REWIND])]
```

**Explanation**

tape-unit       Specifies the tape unit to be used. May be specified as a symbolic name (TAP0 through TAPF) or as a virtual address. The default is TAP1 (virtual address 181). See figure 8-7 for more information on symbolic names.

REWIND          Specifies that the tape should be rewound to the load point after the function is complete. If omitted, the tape remains positioned at the record that follows the VOL1 label when the function is complete.

volser          The one- to six-character volume serial number stored in the VOL1 label and used to identify the tape.

owner           A value (up to eight characters long) that's stored in the owner-id field of the VOL1 label.

---

Figure 10-4      The DVOL1 and WVOL1 functions of the TAPE command

*The DVOL1 and WVOL1 functions of the TAPE command*     In chapter 8, you learned how to use a variety of functions of the TAPE command to handle non-labelled CMS tapes. I mentioned that two of the functions of the TAPE command, DVOL1 and WVOL1, are specifically for handling labelled tapes. The DVOL1 function displays a labelled tape's VOL1 label, and the WVOL1 function writes a VOL1 label.

Figure 10-4 presents the formats of these two functions of the TAPE command. You can use the DVOL1 function to determine whether or not a tape has IBM standard labels. Simply enter the command like this:

```
TAPE DVOL1
```

Here, the tape is mounted on the tape drive at the standard virtual address, 181. If the tape does not have a VOL1 label, a message like this is displayed:

```
'TAP1(181)' VOL1 LABEL MISSING.
```

On the other hand, if a VOL1 label is present, its contents are displayed. Here's what that display might look like:

```
VOL10043610                                    SC1
```

The six-character value in positions 5-10 (here, 004361) is the volume serial number, or volser. The SC1 is the owner-id of the tape.

If a tape is to be used for IBM standard label processing, it must have a VOL1 label. You can write a VOL1 label on tape with the WVOL1 function of the TAPE command.

You supply one or two items of information when you initialize a tape for standard label processing with the WVOL1 command. The first, volser, is the volume serial number that will be stored in the VOL1 label. It's always required. The other, owner, is optional. If you code it, it must be eight or fewer characters long. As a result, you could initialize a tape with the WVOL1 function of the TAPE command like this:

```
TAPE WVOL1 004362 SC2 (183
```

Here, the tape mounted on the tape drive with virtual address 183 is initialized with the volume serial number 004362 and the owner-id SC2.

With either the DVOL1 or WVOL1 function of the TAPE command, you can specify the REWIND option to direct the TAPE command to rewind the tape to its load point after it completes the requested operation. So

```
TAPE WVOL1 004362 SC2 (183 REWIND
```

and

```
TAPE WVOL1 004362 SC2 (183
TAPE REW
```

are equivalent.

***File label processing through the LABELDEF command***     To process file labels (HDR1 and EOF1) as well as volume labels (VOL1), you need to use another command: LABELDEF. Figure 10-5 presents its syntax. The operands you can code on it correspond to fields in VOL1 and HDR1 labels that appear on IBM standard labelled tapes (there are no operands for EOF1 labels).

As with the FILEDEF command, you can display the LABELDEF definitions in effect by entering the command with no operands. Or, to remove all current definitions, you can enter the command followed by an asterisk and the word CLEAR.

When you create a label definition, you must relate the specifications on a given LABELDEF command to a previously defined file. You'll notice that the LABELDEF command doesn't include a way to point to a particular tape unit; that function is performed by the FILEDEF command. As a result, the first operand you code on a LABELDEF command—and the only required operand—is the ddname specified on a previously issued FILEDEF command.

After the ddname, you can code a variety of operands to provide label specifications for the file. One of the operands, VOLID, corresponds to the VOLID operand of the FILEDEF command. You can supply the volser (stored in the tape's VOL1 label) with this operand. If you supply the volser on both the FILEDEF

## The LABELDEF command

**To display current label definitions**

```
LABELDEF
```

**To clear all label definitions**

```
LABELDEF * CLEAR
```

**To supply tape label information**

```
LABELDEF ddname    [FID {?
                         file-identifier}]

                   [VOLID volser]

                   [VOLSEQ vol-seq-number]

                   [FSEQ file-number]

                   [GENN generation-number]

                   [GENV generation-version]

                   [CRDTE creation-date]

                   [EXDTE expiration-date]
```

Figure 10-5    The LABELDEF command (part 1 of 2)

and the LABELDEF commands, the value on the command you entered more recently is in effect.

Each of the other operands of the LABELDEF command corresponds to data in a field of a file's HDR1 label. In this section, though, I'm not going to describe the contents of the label fields in detail. For more information, refer to one of the manuals IBM supplies on tape labels. For VSE systems, start with *VSE/Advanced Functions Tape Labels*; for MVS systems, try *MVS/Extended Architecture Magnetic Tape Labels and File Structure Administration*.

When you're processing a tape as input, the values you supply on the LABELDEF command are checked against the corresponding label fields on the tape; if you don't specify a particular label item, it's ignored in the tape label. For output, the values you supply are written to the new tape label; for values you omit, the defaults in figure 10-5 are used.

**Explanation**

| | |
|---|---|
| ddname | The ddname specified for the file on a FILEDEF command. |
| FID ? | Specifies that you should be prompted for the name of the tape file (that is, the HDR1 label name) to be processed. Use ? if the name is longer than eight characters. The default for output is ddname. |
| FID file-identifier | For file-identifier, code the name of the tape file (the HDR1 label name). Use this form of the FID operand when the name is eight or fewer characters long. The default for output is ddname. |
| VOLID volser | For volser, specify the one- to six-character volume serial number of the tape to be processed. The default for output is CMS001. |
| VOLSEQ vol-seq-number | For vol-seq-number, supply a one- to four-digit number for the volume sequence number. The default for output is 0001. |
| FSEQ file-number | For file-number, supply a one- to four-digit number for the file's sequence number. The default for output is 0001. |
| GENN generation-number | For generation-number, supply a one- to four-digit number. The default for output is spaces. |
| GENV generation-version | For generation-version, supply a one- or two-digit number. The default for output is spaces. |
| CRDTE creation-date | For creation-date, supply a value in the format yyddd. The default for output is the date the label is written. |
| EXDTE expiration-date | For expiration-date, supply a value in the format yyddd. The default for output is the date the label is written. |

Figure 10-5    The LABELDEF command (part 2 of 2)

For example, suppose I want to store the CMS disk file named AR6420B COBOL A on a labelled tape, and I want the name for the file in the tape label to be AR6420. These are the commands I might enter:

```
FILEDEF INMOVE DISK AR6420B COBOL A (RECFM F BLOCK 80 LRECL 80
FILEDEF OUTMOVE TAP1 SL VOLID SLE022 (RECFM FB BLOCK 1600 LRECL 80
LABELDEF OUTMOVE FID AR6420 EXDTE 87365
MOVEFILE
```

Here, I've specified that the disk file, which has 80-character, unblocked, fixed-length records, should be copied to a labelled tape file (SL operand of the FILEDEF command). The tape file should have blocked records; the blocking factor is 20 (twenty 80-character records fit in each 1600-byte block). The volume serial number of the tape to be used is SLE022 (the VOLID operand of the second FILEDEF command), the file will be identified with the name AR6420 (the FID operand of the LABELDEF command), and its expiration date is the last day of 1987 (the EXDTE operand of the LABELDEF command.)

To verify this operation, I rewound the tape, then issued the commands in the screen in figure 10-6. The first FILEDEF command defines an unlabelled tape as the input file; the second specifies that output should be routed to my terminal. When I entered the MOVEFILE command, the file was transferred and the three lines that begin with VOL1, HDR1, and HDR2 appeared.

The first record here is the tape's VOL1 label, the second is the file's HDR1 label (with the information I specified on the LABELDEF command plus defaults for the fields I did not specify), and the third is another label, the HDR2 label. (Its contents are for additional OS tape-processing functions; they're not important in the CMS environment.) Notice that because I treated this labelled tape as an unlabelled tape (by coding LABOFF on the FILEDEF command), the label data was treated as a file and transferred to the output device (the terminal, in this example).

## Discussion

Don't let the information in this chapter intimidate you. If you're called upon to process non-CMS tapes, it's most likely that you'll receive complete specifications about the way you'll have to access those tapes. That kind of information, combined with the concepts and details you've learned in this chapter, will put you in a good position to tackle most tape processing problems. And if your shop makes heavy use of non-CMS tapes, it's likely that standard procedures are in place for handling them. As a result, it should be easy to find out what you need to know to read and write them.

## Terminology

ddname

## Objectives

1. Use the FILEDEF and MOVEFILE commands to read and write files on unlabelled tapes and tapes with IBM standard labels.
2. Use the LABELDEF command to provide file label information for tapes with IBM standard labels.

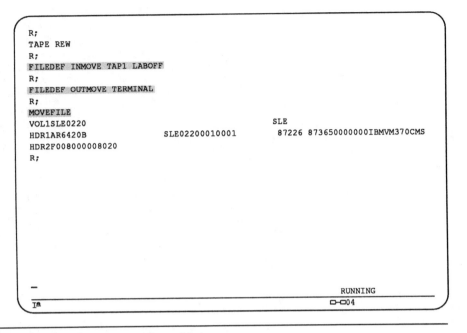

```
R;
TAPE REW
R;
FILEDEF INMOVE TAP1 LABOFF
R;
FILEDEF OUTMOVE TERMINAL
R;
MOVEFILE
VOL1SLE0220                                          SLE
HDR1AR6420B              SLE02200010001               87226 873650000000IBMVM370CMS
HDR2F008000008020
R;
                                                           RUNNING
TA                                                    □-□04
```

Figure 10-6    Displaying the contents of tape labels

# Section 4

Spooling

As part of the virtual machine environment, VM provides simulated unit record devices for your virtual machine and lets you share real unit record devices with other users. Both functions are grouped under the broad term "spooling." In this section, you'll learn basic VM spooling concepts (chapter 11), how to produce and manage spooled print and punch output (chapter 12), and how to retrieve and manage spooled reader input (chapter 13).

# Chapter 11

# VM spooling
# concepts

So far in this book you've learned how VM can allow many users to share a limited number of real disk drives (by dividing their storage into many minidisks) and real tape drives (by allocating tape units to individual virtual machines on demand). In this chapter, you'll see how VM can support the unit record operations of many virtual machines with relatively few real printers, card punches, and card readers. The technique used to provide that support is called *spooling*.

VM unit record processing operates at two levels. At the virtual machine level, virtual readers, punches, and printers are provided. And at the real system level, real readers, punches, and printers are supported. In this chapter, you'll learn how both virtual and real unit record devices work under VM, and you'll see what the relationships are between them.

## How virtual unit record devices work

Part of the configuration of each virtual machine is a set of virtual unit record devices: a virtual card reader, a virtual card punch, and a virtual printer. They all operate in much the same way. But because printing is easiest to understand, I'll introduce spooling by describing how printer output is handled under VM.

In chapter 4, you learned that you can get a printed copy of the contents of a file by issuing the CMS PRINT command. If you happen to issue the PRINT command from a terminal near the printer where the output will be produced, it might seem like the printer starts immediately after you enter the command,

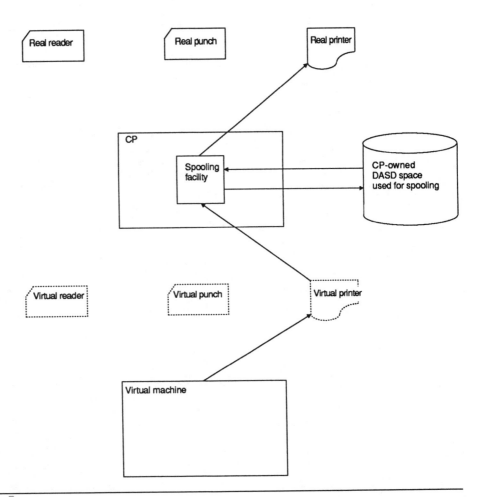

**Figure 11-1**    Spooled printer output

and that the printer is being driven directly by your virtual machine. However, that's not the case.

Figure 11-1 shows what really happens. When your virtual machine produces print output, it's produced on its virtual printer. The Control Program intercepts the print data your virtual machine generates and stores it temporarily in a disk file in a special area of DASD space CP owns. A file that's used to contain a particular item of print output (or card input or output) is called a *spool file*.

When an appropriate real printer is available, CP—not your virtual machine—transfers the contents of the printer spool file to it. Real unit record devices are under the control of CP, not CMS virtual machines.

Why bother to store print output on DASD before passing it to the real printer? Because all the users on the system need to share the few real unit record devices on the system. With spooling, input and output requests for virtual unit record

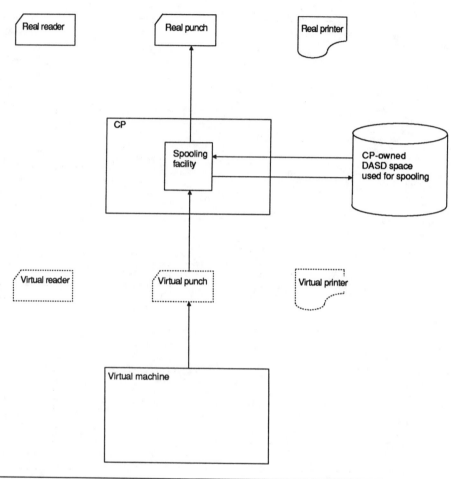

**Figure 11-2**     Spooled card output

devices can be handled by CP so it appears that they're satisfied immediately, regardless of the activity on the corresponding real devices.

So for example, even if a printer is busy producing a long listing, users can produce print output at the same time; CP stores that output in spool files. CP will send the users' output to the printer when the device becomes available. Instead of waiting for the long listing to finish, the users can go ahead and do other work.

The process is similar for card output, as you can see in figure 11-2. The only difference is that a virtual and real card punch are involved instead of a virtual and real printer. For card input, the process is similar, only virtual and real card readers are involved, and the flow of data is toward the virtual machine instead of away from it. Figure 11-3 illustrates spooled card input.

Because virtual unit record device input and output is always stored in spool files, it's possible to perform spooling operations without using a real unit record

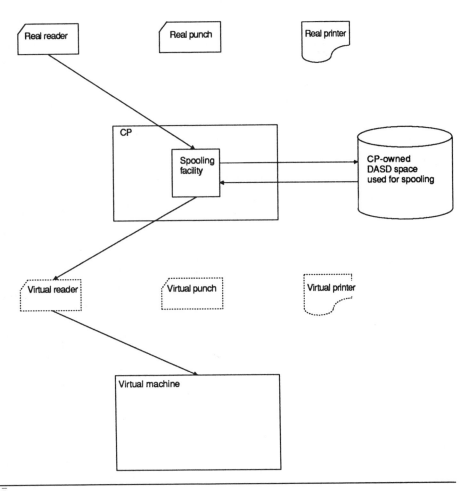

Figure 11-3    Spooled card input

device at all. For example, figure 11-4 shows how virtual card punch output from one virtual machine can be routed to the virtual card reader of a second virtual machine. This is a convenient and common way to transfer data between virtual machines. In fact, you're more likely to do this than to use spooling to access real card devices.

### How virtual unit record devices are defined

Virtual unit record devices are defined in the VM system directory for each virtual machine. If you look at the VM system directory entry in figure 11-5, you'll see three shaded SPOOL statements. Each defines one virtual unit record device. One of the statements,

```
SPOOL 00E 1403 A
```

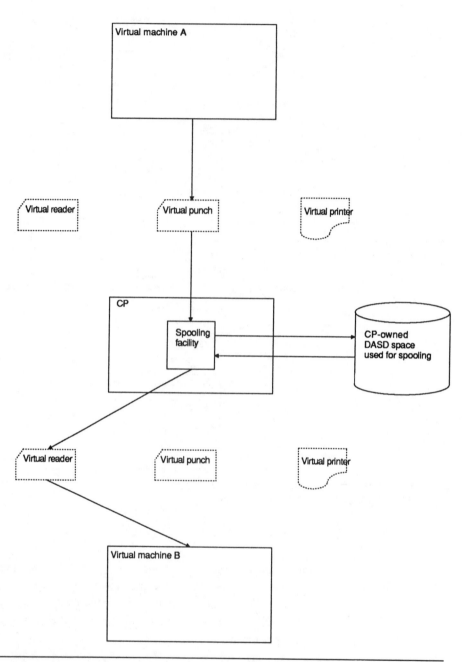

**Figure 11-4**     Spooling from one virtual machine to another

tells VM that for this virtual machine, a spooling device at address 00E should be simulated as a 1403 machine. A 1403 is an IBM printer model that, although not current, is still widely used in virtual machine definitions. (The A is a spooling class for the device; don't worry about it for now; I'll describe it in a moment.)

```
USER STEVE ECKOLS 1M 3M ABCDEG
 IPL CMS
 CONSOLE 009 3215
 SPOOL 00C 2540 READER *
 SPOOL 00D 2540 PUNCH A
 SPOOL 00E 1403 A
 LINK MAINT 190 190 RR
 LINK MAINT 19D 19D RR
 LINK MAINT 19E 19E RR
 LINK DOSVSE 240 240 RR
 LINK DOSVSE 241 241 RR
 MDISK 191 FB-512 041218 003262 VMSRES MW ALL
 MDISK 192 FB-512 000016 001984 VMSEXT MW ALL
```

Figure 11-5   Sample VM directory entry

The result of this statement is that it appears to programs running in this virtual machine that a printer is attached to it at address 00E.

The other two SPOOL statements in the directory entry in figure 11-5 define virtual card devices:

```
SPOOL 00C 2540 READER *
SPOOL 00D 2540 PUNCH A
```

The 2540 is a reader-punch, a card device that contains both an input component (the reader) and an output component (the punch) in one cabinet. The statements specify READER and PUNCH so VM will know which component of the simulated machine should be associated with the given virtual address.

The addresses for the virtual unit record devices in figure 11-5 are almost universally used. Address 00C is almost always a virtual card reader, 00D is almost always a virtual card punch, and 00E is almost always a virtual printer.

For CMS virtual machines, the standard virtual unit record devices are adequate. In some cases, though, particularly for virtual machines that run VSE or MVS as a guest operating system, multiple unit record devices of a given type can be defined. For instance, the VM systems programmer can provide a virtual machine with five virtual printers by coding five SPOOL statements for printers in that machine's directory entry. Because each virtual printer is defined with a different virtual address, CP manages their operations so they are independent of one another.

The last operands in each of the three SPOOL statements in figure 11-5 specify *spooling classes*. CP uses spooling classes to relate virtual unit record activity to real unit record activity. For example, the spooling class for printer output on my virtual machine is A. As a result, when CP receives spooled output from my virtual printer, it routes it to a real printer with the same spooling class.

Spooling classes can be used for a couple of purposes. For one thing, they can be used to insure that output from a particular group of terminal users is routed to real devices at their work site. Or, spooling classes can be used to group output that needs to be routed to devices that contain particular special forms. For instance, class I spooled printer output may be routed to a printer that always has invoice forms mounted in it. Other printers, which can be associated with different spooling classes, can be used for printing on other kinds of forms.

The asterisk for spooling class in the SPOOL statement for the virtual reader in figure 11-5 indicates that the device can process input of any class. This is a typical specification for a virtual reader.

### Spool files

In addition to spooling class, spool files have other characteristics that you need to know about. First, I'll describe spool-ids, the mechanism CP uses to identify spool files. Then, I'll introduce some other characteristics of spool files.

*Spool-ids*     When a spool file is created by any user, VM identifies it with a unique four-digit number in the range 0001 to 9900, called a *spool-id*. (When 9900 is reached, CP starts numbering spool files from 1 again.) Because the same sequence is used for printer, punch, and reader spool files and is shared by all system users, you will notice that the spool-ids assigned to spool files you create will be discontinuous.

For instance, if I print three files in a row with the CMS PRINT command, they might be stored in CMS spool files with spool-ids like 0532, 0537, and 0550. Notice that even though this sequence of spool-ids is discontinuous, each spool-id is different from the others, and each is greater than the one before it.

When you create a printer or punch spool file that (1) is going to be held before it's routed to its destination, (2) is bound for another user's virtual machine, or (3) is to be produced in multiple copies, CP displays a message at your terminal that includes its spool-id. For example, if I print a file and my virtual machine is set up so two copies of it will be produced, a message like

```
PRT FILE 0589   FOR STEVE    COPY 002    NOHOLD
```

appears. Here, 0589 is the spool-id.

Spool-ids are important because you often need to use them to manage your individual spool files. In the chapters on print and punch output (chapter 12) and on reader input (chapter 13), I'll show you how to find out what spool-ids were assigned to your spool files and how to change the characteristics of those files.

In addition to the spool-id, CP records the owner of a spool file. For printer and punch spool files, the owner is the user who created the file; for reader spool files, the owner is the user to whom the file was routed after it was either read by a real card reader or punched by another user.

*Other characteristics of spool files*     Also associated with spool files are several characteristics that determine how CP handles them. To understand these characteristics fully, you need to study them in the context of a particular kind of spool file (printer, punch, or reader). As a result, I'll only mention them here so you'll know what to expect in the next two chapters.

For all kinds of spool files, VM keeps track of whether the file is ready for immediate processing when an appropriate real device becomes available or whether the file should be held until it's explicitly released. These states are called "hold" and "nohold."

For output spool files (printer and punch), the kind of form to be used when the output is sent to the real device is recorded, as is the number of copies of the spool file to be produced.

## CP and CMS commands to manage spooling

Because spooling occurs at two levels under VM, it's also managed at two levels. In the first part of this section, I'll introduce the commands you issue in your virtual machine to control your virtual unit record devices and your spool files. Then, I'll briefly describe how the VM system operator controls the real unit record devices on the system.

*The CMS terminal user manages virtual unit record devices*     Within your virtual machine, you're responsible for controlling the operation of your virtual unit record devices. To do that, several commands are available. Because spooling is a function of CP, the commands you use to manage spooling operations are CP commands. The CMS commands that are used for spooling functions are primarily designed to help you get data from your CMS files into the spooling system, or to retrieve data from spool files and store it in CMS files.

Perhaps the most important CP spooling command you'll need to know is SPOOL. You use it to tailor your virtual machine's spooling environment. With it, you can specify the characteristics that will be applied to newly created spool files. In the next two chapters, I'll describe the CP SPOOL command in detail. (Don't confuse the CP SPOOL command with the SPOOL statement in the VM directory; they aren't the same thing.)

When you issue the CP SPOOL command, you affect how spool files that are created from then on are handled; the CP SPOOL command does not change the characteristics of spool files you've already created. To do that, you can use two other CP commands: CHANGE and PURGE. CHANGE lets you alter the characteristics of an existing spool file, and PURGE lets you delete a spool file. You'll learn how to use these commands for the different kinds of spool files in chapters 12 and 13.

To get information about the spooling system, you use the CP QUERY command. Though you're already familiar with this command, the functions for spooling are new to you.

**The FILES function of the CP QUERY command**

```
QUERY FILES [CLASS class-code] [FORM form-name] [{NOHOLD}]
                                                 [{HOLD  }]
```

**Explanation**

| | |
|---|---|
| QUERY FILES | You may abbreviate the command as Q F. |
| CLASS class-code | Specifies that only spool files with the spooling class indicated by class-code should be counted for the summary. |
| FORM form-name | Specifies that only spool files to be produced on the form indicated by form-name should be counted for the summary. |
| NOHOLD | Specifies that only spool files that are not held should be counted for the summary. |
| HOLD | Specifies that only spool files that are held should be counted for the summary. |

---

**Figure 11-6**    The FILES function of the CP QUERY command

You can use the FILES function of the QUERY command, illustrated in figure 11-6, to display counts of the number of spool files on the system. For example, if you enter simply

```
QUERY FILES
```

or the abbreviation

```
Q F
```

CP displays a line like this on your terminal:

```
FILES: 023 RDR,   NO PRT, 009 PUN
```

In the output line, you can see that the system currently has 23 reader files and 9 punch files, but no printer files. You might be interested in this kind of information, but its use is limited because the totals are for the entire system.

If you want counts for subsets of the spool files that the system currently is maintaining, you can use one of the operands in figure 11-6. For example, you could enter

```
Q F CLASS C HOLD
```

to see counts for all files with spooling class C that are in a held state.

To get information about specific spool files, you can use three other forms of the CP QUERY command: Q RDR, Q PRT, and Q PUN. I'll show you how to use these commands and illustrate their output in the next two chapters.

```
R; T=0.05/0.09 14:05:40
Q V UR
RDR  00C CL *  NOCONT NOHOLD  EOF         READY
PUN  00D CL A  NOCONT NOHOLD COPY 001     READY FORM STANDARD
     00D FOR STEVE    DIST STEVE
PRT  00E CL A  NOCONT NOHOLD COPY 002     READY FORM STANDARD
     00E FOR STEVE    DIST STEVE    FLASHC 000
     00E FLASH        CHAR       MDFY      0 FCB
R; T=0.05/0.12 14:05:43




-
                                                         RUNNING
IA                                                      ▭-▭04
```

**Figure 11-7**   Output of the QUERY VIRTUAL UR command

A third function of the CP QUERY command you might find useful lets you display the current characteristics of your virtual unit record devices. Enter

**QUERY VIRTUAL UR**

or just

**Q V UR**

and you will see a display like the one in figure 11-7. Notice that information for the three standard virtual unit record devices is displayed (a reader at virtual address 00C, a punch at 00D, and a printer at 00E). After you've learned how to use the CP SPOOL command in chapters 12 and 13 to set spooling characteristics, you'll understand the information in this display.

***The VM spooling operator manages real unit record devices***   The real unit record devices of the system are managed by operators called *spool operators*. Spool operators can issue special CP commands that are not available to general users to control real printers, readers, and punches. Although much of the spooling activity of the system is automatic, the spool operator's commands enable him to intervene to override automatic operations or to reset the real devices to correct problems that arise with them.

The spool operator issues commands and completes tasks necessary to keep the real unit record devices running properly. For example, when forms need to be changed in printers, the spool operator probably does it. Or when decks of real punched cards need to be read, the spool operator probably loads them in the reader. And often, the spool operator is responsible for routing print or punch output to its proper destination.

To override the automatic operation of the system, the spool operator can change the number of copies of an output item that are produced, can forward- or backward-space output, or can change the sequence in which output items are routed to their destination real devices. I want you to realize, though, that these activities are exceptions; most spooling is accomplished automatically without operator intervention.

### Discussion

With the background you now have about VM spooling, it should be easy for you to learn the more detailed information about spooling commands that the next two chapters present. Because spooled output (printer and punch operations) is easier to understand than spooled input (reader operations), I've covered spooled output first, in chapter 12. After you've finished that chapter, I don't think you'll have any trouble with the material on spooled input in chapter 13.

### Terminology

spooling
spool file
spooling class
spool-id
spool operator

### Objectives

1. Describe how VM relates virtual unit record input and output to real unit record input and output.
2. Use the CP QUERY command to find how how many spool files are currently stored on your system.
3. Use the CP QUERY command to find out what characteristics are currently being applied to your newly created spool files.

# Chapter 12

## How to print and punch data

In this chapter, you'll learn the commands you need to know to manage spooled output operations: printing and punching. For routine printing and punching, the command elements you need to be familiar with are simple; you'll see them first in this chapter. Then, I'll focus on some more advanced command functions: how to set your spooling defaults and how to manage existing spool files.

### How to use the CMS PRINT, PUNCH, and DISK commands

In this section, you'll learn how to use the CMS PRINT, PUNCH, and DISK commands to transfer the contents of CMS files to virtual printers and punches. Figures 12-1 through 12-3 present the syntax details of these commands.

To create a print spool file, you issue the PRINT command and specify the name of the CMS file to be printed. For example, I'd enter

```
PRINT INV4335 COBOL A
```

to print the contents of the CMS file INV4335 COBOL that's on my A-disk. As with other CMS commands you've learned, if you omit the filemode component of the file identifier, A is assumed. If you code an asterisk for the filemode on the PRINT command, all of your currently accessed minidisks are searched in the standard sequence, and the first file CMS finds that has the filename and filetype your command specified is printed.

**The CMS PRINT command**

```
PRINT fn ft [fm] [ ([CC [HEADER]] [LINECOUN count] [UPCASE] [HEX] ]
```

**Explanation**

| | |
|---|---|
| PRINT | The command may be abbreviated as PR. |
| fn | The filename component of the identifier of the file to be printed. |
| ft | The filetype component of the identifier of the file to be printed. |
| fm | The filemode component of the identifier of the file to be printed. If omitted, A is assumed. You may specify * for fm to cause all of your currently accessed disks to be searched for a file with the fn and ft values you supplied. |
| CC | Specifies that the contents of the first byte in each record of the input file should be interpreted as a carriage-control character and that the PRINT command should not add carriage-control characters to the output it sends to CP for printing. |
| HEADER | Specifies that a second header page should be printed as part of the output file. After the standard VM header page, another follows that contains just the identifier of the file being printed. The HEADER option can only be used when the CC option is in effect. |
| LINECOUN count | For count, code the number of lines that should be printed on each page of the output. You may code values between 0 and 144. If you code 0, the contents of the file are printed continuously; no page breaks occur. The default value for count is 55. |
| UPCASE | Specifies that lowercase letters in the input file should be converted to uppercase letters in the output listing. This option is useful when output will be routed to a printer than cannot print lowercase letters. |
| HEX | Specifies that the contents of the file should be printed in hexadecimal notation. When this option is in effect, the CC and UPCASE options are ignored. |

---

**Figure 12-1**     The CMS PRINT command

When you use the PRINT command, you need to be aware of size restrictions it imposes. Depending on the kind of real printer you'll be using, the maximum record size the PRINT command can handle for routine print operations varies from 132 to 206 bytes. Because most of the files you'll print will have records that are 132 or fewer bytes long, this restriction shouldn't present a problem for you.

The syntax of the PUNCH command is similar for this kind of routine output operation. For instance, the command

```
PUNCH INV4335 COBOL A
```

causes the contents of the file INV4335 COBOL on my A-disk to be copied to my virtual punch and, as a result, into a punch spool file.

**The CMS PUNCH command**

```
PUNCH fn ft [fm] [ (NOH ]
```

**Explanation**

| | |
|---|---|
| PUNCH | The command may be abbreviated as PU. |
| fn | The filename component of the identifier of the file to be punched. |
| ft | The filetype component of the identifier of the file to be punched. |
| fm | The filemode component of the identifier of the file to be punched. If omitted, A is assumed. You may specify * for fm to cause all of your currently accessed disks to be searched for a file with the fn and ft values you supplied. |
| NOH | Specifies that a header control card should not be punched at the beginning of the output deck. |

Figure 12-2    The CMS PUNCH command

The record-size limitations imposed by the PUNCH command are more restrictive than the PRINT command's. Because the PUNCH command works with data in card-image format, it can handle only 80-character records. If a record from a CMS file being processed by the PUNCH command is less than 80 characters long, PUNCH pads it with trailing spaces; if an input record is longer than 80 characters, CMS displays

```
RECORD EXCEEDS ALLOWABLE MAXIMUM.
```

and no spool file is produced.

If you need to transfer a file with records longer than 80 characters to another virtual machine via the spooling system, you can use the DUMP function of the CMS DISK command. Figure 12-3 presents its syntax. The DUMP function of the DISK command causes records longer than 80 bytes to be split into two or more parts, each 80 bytes long. Then, each of those parts is punched as a separate record. When the punch spool file is received through a virtual card reader, the records are reconstructed either with the LOAD function of the DISK command or, more simply, with the RECEIVE command. You'll learn how to use the RECEIVE command in the next chapter.

The other options of the PRINT and PUNCH commands are for specialized spooling functions. One option of the PUNCH command, NOH, lets you specify that an identifying header record *not* be punched at the beginning of the output file. The header record contains information that can make it easier to retrieve the data stored in the card deck, like the name of the CMS file the deck contains. Because the header record directly affects input spooling operations, I'll

**The DUMP function of the CMS DISK command**

```
DISK DUMP fn ft [fm]
```

**Explanation**

fn                    The filename component of the identifier of the file to be dumped.

ft                    The filetype component of the identifier of the file to be dumped.

fm                    The filemode component of the identifier of the file to be dumped. If omitted, A is
                      assumed. You may specify * for fm to cause all of your currently accessed disks
                      to be searched for a file with the fn and ft values you supplied.

---

**Figure 12-3**    The DUMP function of the CMS DISK command

---

describe its effects in the next chapter. In this section, I'll cover just the advanced
options of the PRINT command: CC, LINECOUN, UPCASE, and HEX.

***How to print files with carriage-control characters: The CC option of the PRINT
command***      When records are created in a file that will eventually be sent to
a printer, it's typical for the first byte of each record to contain control information for the printer rather than actual data that will appear on the hard copy.
That first byte is called a *carriage-control character*, and its contents direct the verti-
cal spacing the printer performs (such as when to go to a new page and how
many lines to skip between print records). You don't need to know the specific
values the carriage-control character can have or their functions, but you do need
to know whether a file you want to print contains such characters.

Because most CMS files are not created to be eventual printer output, they
typically do not contain carriage-control characters. As a result, the PRINT command by default adds carriage-control characters to records it reads from a CMS
file before it passes them to CP to be stored in a spool file. Then, when CP routes
that spool file to the destination real printer, the carriage-control characters cause
the output to be spaced properly and page breaks to appear in the right locations.

That's fine for typical CMS files, but if you want to print a file that already
contains carriage-control characters, you need to override the default action of
the PRINT command. To do so, you specify the CC option when you invoke
the PRINT command. CC tells the PRINT command not to add carriage-control
characters to the records it prints.

The chances are that you'll use the CC option only when you want to print
a copy of a file produced by an application program as printer output. When
that's the case, the application program will have already included the right carriage-
control characters in the file. Within CMS, some commands and programs produce such printer files; they have filetype LISTING. These files are a special case.

When you print a file with the filetype LISTING, the CC option is automatically assumed, even though it's not the typical default. Because of this, you shouldn't create a file with the filetype LISTING unless it contains printer data whose records begin with valid carriage-control characters.

When you use the CC option, you can specify a suboption: HEADER. All HEADER does is add a second header page to your output; it simply lists the identifier of the file being printed.

***How to control the number of lines printed on a page: The LINECOUN option of the PRINT command***    As I just mentioned, carriage-control characters specify where page breaks should occur in the hard copy. As a result, when the CC option is in effect, the PRINT command doesn't perform page-checking functions. But if you don't specify CC, the PRINT command has to decide where to place page breaks as it adds carriage-control characters to data it sends to CP for printing.

By default, the PRINT command writes 55 lines to each page of print output when it determines spacing (that is, when the CC option isn't in effect). If you wish, you can override this default with the LINECOUN option. On the LINECOUN option, specify the number of lines that should be printed on each page, from 0 to 144. If you specify 0 lines, CMS prints the file without page breaks.

***How to print the contents of a file in uppercase characters: The UPCASE option of the PRINT command***    If you want to send print output that contains lowercase letters to a printer that can print only uppercase letters, you might need to use the UPCASE option of the PRINT command. When you specify it, any lowercase letters in the input file are translated to uppercase by the PRINT command as it executes. The result is that only uppercase letters are stored in the printer spool file the command produces.

***How to print the contents of a file in hexadecimal: The HEX option of the PRINT command***    If you want to see the values of non-printable characters in a file, you might consider using the HEX option of the PRINT command. As you'd expect, it causes the hexadecimal contents of the file to be routed to the printer.

When you use the HEX option of the PRINT command, records in the input file can be any size up to 65,535 bytes. This is in contrast to the basic operation of the PRINT command, which requires that input records be small enough to fit in one of the output printer's print lines. Also, when you use the HEX option, the UPCASE and CC options are ignored.

The output that results when you use the HEX option can be extensive. As a result, I encourage you to be careful about using it. After all, do you really want to examine dozens of pages of hex values? A better approach might be to narrow the scope of the data you're interested in and use the TYPE command with the HEX option (presented in chapter 5) instead of PRINT.

**The CP SPOOL command functions for printer and punch output**

```
        ⎧ PRINTER         ⎫
SPOOL   ⎨ PUNCH           ⎬   [CLASS class-code]
        ⎩ virtual-address ⎭

                             [⎧FOR⎫  ⎧user-id⎫]
                              ⎩TO ⎭  ⎩  *    ⎭

                             [COPY copies]

                             [FORM form-name]

                             [⎧HOLD  ⎫]
                              ⎩NOHOLD⎭

                             [⎧CONT  ⎫]
                              ⎩NOCONT⎭
```

**Explanation**

| | |
|---|---|
| SPOOL | The command may be abbreviated as SP. |
| PRINTER | Specifies that the characteristics given on this command should apply to all new printer spool files. The keyword may be abbreviated as P or PRT. |
| PUNCH | Specifies that the characteristics given on this command should apply to all new punch spool files. The keyword may be abbreviated as PU. |
| virtual-address | Specifies that the characteristics given on this command should apply to new spool files produced by the unit at virtual-address. |
| CLASS class-code | For class-code, specify the one-character spooling class to be used for all subsequent output produced by the virtual unit record devices for which this command is being issued. You may abbreviate the keyword CLASS as CL. |
| FOR | Indicates that all subsequent output produced by the virtual unit record devices for which this command is being issued should be identified with the user-id of the creator (if * is specified) or with another user (if user-id is specified). |
| TO | Indicates that all subsequent output produced by the virtual unit record devices for which this command is being issued should be routed to the creator (if * is specified) or to another user (if user-id is specified). |
| COPY copies | For copies, code the number of copies (from 1 to 255) to be produced for all subsequent output produced by the virtual unit record devices for which this command is being issued. |
| FORM form-name | For form-name, code the one- to eight-character form-id associated with the form you want to be used with all subsequent output produced by the virtual unit record devices for which this command is being issued. |

---

**Figure 12-4**     The CP SPOOL command functions for printer and punch output (part 1 of 2)

| | |
|---|---|
| HOLD | Indicates that all subsequent output produced by the virtual unit record devices for which this command is being issued should not be automatically routed to its final destination device. |
| NOHOLD | Indicates that all subsequent output produced by the virtual unit record devices for which this command is being issued should be automatically routed to its final destination device. |
| CONT | Indicates that all subsequent output produced by the virtual unit record devices for which this command is being issued should be combined into one continuous spool file. |
| NOCONT | Indicates that all files printed or punched by the virtual unit record devices for which this command is being issued should be stored in separate spool files. |

**Figure 12-4**    The CP SPOOL command functions for printer and punch output (part 2 of 2)

## How to manage your virtual machine's spooling defaults

The characteristics that your print and punch spool files have are determined by default spooling values you can set with the CP SPOOL command. In this section, you'll learn the elements of that command that relate to spooled print and punch output; they're presented in figure 12-4. Specifically, you'll learn how to set your default spooling class, how to produce output on behalf of another user, how to produce spool output that's routed to another user, how to produce multiple copies of your output items, how to associate print and punch output with special forms, how to control the routing of spooled output to its destination real device, and how to combine multiple CMS files into a single output spool file.

As you read the descriptions of these functions, I want you to keep in mind that the specifications you make on the SPOOL command affect files that are created after the SPOOL command is issued. They do not affect existing spool files. To work with existing spool files, you need to use the two CP commands I'll describe at the end of this chapter: PURGE and CHANGE.

***How to find out what your current spooling defaults are: The CP QUERY VIR-TUAL UR command***    Before I show you how to make changes to the individual spooling defaults, I want to describe how to find out what options are in effect. As I showed you in chapter 11, you do that by issuing the CP QUERY command in this format:

```
QUERY VIRTUAL UR
```

or the abbreviated version

```
Q V UR
```

Figure 12-5 presents the output of this command for my virtual machine.

```
R; T=0.05/0.09 14:05:40
Q V UR
RDR  00C CL *  NOCONT NOHOLD     EOF          READY
PUN  00D CL A  NOCONT NOHOLD COPY 001      READY FORM STANDARD
     00D FOR STEVE     DIST STEVE
PRT  00E CL A  NOCONT NOHOLD COPY 002      READY FORM STANDARD
     00E FOR STEVE     DIST STEVE      FLASHC 000
     00E FLASH         CHAR        MDFY        0 FCB
R; T=0.05/0.12 14:05:43




_
                                                    RUNNING
 Iª                                                 ▢–▢04
```

Figure 12-5   Output of the CP QUERY VIRTUAL UR command

As you know, the display contains information for each virtual unit record device in the virtual machine's configuration. In this example, those devices are the standard units: a virtual card reader (RDR) at address 00C, a virtual card punch (PUN) at address 00D, and a virtual printer (PRT) at address 00E. For each device, several items of information appear; they're the spooling defaults you can set with the CP SPOOL command. There are more default settings for printers and punches than there are for readers; that's why you see two lines of information for the output unit record devices in this display, but just one line for the reader. In the sections that follow, I'll describe the important spooling default settings for punch and printer devices.

***How to specify the default spooling class: The CLASS option of the CP SPOOL command*** The first spooling default for both the printer and punch in the display in figure 12-5 is

    CL A

This indicates that the spooling class associated with spool files created by both of these devices will be A. In most shops, A is the spooling class used for routine output, so for routine print and punch tasks, it's appropriate. However, if you want to produce output that will be routed to a real device other than the standard unit(s) defined to handle class A output, you can specify another default spooling class with the CP SPOOL command.

For instance, if you wanted to change your printer's output spooling class to I, you'd enter the SPOOL command like this:

```
SPOOL PRINTER CLASS I
```

or more simply as

```
SPOOL P CL I
```

Then, your subsequent printer output would be created with spooling class I. Remember, though, that the SPOOL command does not affect existing spool files. If you want to change the class of a spool file you've already created, you use the CHANGE command instead of the SPOOL command.

Also, remember that the SPOOL command changes your virtual machine's defaults. So if you issue a command to change the output spooling class, it remains in effect for all subsequent output items produced by that virtual device type. To produce spool files with a different output class, even if it's your installation's standard output class, you need to specify that class by issuing the SPOOL command again.

By the way, as you can see in the syntax of the SPOOL command in figure 12-4, you specify the spooling devices to be affected by a SPOOL command either by type (PRINTER or PUNCH) or by virtual address. So for my virtual machine, the commands

```
SPOOL PRINTER CLASS I
```

and

```
SPOOL 00E CLASS I
```

achieve the same result. When you use a device type on the SPOOL command, your specification affects all devices of that type in your virtual machine's configuration. Because most CMS virtual machines have only one of each of the three kinds of virtual unit record devices, it doesn't matter which form of the command you use. For more complicated virtual machines, such as those used to run guest operating systems (which can require multiple unit record devices), it may be necessary to identify the virtual unit record device to be affected by a SPOOL command with a virtual address so you identify it uniquely.

***How to produce output on behalf of another user: The FOR option of the CP SPOOL command***    In the second line of output for the virtual punch and for the virtual printer in figure 12-5, you can see

```
FOR STEVE
```

This indicates that any spool files produced by these devices are produced "for" the virtual machine with the specified user-id. In other words, the user-id that appears with FOR for a given virtual unit record device will be the owner of any spool files that device produces. Most of the time, you'll see your own user-id with FOR. That's as you'd expect: When you create a spool file, you typically are its owner.

Sometimes, though, you may want to create spooled print or punch files on behalf of another user. When you do, you can change the owner of files produced by a given virtual unit record device with the FOR option of the CP SPOOL command. So I'd enter

```
SPOOL PRT FOR ANNE
```

to indicate that spooled print files produced on my virtual machine should be associated not with my user-id, but rather with the user-id ANNE.

The most tangible result of this option is that the new owner's user-id is printed or punched on the header page CP produces with real output items. That makes it easier for the system operator to route output to the right system user.

If you want to reset the FOR default so output you create is again associated with your user-id, enter the SPOOL command with the FOR operand followed by an asterisk:

```
SPOOL PRINTER FOR *
```

Here, the asterisk refers to the current user. (Don't confuse this with the use of the asterisk in CMS commands, where it typically is a wild-card character that can stand for any value.)

***How to route output to another user: The TO option of the CP SPOOL command***    Another way to put output spool data created by your virtual machine under the control of another user is to pass it to that user's virtual reader. (Remember, when you use the FOR option, spooled output remains as a punch or print spool file.) To send output to a user's virtual reader, you use the SPOOL command to set the TO default. So if I want punch data I create to be sent to the virtual card reader of the user PAT's virtual machine, I'd enter

```
SPOOL PUNCH TO PAT
```

Then, each spool file I create with a CMS PUNCH command is sent directly to the user PAT's virtual reader.

If you want to transfer data directly from one of your own virtual unit record output devices to your own virtual reader, you can enter a command like

```
SPOOL PUNCH TO *
```

Again, the asterisk refers to your own user-id. Although it is possible to route output spool data back to your reader, it's usually not necessary. The only time you'd probably need to do so is in a testing situation.

Notice that it's possible to send not only punch output, but also print output to a virtual reader. For now, just realize that you can do this, and don't let it confuse you. You'll learn more about VM virtual reader operations in the next chapter.

The TO and FOR options of the SPOOL command are mutually exclusive. FOR causes print or punch output you create to be stored in print or punch spool files; TO causes print or punch output you create to be stored in reader spool files. Notice in the output of the Q V UR command in figure 12-5 that there's no indication of a TO setting for either the virtual punch or the virtual printer. That's because FOR settings are in effect for both. If a TO setting had been in place for either, it would have been shown instead of FOR.

***How to produce multiple copies of your output: The COPY option of the CP SPOOL command*** To cause spool files you create to be produced in multiple copies on their destination real devices, you can code a command like

```
SPOOL PRINTER COPY 3
```

This command causes all subsequent print output to be printed three times by the real printer.

The Q V UR command shows what the current COPY setting is for your virtual printer and punch. In figure 12-5, you can see that my virtual punch is set up so only one copy of each output spool file is produced (COPY 001), but my virtual printer is set up so two copies of each output file are printed (COPY 002).

***How to use special forms: The FORM option of the CP SPOOL command***
The kind of computer paper or card to be used for a given output spool file is also determined by a spooling default. In figure 12-5, you can see that

```
FORM STANDARD
```

is indicated for both my virtual punch and my virtual printer. This means that the system makes sure the form called "STANDARD" is mounted in a real printer or punch before a spool file created by either of these virtual devices is routed to it. If the destination output device was last used with a different kind of form, CP prompts the system operator to change the form. (Usually, class A real devices always contain the form called "STANDARD," so operations can proceed automatically without operator intervention.)

If you want to use a special form for a given type of output, enter the SPOOL command with the FORM operand and name the form to be used. For example, if you want to produce printer output not on standard paper, but on three-part carbonless paper, you might enter a command like

```
SPOOL PRINTER FORM CBNLS3PT
```

where CBNLS3PT is the name used for that kind of form. Each shop uses its own form names, so be sure to find out just what you need to specify before you request a special form. And as with the other defaults you can set with the SPOOL command, remember that the alternate form continues to be used for all spool files you create until you explicitly issue another SPOOL command to change back to your shop's usual standard form or still another alternate form.

***How to control the routing of spooled output to its destination: The HOLD and NOHOLD options of the CP SPOOL command***     In figure 12-5, you can see that the condition

```
NOHOLD
```

is in effect for both the virtual punch and printer. That means that output produced by either of those virtual devices is routed automatically to its destination real device as soon as that device is ready for it. In some situations, you might not want the spooled output to be automatically routed to the corresponding real output device. When that's the case, you can change the default to HOLD by entering a command like

```
SPOOL PRINTER HOLD
```

This command causes all spool files produced by your virtual printer to be held until you or the system operator explicitly release them with the CP CHANGE command or delete them with the CP PURGE command. (I'll describe both the CHANGE and PURGE commands in a moment.)

***How to combine multiple CMS files in one spool file: The CONT option of the CP SPOOL command***     The last spooling default I want to discuss in this chapter is that indicated by NOCONT for the printer and punch in the Q V UR output in figure 12-5. This default determines how the data you send to your virtual printer or punch is packaged. Normally, the default condition (NOCONT) is in effect; this means that data coming into the spooling system from your virtual machine's unit record devices is considered to be "non-continuous." In other words, each file you send via your punch or printer is treated as a separate spool file. When the last record is written in such a spool file, the file is closed and is made available for printing or punching.

If the default condition is set to CONT (which stands for continuous) for one of your virtual unit record output devices, CP considers all of the data that comes from that virtual unit record device to be a continuous stream, regardless of how many separate CMS files you punch or print. In effect, CONT causes your output data to be concatenated into a single spool file. To make the file available for processing by a real device, you have to close it by issuing a CP CLOSE command:

```
CLOSE PRINTER
```

or

```
CLOSE PUNCH
```

This is the only situation in which you're likely to use the CLOSE command.

CONT can create some problems, particularly when you send data from your virtual punch to another virtual machine's virtual reader. As a general rule, then, you should avoid continuous spooling. If you do need to use it, you can return to non-continuous spooling by issuing a SPOOL command with the NOCONT option, followed by a CLOSE command.

## How to manage your existing spool files

As I've already said several times, the spooling defaults you set with the CP SPOOL command apply only to spool files created after you issue the SPOOL command. If you want to manage existing, or closed, spool files, you have to use other CP commands. In this section, you'll learn how to get information about your closed spool files with the CP QUERY command, how to use the PURGE command to delete spool files, and how to use the CHANGE command to alter the characteristics of spool files. (By the way, these commands apply not only to your spooled output files, but also to reader spool files.)

***How to get information about your existing spool files: The CP QUERY command***
To find out about your closed output spool files, you use still other options of the CP QUERY command: PRINTER (or its abbreviations P or PRT) and PUNCH (or its abbreviations PU or PUN). The syntax of the CP QUERY command for these options is in figure 12-6. If you specify just PRINTER or PUNCH when you issue the command, the output displayed is for all spool files you own of that type. If you want, you can limit the number of files displayed by requesting only files of a particular class, only files to be used with a particular form, or only files with HOLD or NOHOLD status.

Figure 12-7 shows what the output of the command looks like. One line appears for each spool file that meets the specifications you supplied. As you can see, the output includes the files' spool-ids (in the column labelled FILE), their class, form, record count, number of copies, and hold status. (USER in the column labelled HOLD indicates that these files have been placed in hold status by the user, not the system operator.) You can evaluate this information to determine what spool file management operations you want to perform.

***How to delete a spool file: The CP PURGE command***    To get rid of a spool file, you use the CP PURGE command; figure 12-8 presents its syntax. To refer to a particular spool file, you identify the kind of file it is (PRINTER or PUNCH), then specify its spool-id. So to delete the spool file shown in the list in figure 12-7 with spool-id 1265, I'd enter

```
PURGE PRINTER 1265
```

**The CP QUERY command to get information about existing spool files**

```
QUERY  {PRINTER}  [CLASS class-code] [FORM form-name][{HOLD  }]
       {PUNCH  }                                      {NOHOLD}
```

**Explanation**

QUERY              The command may be abbreviated as Q.

PRINTER            Specifies that only printer spool files should be processed by this command. PRINTER
                   may be abbreviated as PRT or P.

PUNCH              Specifies that only punch spool files should be processed by this command. PUNCH
                   may be abbreviated as PUN or PU.

CLASS class-code   For class-code, specify the one-character class of the spool files for which informa-
                   tion is to be displayed.

FORM form-name     For form-name, specify the one- to eight-character form-id associated with the spool
                   files for which information is to be displayed.

HOLD               Specifies that information should be displayed only for files in a held state.

NOHOLD             Specifies that information should be displayed only for files that are not in a held state.

Figure 12-6        The CP QUERY command functions to get information about existing spool files

```
R; T=15.87/33.76 14:11:41
Q PRT
OWNERID  FILE CLASS RECORDS   CPY HOLD USERFORM OPERFORM
STEVE    1265 A PRT 00000174 001 USER STANDARD STANDARD
STEVE    1271 A PRT 00000241 001 USER STANDARD STANDARD
STEVE    1273 A PRT 00000428 001 USER STANDARD STANDARD
STEVE    1280 A PRT 00001769 001 USER STANDARD STANDARD
STEVE    1306 A PRT 00000030 001 USER STANDARD STANDARD
R; T=0.05/0.12 14:11:44




                                                          RUNNING
                                                          ▢─▢04
```

Figure 12-7        Output of the CP QUERY PRINTER command

## The CP PURGE command

```
         (PRINTER)
PURGE    {PUNCH  }   [spool-id...] [CLASS class-code...] [FORM form-name...] [ALL]
         (ALL    )
```

### Explanation

| | |
|---|---|
| PURGE | The command may be abbreviated as PUR. |
| PRINTER | Specifies that only printer spool files should be processed by this command. PRINTER may be abbreviated as PRT or P. |
| PUNCH | Specifies that only punch spool files should be processed by this command. PUNCH may be abbreviated as PUN or PU. |
| ALL (first operand) | Specifies that spool files of all types should be processed by this command. |
| spool-id | The spool-id of the spool file to be deleted. You may code multiple spool-ids on a single PURGE command. |
| CLASS class-code | For class-code, specify the one-character class of the spool files that should be deleted. You may code multiple occurrences of the keyword CLASS and the class-code value on a single PURGE command. |
| FORM form-name | For form-name, specify the one- to eight-character form-id associated with the spool files that should be deleted. You may code multiple occurrences of the keyword FORM and the form-name value on a single PURGE command. |
| ALL (second operand) | Specifies that all spool files of the indicated type should be deleted. |

---

Figure 12-8    The CP PURGE command

If you want to delete a group of spool files of a particular type, you can identify them in several ways. If you want to delete several specific spool files, you can code the spool-id of each on a single PURGE command. For example,

```
PURGE PRINTER 1265 1271 1273
```

would delete the three named printer spool files.

You can also identify the files to be deleted by CLASS and/or FORM. To delete all of your punch spool files with spooling class K, you'd enter

```
PURGE PUNCH CLASS K
```

When you use the command in this way, all of the files that meet your specification are deleted. Likewise, you can use the FORM operand to indicate that files to be produced with a particular form should be deleted. For instance,

```
PURGE PRINTER FORM NEWINV
```

deletes all printer files that were to be produced on the special form NEWINV.

You can also combine specifications when you use the PURGE command. When you do, any spool file that matches any of the specifications you supply is deleted. So if you enter

```
PURGE PRINTER CLASS I FORM NEWINV
```

all print spool files with class I (regardless of their forms) and all print spool files for form NEWINV (regardless of their classes) are deleted.

You can use the keyword ALL on the PURGE command in two ways. If you code it as the first operand, it indicates that all types of spool files should be processed. For instance,

```
PURGE ALL CLASS A
```

causes all of your reader, printer, and punch spool files with class A to be deleted.

The other way to use ALL is to enter it after the type of file to be processed. When you do that, all files of the indicated type are purged. For example,

```
PURGE PUNCH ALL
```

causes all of your punch spool files to be deleted. Finally, if you enter simply

```
PURGE ALL
```

all of your spool files of all types are deleted.

***How to change a spool file's characteristics: The CP CHANGE command***        You use the CP CHANGE command to alter the characteristics of one or more closed spool files. If you understand the PURGE command, the CHANGE command is easy to master. That's because you identify the files to be processed by the CHANGE command much like you do with the PURGE command. As the command syntax in figure 12-9 shows, you specify the kind of spool file to be processed (PRINTER or PUNCH), then you identify the particular spool file(s) to be affected. You can identify a single file by its spool-id or a group of files by class or form. And, if you want to alter all of the spool files of a given type, you can specify ALL.

After you identify the files to be processed by the command, you specify what change should be applied to them. As figure 12-9 shows, you can specify a new spooling class, a new number of copies to be produced, or a new status (HOLD/NOHOLD). For example, if you want to keep your printer spool files

**The CP CHANGE command**

```
                   (CLASS class-code-1)   (CLASS class-code-2)
          (PRINTER) FORM form-name         COPY count
CHANGE    (PUNCH  ) (spool-id)             HOLD
                   (ALL      )             NOHOLD
```

**Explanation**

CHANGE

The command may be abbreviated as CH.

PRINTER

Specifies that only printer spool files should be processed by this command. PRINTER may be abbreviated as PRT or P.

PUNCH

Specifies that only punch spool files should be processed by this command. PUNCH may be abbreviated as PUN or PU.

CLASS class-code-1

For class-code-1, specify the one-character class of the spool files that should be changed.

FORM form-name

For form-name, specify the one- to eight-character form-id associated with the spool files that should be changed.

spool-id

The spool-id of the spool file to be changed.

ALL

Specifies that all spool files of the indicated type should be changed.

CLASS class-code-2

For class-code-2, specify the one-character class to which the indicated spool files should be changed.

COPY count

For count, specify the number of copies (between 1 and 255) that should be produced of the indicated spool files.

HOLD

Specifies that the status of the indicated spool files should be changed to HOLD.

NOHOLD

Specifies that the status of the indicated spool files should be changed to NOHOLD.

Figure 12-9    The CP CHANGE command

from being routed automatically to the real printer, you can enter

```
CHANGE PRINTER ALL HOLD
```

to change the status of all of your printer files to HOLD. The command

```
CHANGE PRINTER ALL NOHOLD
```

would release them for automatic printing.

## Discussion

You'll use the information in this chapter often as you work with your virtual machine's unit record devices, particularly your virtual printer. Your virtual punch probably won't be used frequently to punch real card decks, so you'll be less concerned with physical card operations. However, virtual card operations, involving your virtual punch and a virtual reader (either yours or another user's), are common. That's the subject of the next chapter.

## Terminology

carriage-control character

## Objectives

1. Use the CMS PUNCH or DISK command to produce a punch spool file.

2. Use the CMS PRINT command to produce a hard copy of the contents of a CMS file. The CMS file may or may not contain carriage-control characters, and the destination printer may or may not be able to print lowercase letters.

3. Use the CMS PRINT command with the LINECOUN option to produce a hard copy of the contents of a CMS file with any supported number of print lines per page.

4. Use the CMS PRINT command with the HEX option to produce a hard copy of the contents of a CMS file in hexadecimal format.

5. Use the CP QUERY V UR command to find out what spooling defaults are in effect for your virtual unit record devices.

6. Use the CP SPOOL command to set the spooling defaults for any virtual printer or punch that's part of your virtual machine's configuration.

7. Use the CP QUERY command with the PRINTER or PUNCH operand to get information about your closed output spool files.

8. Use the CP PURGE command to delete your closed spool files or a subset of them.

9. Use the CP CHANGE command to alter the characteristics of your closed spool files.

# Chapter 13

# How to use
# your virtual reader

Your virtual card reader provides a mechanism through which your virtual machine can receive data from other virtual machines or from a real card reader. As with print and punch spool data, spooled reader data is stored in spool files that CP maintains.

However, reader files are unlike your print and punch files in an important way. As you know, printer and punch files are created by commands you enter; in contrast, your virtual reader files are usually created by other users. You don't even have to be logged on for a reader spool file to be created for you and "stored in" your virtual reader. When you log on, CP displays the number of files in your reader. Then, you can do whatever you want with them. Of course, other users can also create and send files to your virtual reader while you're logged on and working.

In this chapter, you'll learn how to use commands to manage your virtual reader files. First, I'll describe the spooling defaults related to your virtual reader that you need to know about. Then, I'll present commands you can use to examine and delete reader files or to copy their contents to CMS disk files. Next, I'll describe the RDRLIST command; it provides a full-screen reader management facility that works much like FILELIST. Finally, I'll show you how to transfer data from a deck of real cards to your virtual machine.

## Virtual reader spooling defaults

As with your virtual printer and punch, you use the CP SPOOL command to set spooling defaults that apply to your virtual reader. Figure 13-1 presents the

**259**

```
R; T=0.05/0.09 14:05:40
Q V UR
RDR  00C CL *  NOCONT NOHOLD    EOF           READY
PUN  00D CL A  NOCONT NOHOLD COPY 001      READY FORM STANDARD
     00D FOR STEVE    DIST STEVE
PRT  00E CL A  NOCONT NOHOLD COPY 002      READY FORM STANDARD
     00E FOR STEVE    DIST STEVE     FLASHC 000
     00E FLASH        CHAR       MDFY      0 FCB
R; T=0.05/0.12 14:05:43




                                                           RUNNING
 Iª                                                       ▭–▭04
```

---

**Figure 13-1**    Output of the QUERY VIRTUAL UR command

output of the Q V UR command; it shows the defaults in effect for my virtual machine's virtual reader. As you can see, there are fewer defaults for a virtual reader than there are for either a virtual printer or a virtual punch.

The first default, class, is indicated by

```
CL *
```

in the output line for the virtual reader in figure 13-1. The asterisk means the virtual reader can process input of any class. Because you want your virtual reader to be able to process any input that may be sent to your virtual machine, you won't want to change this default.

In fact, there's little reason to change any of the spooling defaults for your virtual reader, with the possible exception of one: hold status. Hold status works differently for a virtual reader than it does for a virtual printer or punch. The normal situation (NOHOLD status) results in reader files being deleted by CP after your virtual machine has received them. As you can see in figure 13-1, the default condition is in effect for my virtual machine.

If you want your reader files to be retained in your reader after you've received them, you need to change your spooling default to HOLD. To do that, you use the CP SPOOL command elements illustrated in figure 13-2. (There are other operands you can use with the CP SPOOL command to set reader spooling defaults, but since I recommend you don't use them, I'm not presenting them here.) As

**The CP SPOOL command for virtual readers**

```
SPOOL  {READER          }  {NOHOLD}
       {virtual-address}  {HOLD  }
```

**Explanation**

| | |
|---|---|
| SPOOL | The command may be abbreviated as SP. |
| READER | Specifies that the characteristic specified on this command should apply to all new virtual reader files. The keyword may be abbreviated as RDR or R. |
| virtual-address | Specifies that the characteristic specified on this command should apply to new reader files associated with the unit at virtual-address. |
| NOHOLD | Indicates that reader files should be deleted after they have been read. |
| HOLD | Indicates that reader files should not be deleted after they have been read. |

**Figure 13-2**  The CP SPOOL command for setting virtual reader hold status

with print and punch files, the SPOOL command only affects reader files that are stored in your reader after the command is issued.

The first operand you code on the command identifies the virtual reader(s) to be affected by the command. If you specify READER (or the abbreviation RDR or R), all of the virtual readers that are part of your virtual machine are affected. If you specify the virtual address of a reader (like 00C), only the device at that address is affected. Because most CMS virtual machines have only one reader, you can probably use the command in either form and achieve the same result. The other operand you code specifies the hold status you want to become the new default.

## How to use basic commands to manage your reader files

This section presents four commands you can use to manage your reader files. The first, the CP QUERY command, displays information about the files in your virtual reader. The second, the CMS RECEIVE command, lets you retrieve a reader file by transferring its contents to a CMS disk file. The third, the CMS PEEK command, lets you examine the contents of spool files on your terminal screen. And the fourth, the CP PURGE command, is the command you use to delete reader files you don't want.

***How to get information about the files in your virtual reader: The CP QUERY command***    To find out what files are in your virtual reader, you can use the CP QUERY command with the READER operand, illustrated in figure 13-3.

**The CP QUERY command to get information about reader files**

```
QUERY READER [CLASS class-code] ⎡⎧NOHOLD⎫⎤
                                 ⎣⎩HOLD  ⎭⎦
```

**Explanation**

| | |
|---|---|
| QUERY | The command may be abbreviated as Q. |
| READER | Specifies that only reader files should be processed by this command. You may abbreviate the keyword as either RDR or R. |
| CLASS class-code | For class-code, specify the one-character spooling class of the reader files for which information is to be displayed. |
| NOHOLD | Specifies that information should be displayed only for reader files with NOHOLD status. |
| HOLD | Specifies that information should be displayed only for reader files with HOLD status. |

**Figure 13-3**   The CP QUERY command functions to get information about reader files

To see all of your virtual reader files, you enter simply

```
Q RDR
```

If you want information about a subset of your virtual reader files, you can use the CLASS, HOLD, or NOHOLD operands. CLASS lets you specify a spooling class; when you use it, only reader files with that class are listed. HOLD and NOHOLD let you display only reader files with a particular hold status value.

The format of the output produced by this version of the QUERY command is like that in figure 12-7. The most important information in the display probably is the spool-id associated with each of your reader files. You use spool-ids when you issue the other commands for reader files this section presents.

*How to transfer a file from your virtual reader to a CMS file: The RECEIVE command*      To capture the data in a reader file and store it in a file on one of your CMS minidisks, you use the RECEIVE command. CMS provides other techniques for transferring the contents of a reader file to disk, but because RECEIVE combines their functions, it's the only command you need to know.

For example, in the last chapter, you learned how to use the CMS DISK command's DUMP function to punch the contents of a CMS file. (Remember, you use the DISK command to punch the contents of a file whose records are longer than 80 characters.) The DISK command also has a LOAD function you can use to restore a CMS disk file from a reader file created by DISK DUMP.

**The CMS RECEIVE command**

```
RECEIVE [spool-id [fn [ft [fm]]]] [ (REPLACE]
```

**Explanation**

spool-id   The spool-id of the reader file to be received. If omitted, the next spool file in your virtual reader will be accessed.

fn   The filename to be used for the new CMS file. If omitted, the filename stored in the reader file's header record will be used. If filename information is not available in a header record and you omit fn, the default READCARD is used.

ft   The filetype to be used for the new CMS file. If omitted, the filetype stored in the reader file's header record will be used. If filetype information is not available in a header record and you omit ft, the default CMSUT1 is used.

fm   The filemode letter of the CMS disk where the new file will be stored. If omitted, A is the default.

REPLACE   Specifies that if a CMS file already exists on the target disk with the filename and filetype to be used for the new file, it should be replaced.

**Figure 13-4**   The CMS RECEIVE command

However, RECEIVE automatically invokes DISK LOAD if it's appropriate for a particular file. As a result, if you know how to use RECEIVE, you don't need to learn DISK LOAD.

As you can see in figure 13-4, the format of the RECEIVE command is simple. You supply one or two items of information: the spool-id of the reader file you want to transfer to disk and the file identifier of the new disk file. For example, the command

```
RECEIVE 1359 AR1400 COBOL A
```

would transfer the contents of a reader file with spool-id 1359 to a CMS file called AR1400 COBOL on the A-disk. If the reader file you're receiving contains identifying file information (either because it was created by the DISK command or because it includes a header card added by the PUNCH command), you can omit the file identifier and the proper name will be used for the file. If you omit the file identifier and the reader file doesn't supply that information either, the new CMS file is called READCARD CMSUT1, and it's stored on your A-disk. Unless you specify the REPLACE option, the RECEIVE command won't overwrite an existing CMS disk file. Finally, if you decide to omit the file identifier, you can also omit the spool-id; in that case, the command will access the next spool file in your virtual reader.

**The CMS PEEK command**

```
PEEK [spool-id] [ ([FROM start-rec] [FOR rec-count] ]
```

**Explanation**

| | |
|---|---|
| spool-id | The spool-id of the reader file to be viewed. If omitted, the next virtual reader file in sequence will be accessed. |
| FROM start-rec | For start-rec, specify the first record in the spool file to be displayed. If omitted, the default is the first record in the file. |
| FOR rec-count | For rec-count, specify the number of records to be displayed. The default is 200; specify * for rec-count if you want to view the entire file and it's longer than 200 records. |

Figure 13-5   The CMS PEEK command

***How to examine a file in your virtual reader: The PEEK command***      If you want to look at the contents of a reader file without transferring it to a CMS file, you can use the CMS PEEK command; figure 13-5 presents its syntax. If you enter the command with no operands, the next spool file in your virtual reader will be displayed. To request a specific reader file, code the spool-id operand on the command. For example,

```
PEEK 778
```

causes the contents of the reader file with the spool-id 778 to be displayed.

Unless you specify otherwise, the PEEK command will display the first 200 records in the reader file it accesses. If you supply the FROM option and a record number, the display will begin not at the first record in the reader file, but at the record you specify. And if you want to display more than 200 records, you can code the FOR option and a count. So if I want to display records 250-500 in the file with spool-id 778, I'd enter

```
PEEK 778 (FROM 250 FOR 251
```

If you want to display all of the records in the file, you can code the asterisk as the FOR option's count value. For example,

```
PEEK 778 (FOR *
```

causes all of the records in that reader file to be displayed, regardless of how many there are.

Figure 13-6 shows how you can use the PEEK command. In part 1 of the figure, I entered

```
Q RDR
```

to display a list of my current reader files. I was interested in the contents of the one with spool-id 1342, so I entered the command

```
PEEK 1342
```

to examine its contents.

The output the command produced is in part 2 of the figure. As you can see, PEEK uses XEDIT facilities to display the contents of the reader file it accesses. As the key assignment values at the bottom of the screen indicate, you can use the PF7 and PF8 keys to scroll backward and forward through the display. You can use PF3 to end the display. And you can use PF9 to invoke the RECEIVE command. For example, if I pressed PF9 from the screen in part 2 of figure 3-6, the reader file would be copied to a CMS disk file, a message like this:

```
FILE SC2C9 COBOL A1 RECEIVED FROM PAT AT * SENT AS SC2C9 COBOL A1
```

would appear on my terminal screen, and the PEEK session would end.

Also, you can delete the spool file you're looking at by keying in

```
DISCARD
```

in the command area of the PEEK screen. As you can see, that's what I did in part 2 of figure 13-6; the DISCARD subcommand is shaded in the figure. When I pressed the enter key, PEEK deleted the file. Then, it displayed the informative message you see in part 3 of the figure and returned to CMS. (The filename in the message in part 3 of the figure is the name of the file stored in the deleted reader spool file; it does not mean that a file with that name on one of my mini-disks was deleted.)

***How to delete a file from your virtual reader: The PURGE command***     If you know you want to delete a reader file, you don't have to PEEK at it first to do so. Instead, you can issue the CP PURGE command and specify the file's spool-id on it. For example,

```
PURGE READER 1342
```

deletes the reader file with spool-id 1342.

As the syntax of the PURGE command for reader files in figure 13-7 shows, you can also delete multiple spool files with one command. All you have to do is key in the spool-ids of the files you want to purge. Or, if you want to delete

The Q RDR command displays a list of your reader files; the PEEK command lets you look at a particular file

```
R; T=0.07/0.19 20:10:44
Q RDR
OWNERID  FILE CLASS RECORDS  CPY HOLD USERFORM OPERFORM
STEVE    1342 A PUN 00000107 001 NONE STANDARD STANDARD
STEVE    1359 A PUN 00000290 001 NONE STANDARD STANDARD
STEVE    1380 A PUN 00000321 001 NONE STANDARD STANDARD
R; T=0.05/0.12 20:10:58




PEEK 1342_
                                                        RUNNING
Iª                                              □─□04
```

---

**Figure 13-6**   How to use the PEEK command (part 1 of 3)

---

The DISCARD subcommand says to delete the file in the PEEK display

```
 1342     PEEK     A0  V 80  TRUNC=80 SIZE=108 LINE=0 COL=1 ALT=0
FILE SC2C9 COBOL FROM PAT AT *.  FORMAT IS PUNCH.
* * * TOP OF FILE * * *
CBL APOST
      IDENTIFICATION DIVISION.
      *
      PROGRAM-ID. PRTLABEL.
      *
      ENVIRONMENT DIVISION.
      *
      INPUT-OUTPUT SECTION.
      *
      FILE-CONTROL.
          SELECT ADDFILE ASSIGN TO SYS020-AS-ADDFILE.
          SELECT MAILIST ASSIGN TO SYS006-UR-1403-S.
      *
      DATA DIVISION.
      *
      FILE SECTION.
1= HELP      2= ADD LINE  3= QUIT     4= TAB     5= CLOCATE   6= ?/CHANGE
7= BACKWARD  8= FORWARD   9= RECEIVE 10= RGTLEFT 11= SPLTJOIN 12=CURSOR

====>DISCARD_
                                                X E D I T  1 FILE
Iª                                              □─□04
```

---

**Figure 13-6**   How to use the PEEK command (part 2 of 3)

When you press the enter key, the file is discarded, and PEEK ends

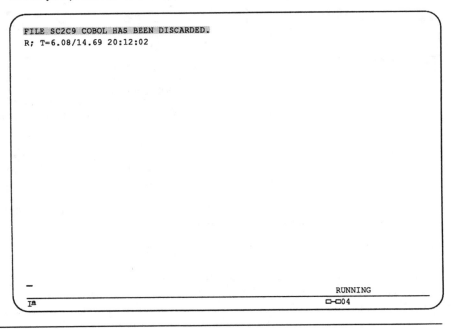

```
FILE SC2C9 COBOL HAS BEEN DISCARDED.
R; T=6.08/14.69 20:12:02




















                                                        RUNNING
 ⌐▪                                                      ◻—◻04
```

**Figure 13-6**      How to use the PEEK command (part 3 of 3)

all of the reader files of a given class, you can use the CLASS operand of the PURGE command. For instance,

```
PURGE READER CLASS B CLASS G
```

deletes all of my reader files with classes B and G. Finally, if you want to delete all your reader files, you can use the ALL operand, like this:

```
PURGE READER ALL
```

or simply omit the second operand and enter

```
PURGE READER
```

## How to use the RDRLIST facility to manage your virtual reader

If you work with lots of reader files, you'll probably find the CMS RDRLIST command a real time-saver. RDRLIST provides a full-screen facility you can use to get information about your reader files and process them. It's much like the FILELIST facility, which you learned in chapter 5. To enter the RDRLIST environment, enter simply

```
RDRLIST
```

**The CP PURGE command for reader files**

```
PURGE READER [CLASS class-code...] [spool-id...] [ALL]
```

**Explanation**

PURGE              The command may be abbreviated as PUR.

READER             Specifies that virtual reader files should be deleted by this command. The keyword
                   may be abbreviated as RDR or R.

CLASS class-code   For class-code, specify the one-character spooling class of the reader files to be
                   deleted. You may code multiple combinations of the keyword CLASS and class- code
                   on a single PURGE command.

spool-id           The spool-id of the reader file to be deleted. You may code multiple spool-ids on a
                   single PURGE command.

ALL                Specifies that all of your reader files should be deleted.

---

Figure 13-7    The CP PURGE command for reader files

or the abbreviation

    RL

from CMS. When you do, the RDRLIST display appears.

*The format of the RDRLIST display*    Part 1 of figure 13-8 presents a typical
RDRLIST display. If you've read the topic on FILELIST in chapter 5, you'll notice
right away that the screens the two commands display are similar. As with both
FILELIST and PEEK, the RDRLIST screen is managed by XEDIT.

Like the FILELIST display, the leftmost column of the RDRLIST screen is
for command entry. The next columns identify reader files. As you can see, reader
files in the RDRLIST display are listed by file identifiers, not by spool-ids. (The
file identifiers are from file data the individual reader files contain.) These file
identifiers can make it easier for you to find particular reader files. The other
information displayed for each reader file on the RDRLIST screen includes the
user who sent you the file, the file's hold status, and the number of records in
the file.

Also as with the FILELIST display, you can use the standard XEDIT keys
to control the RDRLIST display. PF7 and PF8 scroll the display backward and
forward, and PF3 ends the RDRLIST session and returns you to CMS. You can
select from PF4, PF5, and PF6 to change the sequence in which the reader files
appear in the display. And you can use PF9 and PF11 to execute the RECEIVE
and PEEK commands from within the RDRLIST environment.

The beginning RDRLIST display

```
STEVE     RDRLIST  A0  V 108   TRUNC=108 SIZE=4 LINE=1 COL=1 ALT=0
CMD   FILENAME FILETYPE CLASS USER  AT NODE    HOLD  RECORDS  DATE       TIME
      ASM      EXEC     PUN A STEVE    *        NONE      21 08/27   13:18:51
      SC2C9    COBOL    PUN A PAT      *        NONE     107 08/27   14:06:00
      LISTMAST COBOL    PUN A STEVE    *        NONE     290 08/27   14:19:33
      VMUSERS  DIRECT   PUN A MAINT    *        NONE     321 08/27   15:26:17




1= HELP      2= REFRESH   3= QUIT      4= SORT(TYPE) 5= SORT(DATE) 6= SORT(USER)
7= BACKWARD  8= FORWARD   9= RECEIVE  10=           11= PEEK       12=CURSOR

====>_
                                                      X E D I T   1 FILE
 1ª                                                   □─□04
```

Figure 13-8    How to use the RDRLIST command (part 1 of 5)

The DISCARD command says to delete the file on the line where it's entered; in this case, the file is LISTMAST COBOL

```
STEVE     RDRLIST  A0  V 108   TRUNC=108 SIZE=4 LINE=1 COL=1 ALT=0
CMD   FILENAME FILETYPE CLASS USER  AT NODE    HOLD  RECORDS  DATE       TIME
      ASM      EXEC     PUN A STEVE    *        NONE      21 08/27   13:18:51
      SC2C9    COBOL    PUN A PAT      *        NONE     107 08/27   14:06:00
DISCARDISTMAST COBOL    PUN A STEVE    *        NONE     290 08/27   14:19:33
      VMUSERS  DIRECT   PUN A MAINT    *        NONE     321 08/27   15:26:17




1= HELP      2= REFRESH   3= QUIT      4= SORT(TYPE) 5= SORT(DATE) 6= SORT(USER)
7= BACKWARD  8= FORWARD   9= RECEIVE  10=           11= PEEK       12=CURSOR

====>
                                                      X E D I T   1 FILE
 1ª                                                   □─□04
```

Figure 13-8    How to use the RDRLIST command (part 2 of 5)

When you press the enter key, a message appears to tell you the file has been deleted

```
   STEVE     RDRLIST  A0  V 108   TRUNC=108 SIZE=4 LINE=1 COL=1 ALT=0
  CMD    FILENAME FILETYPE CLASS USER  AT NODE      HOLD  RECORDS  DATE       TIME
         ASM      EXEC     PUN A STEVE    *          NONE      21 08/27   13:18:51
         SC2C9    COBOL    PUN A PAT      *          NONE     107 08/27   14:06:00
  *      LISTMAST COBOL    HAS BEEN DISCARDED.
         VMUSERS  DIRECT   PUN A MAINT    *          NONE     321 08/27   15:26:17




  1= HELP      2= REFRESH  3= QUIT     4= SORT(TYPE) 5= SORT(DATE) 6= SORT(USER)
  7= BACKWARD  8= FORWARD  9= RECEIVE  10=           11= PEEK      12=CURSOR

  ====>
                                                      X E D I T  1 FILE
  Iª                                              ▭−▭04
```

Figure 13-8    How to use the RDRLIST command (part 3 of 5)

To invoke the RECEIVE command for a file, position the cursor at the appropriate line in the listing and press PF9

```
   STEVE     RDRLIST  A0  V 108   TRUNC=108 SIZE=4 LINE=1 COL=1 ALT=0
  CMD    FILENAME FILETYPE CLASS USER  AT NODE      HOLD  RECORDS  DATE       TIME
         ASM      EXEC     PUN A STEVE    *          NONE      21 08/27   13:18:51
         SC2C9    COBOL    PUN A PAT      *          NONE     107 08/27   14:06:00
  *      LISTMAST COBOL    HAS BEEN DISCARDED.
  _      VMUSERS  DIRECT   PUN A MAINT    *          NONE     321 08/27   15:26:17




  1= HELP      2= REFRESH  3= QUIT     4= SORT(TYPE) 5= SORT(DATE) 6= SORT(USER)
  7= BACKWARD  8= FORWARD  9= RECEIVE  10=           11= PEEK      12=CURSOR

  ====>
                                                      X E D I T  1 FILE
  Iª                                              ▭−▭04
```

Figure 13-8    How to use the RDRLIST command (part 4 of 5)

A message appears to tell you the file has been received

```
 STEVE      RDRLIST  A0   V 108   TRUNC=108 SIZE=4 LINE=1 COL=1 ALT=0
 CMD    FILENAME FILETYPE CLASS USER  AT NODE     HOLD  RECORDS  DATE      TIME
        ASM      EXEC     PUN A STEVE    *         NONE      21 08/27   13:18:51
        SC2C9    COBOL    PUN A PAT      *         NONE     107 08/27   14:06:00
    *   LISTMAST COBOL    HAS BEEN DISCARDED.
    *   VMUSERS  DIRECT   RECEIVED FROM MAINT AT *.




 1= HELP       2= REFRESH  3= QUIT      4= SORT(TYPE) 5= SORT(DATE) 6= SORT(USER)
 7= BACKWARD   8= FORWARD  9= RECEIVE  10=           11= PEEK       12=CURSOR

 ====>
                                                           X E D I T   1 FILE
  I^                                                  ▭—▭04
```

Figure 13-8    How to use the RDRLIST command (part 5 of 5)

*How to issue commands from the RDRLIST display*      RDRLIST is also like
FILELIST because you can issue commands from its screen to operate on the
files displayed. The three commands you need to know how to use are RECEIVE,
PEEK, and DISCARD.

To delete a reader file from the RDRLIST environment, you position the
cursor in the command field of the line for the file and key in

    DISCARD

Part 2 of figure 13-8 shows how this looks. In this case, I've specified that the
reader file that contains data for the CMS file LISTMAST COBOL should be
erased. (Notice that you can key your command right over the data that's displayed in the line.) When I press the enter key, the command is processed. After
a moment, the acknowledging message in part 3 is displayed.

It's even easier to retrieve or look at a reader file in the RDRLIST environment. For example, to retrieve a file, you position the cursor on the line that
identifies that file and press PF9. To retrieve the file VMUSERS DIRECT from
the reader file that contains it, I move the cursor to the line for that reader file,
as part 4 of figure 13-8 shows. After I press PF9, RDRLIST displays the
acknowledgement in part 5 of the figure.

To invoke PEEK from RDRLIST, you use the same technique. The reader file you select is accessed and displayed in the format shown in part 2 of figure 13-6. You can use the PEEK PF key assignments from that screen, including PF9 to receive the file. You can also issue the DISCARD command from the PEEK screen's command line. When you've finished examining the file, you press PF3 from the PEEK screen, and the RDRLIST screen reappears.

### How to process real card decks

As I've mentioned already, real card devices are more and more uncommon on current computer systems. As a result, it's unlikely that you'll need to be able to read a deck of real cards into your virtual machine. However, it's easy to do.

The only special step you have to take to process a deck of real cards is to include an identification card at the beginning of the deck that tells CP to route the data to your virtual machine's virtual reader. The format of the card is simple: punch the characters ID in columns 1 and 2, then punch your user-id starting in column 4. So to route data from a deck of real cards to my virtual card reader, I'd include a card with the data

```
ID STEVE
```

at the beginning of the deck.

You will probably also want to include a second card in the deck to specify the CMS file identifier to be used for this file when you transfer it to a minidisk. This card begins with a colon in column 1 and the characters READ in columns 2 through 5. Then, starting in column 7, punch the filename and filetype components of the file identifier you want to use. Separate the filename and the filetype with one space. For example, if I punched a card with the data

```
:READ LISTMAST COBOL
```

the file identifier LISTMAST COBOL would be associated with the file when it's stored in my virtual reader. That makes it easier to transfer the reader file to disk with the RECEIVE command. (By the way, this card serves the same function and has the same format as the header card produced when you punch a CMS file with the PUNCH command.)

### Discussion

You'll use the techniques in this chapter often as you work with CMS, particularly for passing data between your virtual machine and others. For instance, if your VM system includes one or more virtual machines that run guest operating systems, you'll probably submit work (jobs) to them and receive output from them through the spooling system.

## Objectives

1. Use the CP SPOOL command to change the hold default for your virtual reader.

2. Use the CP QUERY command to get information about the files in your virtual reader.

3. Use the RECEIVE command to transfer the contents of a file in your virtual reader to a CMS file.

4. Use the PEEK command to examine the contents of a file in your virtual reader.

5. Use the CP PURGE command to delete a file from your virtual reader.

6. Use the RDRLIST facility to display information about the files in your virtual reader.

7. Issue appropriate commands from the RDRLIST environment to delete reader files, examine their contents, or transfer their contents to CMS files.

8. Prepare a real card deck so it can be transferred to your virtual reader and so the data in it can be received into a specific CMS file.

# Index

A-disk, 63, 64, 146
A spooling class, 248
A XEDIT prefix command, 85-86
Abbreviating commands (CMS FILELIST), 107
ACCESS command (CMS), 65-67, 146, 147, 148, 149
    file-identifier operand, 148, 149
    filemode-letter operand, 66, 67, 148
    NOPROF option, 66-67, 148
    parent operand, 147-149
    syntax, 148
    virtual-address operand, 67, 148
Access mechanism, 9, 10, 11
Access mode, 146-147, 150, 151-152
Access-mode operand (CP LINK), 150, 151-152
ACCESS READ option (CMS FSF TDISK USE), 175, 176
ACCESS WRITE option (CMS FSF TDISK USE), 175, 176
Accessing
    another user's minidisks, 150-153
    borrowed FSF minidisks, 175-176
    data communication networks, 26
Activating a virtual machine, 31, 55
Actuator, 9, 10, 11
Add password (FSF), 163, 168, 169, 170
Adding
    lines to a file, 85-86
    tape drives to a virtual machine configuration, 187
ALL operand
    CMS DDR DUMP, 207, 212
    CMS DDR RESTORE, 207, 212
    CMS FSF PATH LIST, 172
    CMS FSF TDISK QUERY, 176
    CP CHANGE, 256, 257
    CP PURGE, 255, 256, 267, 268
Alt-tape operand
    CMS DDR INPUT, 204, 206
    CMS DDR OUTPUT, 204, 206
Altering the sequence of fields in a file, 135-138
Alternate access modes, 152
AMSERV filetype, 71
ANY (FSF password value), 168
APPEND option
    CMS COPYFILE, 126, 129-130
    CMS FILELIST, 98, 114-115
APW option
    CMS FSF PASSWORD, 169
    CMS FSF PATH DEFINE, 170
    CMS FSF STORE, 162, 163
Architecture (processor), 4
Archiving files, 161
AS operand (CP LINK), 150, 151
ASSEMBLE filetype, 71
Assigning filemode letters to minidisks, 65-67
Asterisk
    in CP commands, 32
    in FILEDEF command, 215, 216
    in message commands, 32, 33
    in SPOOL command FOR operand, 250
    as spooling class, 236, 260
Attaching
    devices to a virtual machine, 50
    tape drives to a virtual machine, 184-187

Audio signal, 14
Automatic IPL, 52, 55

Backing up minidisks, 157, 202-213
BASIC filetype, 71
Batch, 19
Batch operating systems, 19-20
Batch processing, 19, 20
Block
    FBA, 48, 49
    file, 8, 11, 12
BLOCK block-size option (CMS FILEDEF), 216, 217, 219, 220, 225
Block commands (XEDIT), 85, 86-87
Block size, 219
Blocking, 8, 180-181, 219
Blocking factor, 181
Borrowed minidisk, 159, 173-177
BPI, 8, 180, 189
BSF function (CMS TAPE), 190, 191, 192-193
BSR function (CMS TAPE), 190, 191, 192-193
Bytes per inch, 8, 180, 189

C XEDIT prefix command, 85, 86-87
Card, 7, 47, 272
    devices, 7-8
    format file, 73
    header, 243, 263, 272
    punch, 7, 235
    reader, 7, 19, 235
Carriage-control character, 244
Cartridge, 8, 180, 189
Case translation, 134
CC option (CMS PRINT), 242, 244-245
Central processing unit, 4, 5, 6
CHANGE command (CP), 237, 249, 256-257
    ALL operand, 256, 257
    CLASS operand, 256, 257
    COPY operand, 257
    FORM operand, 256, 257
    HOLD operand, 256, 257
    NOHOLD operand, 256, 257
    P operand, 256, 257
    PRINTER operand, 256, 257
    PRT operand, 256, 257
    PUN operand, 256, 257
    PUNCH operand, 256, 257
    spool-id operand, 256, 257
    syntax, 257
Changing
    the logical record length of a file, 131-132
    the record format of a file, 132-133
Channel, 4, 5-6, 7, 8, 14, 17, 18
Channel command, 5
Character translation, 134-135, 245
Characteristics of spool files, 237
CKD format, 11, 12, 13
CLASS operand
    CP CHANGE, 256, 257
    CP PURGE, 255, 256, 267, 268
    CP QUERY, 238, 253, 262
    CP SPOOL, 246, 248-249

**275**

CLEAR operand
    CMS FILEDEF, 215, 216
    CMS LABELDEF, 223, 224, 225
Clock time, 35
CLOSE command (CP), 252-253
CMD column (FILELIST display), 105
CMS, 20, 21, 24, 25, 49, 51, 52, 235, 237
    blocks, 72
    environment, 24, 55, 59
    EXEC Facility, 78, 79
    help facility, 101
    ready message, 57, 58
    system residence volume, 51, 55, 63
CMS commands, 24, 59
    ACCESS, 65-67, 146, 147, 148, 149
    COMPARE, 139, 140
    COPYFILE, 74, 76, 110, 124-138
    DDR, 202-213
    DISK, 243, 244, 262-263
    ERASE, 74, 77, 110, 124
    EXEC, 78
    FILEDEF, 214, 215-218, 225
    FILELIST, 75, 97-116
    FORMAT, 154, 156-157
    FSF, 162-177
    FSF ERASE, 166, 167
    FSF GET, 164-165
    FSF LIST, 163-164
    FSF LOCATE, 163-164
    FSF PASSWORD, 168, 169
    FSF PATH DEFINE, 169-170
    FSF PATH DELETE, 172, 173
    FSF PATH LIST, 171-172
    FSF PATH PASSWORD, 170, 171
    FSF RENAME, 166
    FSF STORE, 162, 163
    FSF TDISK BORROW, 174-175
    FSF TDISK QUERY, 176-177
    FSF TDISK RETURN, 177
    FSF TDISK USE, 175-176
    LABELDEF, 223-226
    LISTFILE, 73-75, 97, 125, 128, 131, 132, 133, 134, 219, 220
    MOVEFILE, 214-215, 218, 219, 225
    PEEK, 264-265
    PRINT, 74, 76, 110, 215, 230, 241-245
    PUNCH, 242-245, 263, 272
    QUERY, 59, 60, 78
    RDRLIST, 267-272
    RECEIVE, 243, 262-263, 265
    RELEASE, 66, 67, 149, 153, 157
    RENAME, 74, 76-77, 110-113
    SET, 58
    SORT, 139-144
    TAPE, 189-194, 197-202, 218, 219
    TYPE, 74, 75-76, 107, 117-123
    XEDIT, 81-94, 97, 123, 265, 268
Coaxial cable, 16
COBOL filetype, 69, 71
COL option
    CMS COMPARE, 139, 140
    CMS TYPE, 118-119, 122
Color display, 16
Combining spool output, 252-253
Command line (XEDIT screen), 82

Comment (REXX), 79
Communication
    controller, 14, 15
    line, 14, 15
    network, 13-15
COMPACT option (CMS DDR OUTPUT), 204, 205, 206, 207
COMPARE command (CMS), 139, 140
    COL option, 139, 140
    file-identifier operand, 140
    syntax, 140
Comparing the contents of two files, 139, 140
Compatibility (processor), 3-4
Compressing
    backup data, 204, 205, 206
    files, 133-134
Concatenating
    files, 125, 129-130
    spool output, 252-253
COND ANY option (CMS FSF GET), 164, 165
COND NOU option (CMS FSF GET), 164, 165
COND REP option (CMS FSF STORE), 162, 163
COND UPD option (CMS FSF GET), 165, 168
Configuration
    real machine, 15-19
    virtual machine, 27, 35, 37-42
Connect time, 35
CONSOLE VM directory control statement, 39
CONT operand (CP SPOOL), 246, 247, 252-253
Continuous spooling, 252-253
Control fields, 139-140
Control Program. See CP
Control unit, 6, 7, 8, 17, 18
Control virtual machine (FSF), 160, 161
Conversational Monitor System. See CMS
Co-owner (of a borrowed FSF minidisk), 174, 176
COPY operand
    CP CHANGE, 257
    CP SPOOL, 246, 251
COPYFILE command (CMS), 74, 76, 110, 124-138
    APPEND option, 126, 129-130
    file-identifier operands, 77, 126
    FILL fill-character option, 126, 127, 132-133, 136
    FOR count option, 126, 127, 130-131
    FRLABEL start-text option, 126, 127, 130-131
    FROM start-rec option, 126, 127, 130-131
    LOWCASE option, 126, 127, 134
    LRECL record-length option, 126, 127, 131-132
    NOTRUNC option, 126, 127, 132
    OLDDATE option, 126, 127, 131, 132
    OVLY option, 126, 127, 137-138
    PACK option, 126, 127, 133-134
    RECFM format option, 126, 127, 132
    REPLACE option, 124-125, 126
    SPECS option, 126, 127, 135-138
    syntax, 74, 126-127
    TOLABEL end-text option, 126, 127, 130-131
    TRANS option, 126, 127, 134-135
    TYPE option, 125, 126, 128-129
    UNPACK option, 126, 127, 133-134
    UPCASE option, 126, 127, 134
Copying
    a file onto itself, 131
    lines in a file, 85, 86-87
    a minidisk to tape, 202-213

Copying (continued)
  multiple files, 125, 127-128
  over an existing file, 124-125
  part of a file, 130-131
Count area, 11, 12, 13
Count-key-data format, 11, 12, 13
Count option (CMS TAPE), 190, 191
CP, 23-25, 26, 27, 32, 33, 37, 42, 47, 50, 55, 59, 63, 187,
    231-232, 236, 237
  environment, 24-25
  owned DASD space, 47, 231
CP commands, 24
  CHANGE, 237, 249, 256-257
  CLOSE, 252-253
  DEFINE, 39, 154-155
  DETACH, 149, 153, 157, 187
  IPL, 51-52, 55
  LINK, 150-153
  LOGOFF, 31, 59-60
  LOGON, 27-31, 55-56
  MESSAGE, 32-33, 184-187, 188
  PURGE, 237, 253-256, 265-267
  QUERY, 33-35, 61, 237-239, 253, 254, 261-263
  SPOOL, 237, 246-253, 259-261
CP READ terminal status message, 42, 43, 44
CPU, 4, 5, 6
CPY filetype, 77
CRDTE operand (CMS LABELDEF), 224, 225
Creating a path (FSF), 169-170
Creation date, 75, 224, 225
Current line (XEDIT screen), 82, 83
Cursor, 27
Cylinder, 9-10, 145, 154, 155

D-disk, 64, 146
D XEDIT prefix command, 85, 86
DASD, 7, 8-13, 62
DASD Dump and Restore program, 202-213. *See also* DDR
    command
Data area, 11, 12, 13
Data communication
  devices, 13-15
  network, 13-15
Data Space and Sharing Facility, 159, 160, 161-173
Date and time stamping for CMS files, 131
DATE option (CMS FSF TDISK BORROW), 174, 175
Ddname, 215, 216, 217, 223, 224, 225
Ddname operand
  CMS FILEDEF, 216, 217, 225
  CMS LABELDEF, 223, 224, 225
DDR command (CMS), 202-213
  DUMP control statement, 206-207, 212
    ALL operand, 207, 212
  file-identifer operand, 203, 212
  INPUT control statement, 203-206, 207, 212
    alt-tape operand, 204, 206
    device-type operand, 204, 205, 207, 212
    disk-label operand, 204, 205
    SCRATCH operand, 204, 205
    syntax, 204-205
    virtual-address operand, 204, 205, 207, 212
  OUTPUT control statement, 203-206, 207, 212
    alt-tape operand, 204, 206
    COMPACT option, 204, 205, 206, 207

DDR command (CMS) (continued)
    device-type operand, 204, 205, 207, 212
    disk-label operand, 204, 205, 212
    MODE option, 204, 205, 206
    SCRATCH operand, 204, 205
    syntax, 204-205
    virtual-address operand, 204, 205, 207, 212
  RESTORE control statement, 206-207, 212
    ALL operand, 207, 212
  syntax, 203
Deactivating a virtual machine, 31
Default filemode letter assignments, 63-64
Default spooling values, 246-253
DEFINE command (CP), 39, 154-155, 159
  real-device-type operand, 154, 155
  storage operand, 154, 155
  syntax, 155
  virtual-address operand, 154, 155
Defining virtual unit record devices, 233-236
Delete password (FSF), 170
Deleting
  a CMS file, 77, 107-109
  an FSF file, 166-167
  lines in a file, 85, 86
  a reader file, 265, 266, 267, 268
  a spool file, 253-256
DEN option (CMS TAPE), 190, 191
Density, 8, 180, 189-192, 204, 205, 206
DETACH command (CP), 149, 153, 157
  syntax, 153
  virtual-address operand, 153
Device address (real), 17-19
Device-type operand
  CMS DDR INPUT, 204, 205, 207, 212
  CMS DDR OUTPUT, 204, 205, 207, 212
Dial-up line, 26, 31
Digital signal, 14
Direct access storage device, 7, 8-13, 62
Directory control statements
  CONSOLE, 39
  IPL, 52
  LINK, 48-49, 62-63, 146, 150
  MDISK, 48, 62-63, 145-146
  SPOOL, 233-236
  USER, 38
DISCARD subcommand
  CMS FILELIST, 107
  CMS PEEK, 265, 266
  CMS RDRLIST, 271, 272
Disk
  capacity, 10-12
  format, 11-12
  pack, 9
DISK command (CMS), 243, 244, 262-263
  DUMP operand, 243, 244, 262-263
  file-identifier operand, 243
  LOAD operand, 243, 262-263
  syntax, 244
Disk-label operand
  CMS DDR INPUT, 204, 205
  CMS DDR OUTPUT, 204, 205, 212
Disk-name operand
  CMS FSF TDISK BORROW, 174, 175
  CMS FSF TDISK QUERY, 176

Disk-name operand (continued)
   CMS FSF TDISK RETURN, 177
   CMS FSF TDISK USE, 175
DISK operand
   CMS FILEDEF, 216
   CMS QUERY, 59, 60, 64-65, 66
Disk Operating System (DOS), 19-20
DISK option
   CMS TAPE DUMP, 197
   CMS TAPE LOAD, 200
   CMS TAPE SCAN, 202
   CMS TAPE SKIP, 202
Displaying
   part of a file, 117, 119, 120-121
   tape labels, 226, 227
DOS, 24, 64
   operating systems, 19-20
   simulation functions, 49
DOS/VS, 19
DOS/VSE, 19
DOWN command (XEDIT), 83-84
DPW option
   CMS FSF PATH DEFINE, 170
   CMS FSF PATH DELETE, 172, 173
   CMS FSF PATH PASSWORD, 171
DSSF, 159, 160, 161-173
DUMP control statement (CMS DDR), 206-207, 212
DUMP function (CMS TAPE), 197-199
DUMP operand (CMS DISK), 243, 244, 262-263
Duplicating lines in a file, 85, 86
DVOL1 function (CMS TAPE), 190, 191, 194, 222
Dynamically created minidisks, 154-156

EBCDIC format, 117, 119
EDIT (CMS), 81
Editor, 81-94
End-of-file label, 184
End-of-volume label, 184
Ending an editing session, 84, 87
EOF option
   CMS TAPE LOAD, 200, 201
   CMS TAPE SCAN, 202
   CMS TAPE SKIP, 202
EOF1 label, 184, 226
EOT option
   CMS TAPE LOAD, 200, 201
   CMS TAPE SCAN, 202
   CMS TAPE SKIP, 202
EOV1 label, 184
EPW option
   CMS FSF PATH DEFINE, 170
   CMS FSF PATH PASSWORD, 171
Equal sign
   in CMS commands, 124-125, 129, 130
   in the FILELIST environment, 107
ERASE command (CMS), 74, 77, 110, 124
   file-identifier operand, 77
   syntax, 74
Exclusive read/write access mode, 151-152
EXDTE operand (CMS LABELDEF), 224, 225
EXEC command (CMS), 78
EXEC filetype, 71
EXEC procedure, 78-79
EXEC2 processor, 78, 79

Expanding a compressed file, 133-134
Expiration date, 224, 225
Extending a FILELIST display, 114-115
Extension, 63, 147-149
Extension password (FSF), 170
Extent, 48, 62

F XEDIT prefix command, 85, 86-87
FBA block, 154, 155
FBA DASD, 48, 62, 154, 155
FID operand (CMS LABELDEF), 224, 225
Field attribute characters, 119-121, 122
File
   area (XEDIT screen), 82, 83, 84
   identification line (XEDIT screen), 81, 82
   identifier, 69-72
   sequence number, 224, 225
   size, 75
   tape, 182, 183, 184
FILE command (XEDIT), 87, 88
File-header label (HDR1 label), 184
File-identifier operand
   CMS ACCESS, 148-149
   CMS DDR, 203, 212
   CMS COMPARE, 140
   CMS COPYFILE, 77, 126
   CMS DISK, 243
   CMS ERASE, 77
   CMS FILEDEF, 216
   CMS FILELIST, 97-99
   CMS FSF ERASE, 166, 167
   CMS FSF GET, 164, 165
   CMS FSF LIST, 164
   CMS FSF LOCATE, 164
   CMS FSF PASSWORD, 168, 169
   CMS FSF RENAME, 166
   CMS FSF STORE, 162, 163
   CMS LISTFILE, 73-75
   CMS PRINT, 76, 241, 242
   CMS PUNCH, 242, 243
   CMS RECEIVE, 263
   CMS RENAME, 76-77
   CMS SORT, 139, 141
   CMS TAPE DUMP, 197, 198
   CMS TAPE LOAD, 199, 200
   CMS TAPE SCAN, 202
   CMS TAPE SKIP, 202
   CMS TYPE, 75, 118
   CMS XEDIT command, 81
File-position operand (CMS FILEDEF), 216, 217
File Storage Facility, 159-177
FILEDEF command (CMS), 214, 215-218, 225
   BLOCK block-size option, 216, 217, 219, 220, 225
   ddname operand, 216, 217, 225
   DISK operand, 216
   file-identifier operand, 216
   file-position operand, 216, 217
   LABOFF operand, 216, 217, 218, 226
   LRECL rec-length option, 216, 217, 219, 220, 225
   RECFM rec-format option, 216, 217, 219, 220, 225
   SL operand, 216, 221
   syntax, 216-217
   TAPn operand, 216, 217
   TERMINAL operand, 216

FILEDEF command (CMS) (continued)
    VOLID volser operand, 216, 217, 221
    * CLEAR operand, 215, 216
FILELIST command (CMS), 75, 97-116
    abbreviating commands, 107
    APPEND option, 98, 114-115
    DISCARD subcommand, 107
    display, 99-100
    file-identifier operand, 97-99
    FILELIST option, 98, 113-114
    format of the display, 99-100
    invoking XEDIT from FILELIST, 102-107
    PF keys, 100-105
    resequencing the display, 101-102
    selecting a subset of files for display, 102, 104-105
    SLREC subcommand, 102
    SMODE subcommand, 102
    SNAME subcommand, 102, 103
    SRECF subcommand, 102
    syntax, 98
FILELIST option (CMS FILELIST), 98, 113-114
Filemode
    component of file identifier, 69, 70, 71
    extensions, 147-149
    letter, 63-67, 146
    number, 70-72
Filemode-letter operand
    CMS ACCESS, 66, 67, 148
    CMS FORMAT, 156, 157
    CMS FSF GET, 164, 165
    CMS FSF TDISK USE, 175, 176
    CMS RELEASE, 66, 67
Filename, 69, 70
FILES operand (CP QUERY), 237-238
Filetype, 69, 70, 71, 73
Fill character, 132-133
FILL fill-character option (CMS COPYFILE), 126, 127, 132-133, 136
First-rec operand (CMS TYPE), 117, 118
Fixed Block Architecture format, 11, 12
Fixed disk pack, 9, 12
Fixed-head storage, 10
Fixed-length
    block, 11, 72
    record, 72, 132-133
Fixed-pack DASD, 16, 17
FOR count option (CMS COPYFILE), 126, 127, 130-131
FOR operand (CP SPOOL), 246, 249-250
FOR option (CMS PEEK), 264
FORM operand
    CP CHANGE, 256, 257
    CP PURGE, 255, 256
    CP QUERY, 238, 254
    CP SPOOL, 246, 251-252
FORMAT command (CMS), 154, 156-157
    filemode-letter operand, 156, 157
    syntax, 157
    virtual-address operand, 156, 157
Forms (for spooled output), 237, 238, 239-240, 251-252, 253
FORTRAN filetype, 71
FREEFORT filetype, 71
FRLABEL start-text option (CMS COPYFILE), 126, 127, 130-131
FROM option (CMS PEEK), 264
FROM start-rec option (CMS COPYFILE), 126, 127, 130-131
FSEQ operand (CMS LABELDEF), 224, 225

FSF command (CMS), 162-177
    ERASE function, 166, 167
        file-identifier operand, 166, 167
        NODE option, 167
        path operand, 167, 171
        syntax, 167
        WPW option, 167, 168
    GET function, 164-165
        COND ANY option, 164, 165
        COND NOU option, 164, 165
        COND UPD option, 165, 168
        file-identifier operand, 164, 165
        filemode-letter operand, 164, 165
        NODE option, 165
        path operand, 165, 171
        RPW option, 165, 167, 168
        syntax, 163
        WPW option, 164, 165, 168
    LIST function, 163-164
        file-identifier operand, 164
        NODE option, 164
        path operand, 164, 171
        RPW option, 164, 167
        syntax, 164
    LOCATE function, 163-164
        file-identifier operand, 164
        NODE option, 164
        path operand, 164, 171
        RPW option, 164, 167
        syntax, 164
    PASSWORD function, 168, 169
        APW option, 169
        file-identifier operand, 168, 169
        NODE option, 169
        OPW option, 168, 169
        path operand, 169
        RPW option, 169
        syntax, 169
        WPW option, 168, 169
    PATH DEFINE function, 169-170
        APW option, 170
        DPW option, 170
        EPW option, 170
        NODE option, 170
        path operand, 170
        syntax, 170
    PATH DELETE function, 172, 173
        DPW option, 172, 173
        NODE option, 172, 173
        path operand, 172, 173
        syntax, 173
    PATH LIST function, 171-172
        ALL operand, 172
        NODE option, 172
        path-mask operand, 171, 172
        syntax, 172
    PATH PASSWORD function, 170, 171
        DPW option, 171
        EPW option, 171
        NODE option, 171
        OPW option, 170, 171
        path operand, 170, 171
        syntax, 171

FSF command (CMS) (continued)
    RENAME function, 166
        file-identifier operand, 166
        NODE option, 166
        path operand, 166, 171
        syntax, 166
        WPW option, 166, 168
    STORE function, 162, 163
        APW option, 162, 163
        COND REP option, 162, 163
        file-identifier operand, 162, 163
        NODE option, 162, 163
        path operand, 162, 163, 171, 172
        RPW option, 162, 163, 167, 168
        syntax, 163
        WPW option, 162, 163, 168
    TDISK BORROW function, 174-175
        DATE option, 174, 175
        disk-name operand, 174, 175
        size operand, 174, 175
        syntax, 174
        TIME option, 174, 175
    TDISK QUERY function, 176-177
        ALL operand, 176
        disk-name operand, 176
        syntax, 176
    TDISK RETURN function, 177
        disk-name operand, 177
        syntax, 177
    TDISK USE function, 175-176
        ACCESS READ option, 175, 176
        ACCESS WRITE option, 175, 176
        disk-name operand, 175
        filemode-letter operand, 175, 176
        syntax, 175
FSF function (CMS TAPE), 190, 191, 192-193, 201, 218, 219, 221
FSFPATHS file, 173
FSR function (CMS TAPE), 190, 191, 192-193
Functional control statements (CMS DDR), 206-207

Gap, 11-12
Generations, 224, 225
GENN operand (CMS LABELDEF), 224, 225
GENV operand (CMS LABELDEF), 224, 225
Getting information about
    borrowed FSF minidisks, 176-177
    closed spool files, 253
    CMS files, 73-75, 97-116
    FSF files, 163-164
    minidisks, 59, 60
    spooling defaults, 247-248, 259-260
    spooling system, 237-239
Grouping
    commands, 78-79
    spooled output, 236
Guest operating system, 20, 49, 51-52

HDR1 label, 224, 226
Header card, 243, 263, 272
HEADER option (CMS PRINT), 242, 245
Help files, 49
HEX option
    CMS PRINT, 242, 245
    CMS TYPE, 118, 119-121, 122

Hexadecimal, 17, 119-121, 122, 134, 245
High-level qualifier, 159
HOLD operand
    CP CHANGE, 256, 257
    CP LOGOFF, 31
    CP QUERY, 238, 253, 254, 262
    CP SPOOL, 246, 247, 252, 261
Hold status (spool file), 237, 238, 252, 253, 256, 257, 260, 261
HOLDING terminal status message, 43, 44
Host system, 14, 15
HT immediate command, 76, 117, 120-121

I XEDIT prefix command, 85-86
IBG, 8, 180, 181
IBM standard label tapes, 183-184, 194, 223-226
ID card, 272
Identification card, 272
Identifying FSF paths by number, 172-173
Immediate command, 76, 117, 120-121
Impact printer, 7
IMPEX ON (CMS SET), 78
IMPEX option (CMS QUERY), 78
Implied execution option, 78
Independence of a virtual machine, 23
Initial program load, 50-52, 55, 57, 58, 63
Initializing a labelled tape, 222-223
INMOVE ddname, 215, 216, 218, 219
INPUT control statement (CMS DDR), 203-206, 207, 212
Input-ddname operand (CMS MOVEFILE), 215
Input/output device, 2, 4, 5, 6, 7-14, 15, 17, 18
Inserting lines in a file, 85-86
Inter-block gap, 8, 180, 181
Inter-record gap, 8, 180, 181
I/O definition control statements (CMS DDR), 203-206
I/O device, 2, 4, 5, 6, 7-14, 15, 17, 18
IPL, 50-52, 55, 57, 58, 63
IPL command (CP), 51-52, 55
    saved-system-name operand, 51
    syntax, 51
    virtual-address operand, 51
IPL VM directory control statement, 52
IRG, 8, 180, 181
Issuing CP commands from CMS, 59, 60

Job, 19, 20, 21

K, 37, 174
Key area, 11, 12, 13
Keywords (in syntax), 27
Kilobyte, 37, 174

LABEL option (CMS LISTFILE), 74-75
LABELDEF command (CMS), 223-226
    CRDTE operand, 224, 225
    ddname operand, 223, 224, 225
    EXDTE operand, 224, 225
    FID operand, 224, 225
    FSEQ operand, 224, 225
    GENN operand, 224, 225
    GENV operand, 224, 225
    syntax, 224-225
    VOLID operand, 224, 225
    VOLSEQ operand, 224, 225
    * CLEAR operand, 223, 224, 225

Labelled tape, 183-184, 194, 221-227
Labels (tape), 182-184
LABOFF operand (CMS FILEDEF), 216, 217, 218, 226
Laser printer, 7-8
Last-col option (CMS TYPE), 118, 119-121, 122
Last-rec operand (CMS TYPE), 117, 118
Leased line, 26
LINECOUN option (CMS PRINT), 242, 245
LINK command (CP), 150-153
    access-mode operand, 150, 151-152
    AS operand, 150, 151
    PASS operand, 150, 152-153
    syntax, 150
    TO user-id operand, 150, 151
    virtual-address operand, 150, 151
LINK VM directory control statement, 48-49, 62-63, 146, 150
LISTFILE command (CMS), 73-75, 97, 125, 128, 131, 132, 133, 134, 219, 220
    file-identifier operand, 73-75
    LABEL option, 74-75
    syntax, 74
LISTING filetype, 71, 244-245
Literals (in syntax), 27
LMF, 159, 160, 173-177
LOAD function (CMS TAPE), 199-201
LOAD operand (CMS DISK), 243, 262-263
Load point, 192
Loading an operating system in a virtual machine, 30, 50-52
LOADLIB filetype, 71
Loaned Minidisk Facility, 159, 160, 173-177
Local terminal, 13, 26
Local 3270 system, 16, 17
Logging on the VM system, 26-31, 55-57
Logical record, 181, 182
Logo, 26, 28
LOGOFF command (CP), 31, 59-60
    HOLD operand, 31
    syntax, 31
LOGON command (CP), 27-31, 55-56
    NOIPL operand, 30-31, 52
    password operand, 30-31
    syntax, 30
    user-id operand, 27, 30
LOWCASE option (CMS COPYFILE), 126, 127, 134
LRECL rec-length option
    CMS COPYFILE, 126, 127, 131-132
    CMS FILEDEF, 216, 217, 219, 220, 225

M, 6, 16, 38, 39
M access mode, 151, 152
M XEDIT prefix command, 85, 86-87
MACLIB filetype, 71
MACRO filetype, 71
Magnetic tape, 8, 180
Magnetic tape drive, 7, 8, 50, 180
Main memory, 6
Main storage, 4
Mainframe computer system, 2, 15-19
MAINT user-id, 49, 55, 63
Major control field, 140
Managing existing spool files, 253-257
Mask, 99
MDISK VM directory control statement, 48, 62-63, 145-146
Megabyte, 6, 16, 38, 39

MEMO filetype, 71
MESSAGE command (CP), 32-33, 184-187, 188
    asterisk (*) operand, 32, 33
    OPERATOR keyword operand, 32, 33
    syntax, 33
    user-id operand, 32, 33
Message from CP, 236
Metal oxide, 8, 9, 180
Minidisk, 48-49, 55, 59, 60, 62-68, 69, 145-157, 159, 160, 161, 204, 205
    directories, 149
    label, 204, 205
    password, 152-153
    search order, 64-65, 147-148, 156
MODE option (CMS DDR OUTPUT), 204, 205, 206
Modem, 14, 15, 16, 17
MODESET function (CMS TAPE), 189-192
MODULE filetype, 71
MORE terminal status message, 43, 44, 58, 76, 117, 120
MOVEFILE command (CMS), 214-215, 218, 219, 225
    input-ddname operand, 215
    output-ddname operand, 215
    syntax, 215
Moving lines in a file, 85, 86-87
MR access mode, 151, 152
MSG command (CP), 32-33, 184-187, 188
    asterisk (*) operand, 32, 33
    OPERATOR keyword operand, 32, 33
    syntax, 33
    user-id operand, 32, 33
Multi-file volume, 182, 183, 184
Multiple copies of spooled output, 251
Multiple password, 152-153
Multiprocessing, 4
Multiprocessor system, 4
Multi-volume file, 182, 183
MVS, 20, 235
MVS/SP, 20
MVS/XA, 20
MW access mode, 151, 152

Naming restrictions
    ddname, 217
    filename, 69, 70
    filetype, 69, 70
    FSF path, 169-170
National character, 217
Network, 13-15
NOCONT operand (CP SPOOL), 246, 247, 252-253
Node (FSF), 160, 163, 164
NODE option
    CMS FSF ERASE, 167
    CMS FSF GET, 165
    CMS FSF LIST, 164
    CMS FSF LOCATE, 164
    CMS FSF PASSWORD, 169
    CMS FSF PATH DEFINE, 170
    CMS FSF PATH DELETE, 172, 173
    CMS FSF PATH LIST, 172
    CMS FSF PATH PASSWORD, 171
    CMS FSF RENAME, 166
    CMS FSF STORE, 162, 163
NOH option (CMS PUNCH), 243

NOHOLD operand
    CP CHANGE, 256, 257
    CP QUERY, 238, 253, 254, 262
    CP SPOOL, 246, 247, 252, 261
No-hold status (spool file), 237, 238, 252, 260
NOIPL operand (CP LOGON), 30-31, 52
Non-impact printer, 7-8
Non-removable disk pack, 9, 12
NOPRINT option
    CMS TAPE DUMP, 197
    CMS TAPE LOAD, 200
    CMS TAPE SCAN, 202
    CMS TAPE SKIP, 202
NOPROF option (CMS ACCESS), 66-67, 148
NOT ACCEPTED terminal status message, 43, 44
NOTRUNC option (CMS COPYFILE), 126, 127, 132

OLDDATE option (CMS COPYFILE), 126, 127, 131, 132
Operand, 27, 59
Operating system, 19, 24, 25, 50-52
OPERATOR keyword operand (CP MESSAGE), 32, 33
Option format (FSF commands), 162
Optional operands (in syntax), 31
Option (syntax), 66
OPW option
    CMS FSF PASSWORD, 168, 169
    CMS FSF PATH PASSWORD, 170, 171
OS file, 215
OS format data set, 72
OS/MFS, 20
OS/MVT, 20
OS operating systems, 19, 20, 24, 64, 72, 169
OS/VS1, 20
OS/VS2, 20
OUTMOVE ddname, 215, 217, 218, 219
OUTPUT control statement (CMS DDR), 203-206, 207, 212
Output-ddname operand (CMS MOVEFILE), 215
Overriding CMS defaults at IPL, 58
OVLY option (CMS COPYFILE), 126, 127, 137-138
Owned minidisk, 48, 62, 159
OWNER (FSF password value), 168
Owner of a spool file, 236, 250, 253
Owner operand (CMS TAPE WVOL1), 222, 223

P operand
    CP CHANGE, 256, 257
    CP PURGE, 253, 255, 256
    CP QUERY, 238, 253-254, 261-262
    CP SPOOL, 246, 249
P XEDIT prefix command, 85, 86-87
PACK option (CMS COPYFILE), 126, 127, 133-134
Pad character, 132-133
Padding a file's records, 132
Page length (printer output), 245
Parent minidisk, 147, 148
Parent operand (CMS ACCESS), 147-149
PASS operand (CP LINK), 150, 152-153
Password
    FSF, 166-168, 169, 170, 171
    suppression facility, 153
    VM, 30, 38, 55
Password operand (CP LOGON), 30-31
Path (FSF), 163, 168-173
Path-mask operand (CMS FSF PATH LIST), 171, 172

Path operand
    CMS FSF ERASE, 167, 171
    CMS FSF GET, 165, 171
    CMS FSF LIST, 164, 171
    CMS FSF LOCATE, 164, 171
    CMS FSF PATH DEFINE, 170
    CMS FSF PATH DELETE, 172, 173
    CMS FSF PATH PASSWORD, 170, 171
    CMS FSF RENAME, 166, 171
    CMS FSF STORE, 162, 163, 171, 172
PA2 key, 43, 44, 58, 76, 117, 120
PEEK command (CMS), 264-265
    DISCARD subcommand, 265, 266
    FOR option, 264
    FROM option, 264
    invoking from RDRLIST, 268-271
    spool-id operand, 264, 265
    syntax, 264
Percent sign in FILELIST command, 98, 99
Performance of the system, 4, 5
Permanent
    link, 150
    minidisk, 146, 154
PF key assignments
    FILELIST, 100-105
    XEDIT, 83-84
PF1 key (FILELIST), 101
PF2 key (FILELIST), 101, 107
PF3 key
    FILELIST, 100, 101
    RDRLIST, 268
    XEDIT, 84
PF4 key
    FILELIST, 101-102
    RDRLIST, 268
PF5 key
    FILELIST, 101-102
    RDRLIST, 268
PF6 key
    FILELIST, 101-102
    RDRLIST, 268
PF7 key
    FILELIST, 100, 101
    RDRLIST, 268
    XEDIT, 83-84
PF8 key
    FILELIST, 100, 101
    RDRLIST, 268
    XEDIT, 83-84, 87
PF9 key
    FILELIST, 102
    RDRLIST, 268
PF11 key
    FILELIST, 102-105
    RDRLIST, 268
Physical
    file, 198-199, 200-201
    record, 181
Platter, 9
PLI filetype, 71
PLIOPT filetype, 71
Positional operand, 31
Positioning a tape, 192-193
Prefix area (XEDIT screen), 82, 83

Prefix commands (XEDIT), 83, 84-87
   A, 85-86
   C, 85, 86-87
   D, 85, 86
   F, 85, 86-87
   I, 85-86
   M, 85, 86-87
   P, 85, 86-87
   ", 85, 86
Preliminary logon, 26
Primary data minidisk, 64
Primary multiple access mode, 152
Primary read/only access mode, 152
PRINT command (CMS), 74, 76, 110, 215, 230, 241-245
   CC option, 242, 244-245
   file-identifier operand, 76, 241, 242
   HEADER option, 242, 245
   HEX option, 242, 245
   LINECOUN option, 242, 245
   size restrictions, 242
   syntax, 74, 242
   UPCASE option, 242, 245
PRINT option
   CMS TAPE DUMP, 197
   CMS TAPE LOAD, 200
   CMS TAPE SCAN, 202
   CMS TAPE SKIP, 202
Print output routed to a reader, 251
Printer, 7-8, 14
PRINTER operand
   CP CHANGE, 256, 257
   CP PURGE, 253, 255, 256
   CP QUERY, 238, 253-254, 261-262
   CP SPOOL, 246, 249
Printer spool file, 236, 238
Printing files, 76
   with and without carriage-control characters, 244-245
Private file, 71
Procedure, 78-79
Processor, 2, 14, 15
PRT operand
   CP CHANGE, 256, 257
   CP PURGE, 253, 255, 256
   CP QUERY, 238, 253-254, 261-262
   CP SPOOL, 246, 249
PUN operand
   CP CHANGE, 256, 257
   CP PURGE, 255, 256
   CP QUERY, 238, 253, 254
   CP SPOOL, 246, 249
PUNCH command (CMS), 242-245, 263, 272
   file-identifier operand, 242, 243
   NOH option, 243
   size restrictions, 243
   syntax, 243
PUNCH operand
   CP CHANGE, 256, 257
   CP PURGE, 255, 256
   CP QUERY, 238, 253, 254
   CP SPOOL, 246, 249
Punch spool file, 236, 238
Punching files with records larger than 80 characters, 243
PURGE command (CP), 237, 253-256, 265-267
   ALL operand, 255, 256, 267, 268

PURGE command (CP) (continued)
   CLASS operand, 255, 256, 267, 268
   FORM operand, 255, 256
   P operand, 253, 255, 256
   PRINTER operand, 253, 255, 256
   PRT operand, 253, 255, 256
   PUN operand, 255, 256
   PUNCH operand, 255, 256
   R operand, 265, 267, 268
   RDR operand, 265, 267, 268
   READER operand, 265, 267, 268
   spool-id operand, 253, 265, 268
   syntax, 255, 268
Putting a file under the control of FSF, 162-163

Qualified data set name, 169
QUERY command (CMS), 59, 60
   DISK operand, 59, 60, 64-65, 66
   IMPEX, 78
   SEARCH operand, 59, 60, 64, 65
   syntax, 60
QUERY command (CP), 33-35, 61, 237-239, 253, 254, 261-263
   CLASS operand, 238, 253, 262
   FILES operand, 237-238
   FORM operand, 238, 254
   HOLD operand, 238, 253, 254, 262
   NOHOLD operand, 238, 253, 254, 262
   P operand, 238, 253-254, 261-262
   PRINTER operand, 238, 253-254, 261-262
   PRT operand, 238, 253-254, 261-262
   PUN operand, 238, 253, 254
   PUNCH operand, 238, 253, 254
   R operand, 238
   RDR operand, 238
   READER operand, 238
   syntax, 34, 238, 254, 262
   TIME operand, 34, 35
   USERID operand, 33, 34
   VIRTUAL address operand, 35
   VIRTUAL CHANNELS operand, 35
   VIRTUAL CONSOLE operand, 35, 39-42, 44
   VIRTUAL DASD operand, 35, 49
   VIRTUAL GRAF operand, 35
   VIRTUAL operand, 34, 35
   VIRTUAL STORAGE operand, 35, 38-39, 44
   VIRTUAL TAPES operand, 35, 188
   VIRTUAL UR operand, 35, 44-47, 239, 247-248
QUIT command (XEDIT), 84, 87

R access mode, 151, 152
R operand
   CP PURGE, 265, 267, 268
   CP QUERY, 238
   CP SPOOL, 260, 261
RDR operand
   CP PURGE, 265, 267, 268
   CP QUERY, 238
   CP SPOOL, 260, 261
RDRLIST command (CMS), 267-272
   DISCARD subcommand, 271, 272
   format of the display, 268
   PF keys, 268
   resequencing the display, 268
RDYMSG LMSG operand (CMS SET), 58

RDYMSG SMSG operand (CMS SET), 58
Read minidisk password, 152-153
Read password (FSF), 163, 167-168, 169
Read/only access mode, 49, 55, 64, 65, 146-147, 148, 149, 151-152, 176
Read/write access mode, 49, 55, 64, 65, 146-147, 149, 151-152, 176
Read/write head, 9, 10, 11, 13
READCARD CMSUT1 file identifier, 263
READER operand
    CP PURGE, 265, 267, 268
    CP QUERY, 238
    CP SPOOL, 260, 261
Reader/punch device, 7
Reader spool file, 236, 238
Real
    address, 41, 42
    card reader, 47
    cards, 272
    system, 23, 41
    unit record devices, 230, 231, 232-233
Real-device-type operand (CP DEFINE), 154, 155
RECEIVE command (CMS), 243, 262-263, 265
    file-identifier operand, 263
    invoking from RDRLIST, 268-271
    REPLACE option, 263
    spool-id operand, 263
    syntax, 263
RECFM option
    CMS COPYFILE, 126, 127, 132
    CMS FILEDEF, 216, 217, 219, 220, 225
Record, 6, 8, 181, 182
    format, 72, 75, 219
    length, 75, 219
Reel, 8, 180, 189
Refreshing
    FILELIST display, 101
    minidisk directory image, 149
RELEASE command (CMS), 66, 67, 149, 153, 157
    filemode-letter operand, 66, 67
    syntax, 67
    virtual address operand, 66, 67
Remote
    terminal, 13-14, 26
    3270 system, 16, 17
Removable disk pack, 9, 12
Removing
    minidisks from a virtual machine's configuration, 149, 153
    tape drives from a virtual machine's configuration, 187
RENAME command (CMS), 74, 76-77, 110-113
    file-identifier operand, 76-77
    syntax, 74
Renaming
    CMS files, 76-77
    FSF files, 166
REPLACE option
    CMS COPYFILE, 124-125, 126
    CMS RECEIVE, 263
Replacing
    CMS files, 124-125
    FSF files, 162, 163
Resequencing the records in a file, 139-144
Reserved filetypes, 69, 71
RESTORE control statement (CMS DDR), 206-207, 212
Restoring a backed up minidisk from tape, 202-213

Restructured Extended Executor, 79
Retrieving an FSF file, 164-165
Returning a borrowed FSF minidisk, 177
REW function (CMS TAPE), 190, 191, 193, 218, 219
REWIND option
    CMS TAPE DVOL1, 222
    CMS TAPE WVOL1, 222, 223
REXX, 79
RPW option
    CMS FSF GET, 165, 167, 168
    CMS FSF LIST, 164, 167
    CMS FSF LOCATE, 164, 167
    CMS FSF PASSWORD, 169
    CMS FSF STORE, 162, 163, 167, 168
RR access mode, 151, 152
RUN function (CMS TAPE), 190, 191, 193
RUNNING terminal status message, 42, 43

S-disk, 63, 64
SAVE command (XEDIT), 87
Saved system, 52
Saved-system-name operand (CP IPL), 51
Saving
    edited file, 87
    FILELIST display, 113-114
Scale line (XEDIT screen), 82
SCAN function (CMS TAPE), 201-202
SCRATCH operand
    CMS DDR INPUT, 204, 205
    CMS DDR OUTPUT, 204, 205
SCRIPT filetype, 71
Scrolling text (XEDIT), 83
SEARCH operand (CMS QUERY), 59, 60, 64, 65
Search order (minidisk), 64-65, 147-148, 156
Secondary storage, 7
Security, 30
Selecting a subset of files for display (CMS FILELIST), 102, 104-105
Sending a message to a user, 32-33
Sequencing the FILELIST display, 101-102
Sequential processing, 8, 72
SET command (CMS), 58
    IMPEX ON, 78
    RDYMSG LMSG, 58
    RDYMSG SMSG, 58
Setting
    input spooling defaults, 259-261
    output spooling defaults, 246-253
    page length, 245
Shared minidisks, 48, 63, 147, 150-153
Sierra system, 3-4
Single-file volume, 182, 183
Size of a minidisk, 65 ,66
Size operand (CMS FSF TDISK BORROW), 174, 175
SKIP function (CMS TAPE), 201-202
SL operand (CMS FILEDEF), 216, 221
SLREC subcommand (CMS FILELIST), 102
SMODE subcommand (CMS FILELIST), 102
SNAME subcommand (CMS FILELIST), 102, 103
SORT command (CMS), 139-144
    file-identifier operand, 139, 141
    syntax, 141
Sorting a file, 139-144
Special forms. *See* Forms
SPECS option (CMS COPYFILE), 126, 127, 135-138

SPOOL command (CP), 237, 246-253, 259-261
    CLASS operand, 246, 248-249
    CONT operand, 246, 247, 252-253
    COPY operand, 246, 251
    FOR operand, 246, 249-250
    FORM operand, 246, 251-252
    HOLD operand, 246, 247, 252, 261
    NOCONT operand, 246, 247, 252-253
    NOHOLD operand, 246, 247, 252, 261
    P operand, 246, 249
    PRINTER operand, 246, 249
    PRT operand, 246, 249
    PUN operand, 246, 249
    PUNCH operand, 246, 249
    R operand, 260, 261
    RDR operand, 260, 261
    READER operand, 260, 261
    syntax, 246-247, 261
    TO operand, 246, 250-251
    virtual-address operand, 246, 249, 261
Spool file, 47, 231, 232, 233, 236-237, 238, 244, 259
Spool-id, 236, 253
Spool-id operand
    CMS PEEK, 264, 265
    CMS RECEIVE, 263
    CP CHANGE, 256, 257
    CP PURGE, 253, 265, 268
Spool operator, 239-240, 252
SPOOL VM directory control statement, 233-236
Spooled
    card operations, 232-233
    printing, 230-232
Spooling, 47, 230-240
Spooling class, 234, 235-236, 238, 248-249, 253, 260, 262, 267, 268
SRECF subcommand (CMS FILELIST), 102
Standard labels, 183-184, 194
Standard node (FSF), 160, 162, 163, 168
Statistics for a terminal session, 35
Storage control, 13
Storage operand (CP DEFINE), 154, 155
Storing a file with FSF, 162-163
String, 13, 16
String controller, 12-13
Switched line, 26
Symbolic names (tape units), 188, 189, 190, 191
Syntax, 27
    ACCESS (CMS), 148
    CHANGE (CP), 257
    COMPARE (CMS), 140
    COPYFILE (CMS), 74, 126-127
    DDR (CMS), 203
    DDR INPUT (CMS), 204-205
    DDR OUTPUT (CMS), 204-205
    DEFINE (CP), 155
    DETACH (CP), 153
    DISK (CMS), 244
    ERASE (CMS), 74
    FILEDEF (CMS), 216-217
    FILELIST (CMS), 98
    FORMAT (CMS), 157
    FSF ERASE (CMS), 167
    FSF GET (CMS), 163
    FSF LIST (CMS), 164
    FSF LOCATE (CMS), 164

Syntax (continued)
    FSF PASSWORD (CMS), 169
    FSF PATH DEFINE (CMS), 170
    FSF PATH DELETE (CMS), 173
    FSF PATH LIST (CMS), 172
    FSF PATH PASSWORD (CMS), 171
    FSF RENAME (CMS), 166
    FSF STORE (CMS), 163
    FSF TDISK BORROW (CMS), 174
    FSF TDISK QUERY (CMS), 176
    FSF TDISK RETURN (CMS), 177
    FSF TDISK USE (CMS), 175
    IPL (CP), 51
    LABELDEF (CMS), 224-225
    LINK (CP), 150
    LISTFILE (CMS), 74
    LOGOFF (CP), 31
    LOGON (CP), 30
    MESSAGE (CP), 33
    MOVEFILE (CMS), 215
    PEEK (CMS), 264
    PRINT (CMS), 74, 242
    PUNCH (CMS), 243
    PURGE (CP), 255, 268
    QUERY (CMS), 60
    QUERY (CP), 34, 238, 254, 262
    RECEIVE (CMS), 263
    RELEASE (CMS), 67
    RENAME (CMS), 74
    SORT (CMS), 141
    SPOOL (CP), 246-247, 261
    TAPE (control functions) (CMS), 190-191
    TAPE DUMP (CMS), 197
    TAPE DVOL1 (CMS), 222
    TAPE LOAD (CMS), 200
    TAPE SCAN (CMS), 202
    TAPE SKIP (CMS), 202
    TAPE WVOL1 (CMS), 222
    TYPE (CMS), 74, 118
    XEDIT (CMS), 74
System
    administrator, 27, 30, 37, 51, 55, 64, 145-146, 152
    directory, 37, 146, 233-236
    operator, 32, 33, 50, 184-187, 237, 239-240, 252
    residence volume, 50-52
    software, 19
System Product Editor, 81-94
System Product Interpreter, 79
System/360 processor, 3-4, 19
System/360-370-family processors, 2-4, 20
System/370 processor, 3-4, 14, 15, 19

T-disk, 175
Tailoring spooling operations, 237
TAPE command (CMS), 189-194, 218, 219
    BSF function, 190, 191, 192-193
    BSR function, 190, 191, 192-193
    count option, 190, 191
    DEN option, 190, 191
    DUMP function, 197-199
        DISK option, 197
        file-identifier operand, 197, 198
        NOPRINT option, 197
        PRINT option, 197

TAPE command (continued)
    tape-unit option, 199
    WTM option, 197, 199
  DVOL1 function, 190, 191, 194, 222
    REWIND option, 222
    syntax, 222
    tape-unit option, 222
  FSF function, 190, 191, 192-193, 201, 218, 219, 221
  FSR function, 190, 191, 192-193
  LOAD function, 199-201
    DISK option, 200
    EOF option, 200, 201
    EOT option, 200, 201
    file-identifier operand, 199, 200
    NOPRINT option, 200
    PRINT option, 200
    tape-unit option, 200
  MODESET function, 189-192
  REW function, 190, 191, 193, 218, 219
  RUN function, 190, 191, 193
  SCAN function, 201-202
    DISK option, 202
    EOF option, 202
    EOT option, 202
    file-identifier operand, 202
    NOPRINT option, 202
    PRINT option, 202
    tape-unit option, 202
  SKIP function, 201-202
    DISK option, 202
    EOF option, 202
    EOT option, 202
    file-identifier operand, 202
    NOPRINT option, 202
    PRINT option, 202
    tape-unit option, 202
  syntax (tape-control functions), 190-191, 197, 200, 202
  tape-unit option, 190, 191
  WTM function, 190, 191, 193, 199
  WVOL1 function, 190, 191, 194, 222, 223
    owner operand, 222, 223
    REWIND option, 222, 223
    syntax, 222
    tape-unit option, 222, 223
    volser operand, 222, 223
Tape drive, 7, 8, 50, 180
TAPE MAP file identifier, 197
Tape-unit option
  CMS TAPE, 190, 191
  CMS TAPE DUMP, 199
  CMS TAPE DVOL1, 222
  CMS TAPE LOAD, 200
  CMS TAPE SCAN, 202
  CMS TAPE SKIP, 202
  CMS TAPE WVOL1, 222, 223
Tapemark, 182, 183, 193, 198-199, 201, 219
TAPn operand (CMS FILEDEF), 216, 217
TAP0-TAPF symbolic names, 188, 189, 190, 191, 218
Task virtual machine (FSF), 160, 161
Telecommunications
  access method, 26
  devices, 7
  network, 26

Temporary
  file, 72
  link, 150-151, 152
  minidisk, 146, 154-156, 173
Terminal, 7, 14, 15, 21
TERMINAL operand (CMS FILEDEF), 216
Terminal status message, 42-44
  CP READ, 42, 43, 44
  HOLDING, 43, 44
  MORE, 43, 44, 58, 76, 117, 120
  NOT ACCEPTED, 43, 44
  RUNNING, 42, 43
  VM READ, 42-43, 57, 58
Terminal system, 14, 15
TEST filetype, 71
TIME operand (CP QUERY), 34, 35
TIME option (CMS FSF TDISK BORROW), 174, 175
TO operand (CP SPOOL), 246, 250-251
TO user-id operand (CP LINK), 150, 151
TOLABEL end-text option (CMS COPYFILE), 126, 127, 130-131
Total CPU time, 35
Track, 9-10, 11, 12, 145
TRANS option (CMS COPYFILE), 126, 127, 134-135
Transferring data between virtual machines, 233
Translating characters, 134-135
Tree-structured directories, 169
Truncating a file's records, 132
TXTLIB filetype, 71
TYPE command (CMS), 74, 75-76, 107, 117-123
  COL option, 118-119, 122
  file-identifier operand, 75, 118
  first-rec operand, 117, 118
  HEX option, 118, 119-121, 122
  last-col option, 118, 119-121, 122
  last-rec operand, 117, 118
  syntax, 74, 118
TYPE option (CMS COPYFILE), 125, 126, 128-129

Unit record device, 7-8
Unlabelled tape, 182-183, 184, 218-221
Unload (a tape), 193
UNPACK option (CMS COPYFILE), 126, 127, 133-134
UP command (XEDIT), 83-84
UPCASE option
  CMS COPYFILE, 126, 127, 134
  CMS PRINT, 242, 245
Update-in-place file, 72
Update status (FSF), 165
User-id operand
  CP LOGON, 27, 30
  CP MESSAGE, 32, 33
User identification, 27, 29, 32, 33, 34, 38, 48, 55, 167, 168, 170, 250
User profile, 63, 146
USER VM directory control statement, 38
USERID operand (CP QUERY), 33, 34

Variable (in syntax), 27
Variable-length
  block, 11
  records, 72, 132-133
Viewing the contents of a reader file, 264-265

Virtual
    address, 39, 40, 42, 44, 63, 188, 189, 190, 191, 233, 234, 235
        009, 39
        00C, 44, 235, 238, 248, 261
        00D, 44, 235, 238, 248
        00E, 44, 233-234, 235, 238, 248
        180-187, 188, 189
        181, 188, 189, 190, 191, 196, 218
        190, 48, 49, 52, 55, 63
        191, 48, 49, 63, 64, 146
        192, 48, 49, 64, 146
        19D, 49
        19E, 49, 63, 64
        288-28F, 188, 189
        333, 175
    address space, 37, 38-39
    card punch, 23, 37, 44, 47, 230, 232, 233, 238, 248
    card reader, 23, 37, 44, 47, 230, 232, 233, 238, 248, 259-272
    console, 23, 37, 39, 42
    DASD, 23, 37, 47-49
    machine, 20, 23-25, 37-52, 62, 145, 146, 160, 161
    Machine/System Product, 20, 58
    printer, 23, 37, 44, 230-232, 235, 238, 248
    processor, 23, 37, 39
    processor time, 35
    punch, 23, 37, 44, 47, 230, 232, 233, 238, 248
    reader, 23, 37, 44, 47, 230, 232, 233, 238, 248, 259-272
    unit record device, 23, 37, 230-240
Virtual-address operand
    CMS ACCESS, 67, 148
    CMS DDR INPUT, 204, 205, 207, 212
    CMS DDR OUTPUT, 204, 205, 207, 212
    CMS FORMAT, 156, 157
    CMS RELEASE, 66, 67
    CP DEFINE, 154, 155
    CP DETACH, 153
    CP IPL, 51
    CP LINK, 150, 151
    CP QUERY, 35
    CP SPOOL, 246, 249, 261
VIRTUAL CHANNELS operand (CP QUERY), 35
VIRTUAL CONSOLE operand (CP QUERY), 35, 39-42, 44
VIRTUAL DASD operand (CP QUERY), 35, 49
VIRTUAL GRAF operand (CP QUERY), 35
Virtual Machine/System Product, 20, 58
VIRTUAL operand (CP QUERY), 34, 35
VIRTUAL STORAGE operand (CP QUERY), 35, 38-39, 44
VIRTUAL TAPES operand (CP QUERY), 35, 188
VIRTUAL UR operand (CP QUERY), 35, 44-47, 239, 247-248
VM File Storage Facility, 159-177
VM READ terminal status message, 42-43, 57, 58
VM/SP, 20, 58
VMFSF, 159-177
VOLID operand
    CMS FILEDEF, 216, 217, 221
    CMS LABELDEF, 224, 225
VOLSEQ operand (CMS LABELDEF), 224, 225
Volser, 17, 18, 48, 49, 62, 75, 156, 183, 184, 221, 222, 223
Volser operand (CMS TAPE WVOL1), 222, 223
Volume, 9, 10, 48, 182
    label, 183, 184, 194, 221, 223, 226
    sequence number, 224, 225
    serial number, 17, 18, 48, 49, 62, 75, 156, 183, 184, 221,
        222, 223

VOL1 label, 183, 184, 194, 221, 223, 226
VSBASIC filetype, 71
VSE, 20, 21, 49, 51-52, 235
    file, 215
VSE/AF, 19
VSE/SP, 19
VTAM, 26

W access mode, 151-152
Wild-card character, 73-74, 75, 76, 77, 97, 125, 163, 198, 199, 250
WPW option
    CMS FSF ERASE, 167, 168
    CMS FSF GET, 164, 165, 168
    CMS FSF PASSWORD, 168, 169
    CMS FSF RENAME, 166, 168
    CMS FSF STORE, 162, 163, 168
WR access mode, 151, 152
Write minidisk password, 152-153
Write password (FSF), 163, 168, 169
Writing a tapemark on tape, 193
WTM function
    CMS TAPE, 190, 191, 193, 199
    CMS TAPE DUMP, 197, 199
WVOL1 function (CMS TAPE), 190, 191, 194, 222, 223

XEDIT command (CMS), 81-94, 97, 123, 265, 268
    file-identifier operand, 81
    syntax, 74
XEDIT screen, 81-83
XEDIT subcommands
    A prefix command, 85-86
    C prefix command, 85, 86-87
    D prefix command, 85, 86
    DOWN, 83-84
    F prefix command, 85, 86-87
    FILE, 87, 88
    I prefix command, 85-86
    M prefix command, 85, 86-87
    P prefix command, 85, 86-87
    Prefix commands, 83, 84-87
    QUIT, 84, 87
    SAVE, 87
    UP, 83-84
    " prefix command, 85, 86

Y-disk, 63, 64

009 virtual address, 39
00C virtual address, 44, 235, 238, 248, 261
00D virtual address, 44. 235, 238, 248
00E virtual address, 44, 233-234, 235, 238, 248
180-187 virtual addresses, 188, 189
181 virtual address, 188, 189, 190, 191, 196, 218
190 virtual address, 48, 49, 52, 55, 63
191 virtual address, 48, 49, 63, 64, 146
192 virtual address, 48, 49, 64, 146
19D virtual address, 49
19E virtual address, 49, 63, 64
288-28F virtual addresses, 188, 189
333 virtual address, 175
1403 printer, 234
2314 DASD, 155
2319 DASD, 155
2540 reader-punch, 235

303X processor, 6
3080 processor, 3-4
3081 processor, 6
3084 processor, 6
3090 processor, 3-4, 5, 6
3178 terminal, 14, 15, 16, 18, 26, 41, 42
3179 terminal, 26
3191 terminal, 14
3193 terminal, 26
3194 terminal, 26
3215 terminal, 39
3262 printer, 16, 18, 41
3270 Information Display System, 14, 15, 26
3270 printer, 14
3270 terminal, 14, 15, 83
3274 terminal controller, 14, 15
3278 terminal, 26
3278-2A console, 16, 18, 41
3279 terminal, 16, 18, 26
3287 printer, 16, 18, 41
3310 DASD, 12, 16, 18, 41, 49
3330-1 DASD, 12, 155
3330-11 DASD, 12, 155
3340-35 DASD, 12, 155
3340-70 DASD, 12, 155
3350 DASD, 12, 16, 17, 155
3370 DASD, 12
3375 DASD, 12, 155
3380 DASD, 12, 155
3380-E DASD, 12, 155
3420 magnetic tape drive, 16, 17
3725 communication controller, 15
3800 Printing Subsystem, 7-8
3880 Storage Control, 13
4300 processor, 3-4
4331 processor, 16, 18, 41
4341 processor, 6
4361 processor, 6
4381 processor, 6, 16, 17
8809 magnetic tape drive, 16, 18, 41
9370 processor, 3-4, 16

" XEDIT prefix command, 85, 86
#CP prefix, 59-61
&TRACE (EXEC2), 79
* CLEAR operand
    CMS FILEDEF, 215, 216
    CMS LABELDEF, 223, 224, 225

# Comment Form

## Your opinions count

If you have comments, criticisms, or suggestions, I'm eager to get them. Your opinions today will affect our products of tomorrow. If you have questions, you can expect an answer within one week of the time we receive them. And if you discover any errors in this book, typographical or otherwise, please point them out so we can make corrections when the book is reprinted.

Thanks for your help.

**Mike Murach**
**Fresno, California**

**Book title:** VM/CMS: Commands and Concepts

Dear Mike: _____
_____
_____
_____
_____
_____
_____
_____
_____
_____
_____
_____
_____
_____
_____
_____
_____
_____

Name & Title _____
Company (if company address) _____
Address _____
City, State, Zip _____

Fold where indicated and tape closed.
No postage necessary if mailed in the U.S.

## BUSINESS REPLY MAIL
FIRST-CLASS MAIL      PERMIT NO. 3063      FRESNO, CA

POSTAGE WILL BE PAID BY ADDRESSEE

**Mike Murach & Associates, Inc.**

4697 West Jacquelyn Avenue
Fresno, CA 93722-9986

fold

fold

fold

fold

# Order Form

## Our Unlimited Guarantee

**To our customers who order directly from us:** You must be satisfied. Our books must work for you, or you can send them back for a full refund . . . no matter how many you buy, no matter how long you've had them.

Name & Title _____

Company (if company address) _____

Address_____

City, State, Zip _____

Phone number (including area code) _____

| Qty | Product code and title | *Price |
|-----|-----------------------|--------|

### VM Subjects

| Qty | Product code and title | *Price |
|-----|-----------------------|--------|
| _____ | VMCC  VM/CMS: Commands and Concepts | $25.00 |
| _____ | VMXE  VM/CMS: XEDIT | 25.00 |

### OS/MVS Subjects

| _____ | MJCL  MVS JCL | $34.50 |
| _____ | TSO   MVS TSO | 27.50 |
| _____ | MBAL  MVS Assembler Language | 36.50 |
| _____ | OSUT  OS Utilities | 17.50 |

### DOS/VSE Subjects

| _____ | VJLR  DOS/VSE JCL (Second Edition) | $34.50 |
| _____ | ICCF  DOS/VSE ICCF | 31.00 |
| _____ | VBAL  DOS/VSE Assembler Language | 36.50 |

### VSAM

| _____ | VSMX  VSAM: Access Method Services and Application Programming | $27.50 |
| _____ | VSMR  VSAM for the COBOL Programmer (Second Edition) | 17.50 |

### CICS

| _____ | CIC1  CICS for the COBOL Programmer: Part 1 | $31.00 |
| _____ | CIC2  CICS for the COBOL Programmer: Part 2 | 31.00 |
| _____ | CREF  The CICS Programmer's Desk Reference | 36.50 |

### Data Base Processing

| _____ | IMS1  IMS for the COBOL Programmer Part 1: DL/I Data Base Processing | $34.50 |
| _____ | IMS2  IMS for the COBOL Programmer Part 2: Data Communications and MFS | 36.00 |

### COBOL Language Elements

| _____ | SC1R  Structured ANS COBOL: Part 1 | $31.00 |
| _____ | SC2R  Structured ANS COBOL: Part 2 | 31.00 |
| _____ | RW    Report Writer | 17.50 |
| _____ | VC2R  VS COBOL II (Second Edition) | 27.50 |

### COBOL Program Development

| _____ | DDCP  How to Design and Develop COBOL Programs | $34.50 |
| _____ | CPHB  The COBOL Programmer's Handbook | 25.00 |

☐ Bill me the appropriate price plus UPS shipping and handling (and sales tax in California) for each book ordered.

☐ Bill the appropriate book prices plus UPS shipping and handling (and sales tax in California) to my
_____VISA _____MasterCard:

Card number_____

Valid thru (month/year)_____

Cardowner's signature_____
                        (not valid without signature)

☐ I want to **save** UPS shipping and handling charges. Here's my check or money order for $_____. California residents, please add 6¼% sales tax to your total. (Offer valid in the U.S. only.)

**\*Prices are subject to change.**
**Please call for current prices.**

## To order more quickly,

Call **toll-free** 1-800-221-5528

(Weekdays, 8:30 to 5 Pacific Std. Time)

### Mike Murach & Associates, Inc.

4697 West Jacquelyn Avenue
Fresno, California 93722
(209) 275-3335
Fax: (209) 275-9035

fold

fold

fold

fold